AROUND THE
SHABBAT TABLE

AROUND THE SHABBAT TABLE

A GUIDE TO FULFILLING AND MEANINGFUL
SHABBAT TABLE CONVERSATIONS

ARYEH BEN DAVID

JASON ARONSON INC.
Northvale, New Jersey
Jerusalem

This book was set in 11 point Garamond by Pageworks, Old Saybrook and Lyme, CT and printed and bound by Book-mart Press, Inc. of North Bergen, NJ.

Library of Congress Cataloging-in-Publication Data

Ben David, Aryeh.
 Around the Shabbat table: a guide to fulfilling and meaningful
 Shabbat table conversations / by Aryeh Ben David.
  p. cm.
 ISBN 0-7657-6124-6
 1. Bible O.T. Pentateuch—Commentaries. 2. Bible
O.T. Pentateuch—Meditations. 3. Legends, Jewish. I. Title.
BS1224.3.D379 2000
296.4'1 21—dc21   99-041841

Printed in the United States of America on acid-free paper. For information and catalog write to Jason Aronson Inc., 230 Livingston Street, Northvale, NJ 07647-1726, or visit our website: www.aronson.com

To my parents,
Alan and Magda Nemlich,
whose love and support transcend oceans.

The author would like to thank Pantheon Books for permission to reprint from the following books:

Samuel Dresner, *Tzaddik*, © 1960 by Samuel Dresner.

Hannah Senesh, *Hannah Senesh: Her Life and Diary*, © 1966 by Hakibbutz Hameuchad Publishing House Ltd.

Jack Reimer, *Jewish Reflections on Death*, © 1974 by Schocken Books Inc.

The author would like to thank Penguin Putnam Inc. for permission to reprint from the following books:

Gold Meir, *My Life*, © 1975 by Golda Meir.

Larry Collins and Dominique LaPierre, *O Jerusalem*, © 1972 by Larry Collins and Dominique LaPierre.

The author would like to thank Random House Inc. for permission to reprint from the following book:

Natan Sharansky, *Fear No Evil*, © 1988, 1989 by Random House, Inc.

The author would like to thank the Breslov Research Institute for permission to reprint from the following book:

Rabbi Chaim Kramer, *Rabbi Nachman's Stories*, © 1983 by Breslov Research Institute.

The author would like to thank Simcha Raz for permission to reprint from the following book:

Simcha Raz, *A Tzaddik in Our Time*, © 1976 by Rabbi Isaiah Dvorkas.

The author would like to thank Naomi Rosen (Jaffe) for permission to reprint from the following book:

Rabbi Moshe Zvi Neriyah, *Celebration of the Soul*, translated by Pesach Jaffe, © 1992 by Pesach Jaffe.

The author would like to thank Dr. Avraham Twersky for permission to reprint from the following book:

Abraham J. Twerski, *From Generation to Generation*, © 1985, 1987, 1989 by Abraham J. Twerski, Traditional Press.

Contents

Exodus

Leviticus

Numbers

Deuteronomy

Preface

During the last fifteen years, I have been privileged to be associated with two very special institutions that deal with Jewish learning and identity: the Pardes Institute and Livnot U'Lehibanot. Both of these Jerusalem centers seek to address the intellectual and spiritual needs of postcollege adults, offering them open and inspiring environments in which they can explore and develop their Jewish identities. Common to both programs is the respect and care given to their participants; they neither mold nor indoctrinate and offer a plethora of experiences and views that enable students to choose their own course of Jewish growth and expression.

Through countless conversations over the years, many of which lasted well into the night, I discovered that most of my students were enchanted by the experience of *Shabbat*. Often trapped in their concerns for developing their personal relationships and beginning their careers, these young people found that *Shabbat* offered them the opportunity to tap into their deeper and more spiritual selves.

My contact with alumni, however, revealed that once they left their study programs, *Shabbat* sometimes turned into a bittersweet occurrence. The blissful and meaningful *Shabbat* experiences they had shared in their communities of learning often were not replicated elsewhere. While the students were able to provide the external signs of *Shabbat*—wearing special clothes, eating *Shabbat* foods, singing *Shabbat* songs—they were unable to supply the content to replicate the meaningful *Shabbat* conversations that we had once shared.

This book is really for them or for anyone else who has ever had the experience—either late on a Friday night, or on *Shabbat* day, or as *Shabbat* is about to depart—of yearning for the special thoughts and connections with others that only *Shabbat* seems able to offer. It was written with a deep sense of gratitude for everything that my students have given to me and my family during the last fifteen years. You have enhanced our *Shabbat* table; I hope that this enriches yours.

Many people assisted in bringing this book to its present stage.

First of all, I am grateful for the wisdom and caring of my teachers and colleagues—Dov Berkovits and Meir Schweiger from Pardes, and Aharon Botzer and Gabi Nachmani from Livnot.

Deborah Shapira, Tovah Leah Nachmani, and Valerie Feldman provided thoughtful editing. Yehoshua Rubin offered inspiring stories. Sara Heitler carefully proofread. Mick Weinstein edited many sections and prepared the glossary.

Words cannot express my gratitude and deep respect for the book's final editor, Shira Pasternak Be'eri, whose insights, professionalism, and sense of humor all proved to be invaluable.

Most of all, *Todah* to those closest to me who waited patiently while I sat and thought and typed: my children—Shachar, Ma'ayan, Amichai, Yaniv, Ra'aya, and Lilach—and my wife, the most special of women, Sara Yehudit.

Aryeh Ben David

Introduction

The pace and pressures of the work week often do not afford us the freedom to discuss essential or personal questions. In his book, *The Sabbath*, Abraham Joshua Heschel described life as a "tempestuous ocean of time and toil in which there are islands of stillness." "The island," he wrote, "is the seventh day, *Shabbat*, a day of detachment from things, instruments, and practical affairs, as well as of attachment to the spirit."

Yet sometimes the opportunity to reclaim this "island of time" is not fully realized. Sometimes, the splendor of *Shabbat* fades. Small-talk and sluggish fatigue surround the *Shabbat* table, instead of engaging dialogue and revitalizing conversation. Despite our best intentions, the lack of time and sufficient resources may preclude in-depth grappling with more significant and meaningful issues.

This book is intended to serve as a springboard for more personally stimulating and meaningful *Shabbat* conversations. The ideas presented are designed for Jewish adults of all backgrounds and religious denominations. They reflect a philosophy that the Torah belongs to and should be accessible to all Jews, whatever they think or believe, wherever they may be. Each unit can be read directly at the *Shabbat* table. No prior knowledge or preparation is necessary.

In this book, each weekly *parsha* (Torah portion) is divided into three independent sections, one for each of the three *Shabbat* meals.

The three sections reflect the different moods that characterize each of the three traditional *Shabbat* meals:

1. The first *Shabbat* meal (Friday night) focuses on a central theme stemming from the week's *parsha*.

2. The second *Shabbat* meal (Saturday lunch) discusses a human quality or an aspect of interpersonal behavior that emerges from the *parsha*.

3. The third *Shabbat* meal (*Seuda Shlishit*) retells an anecdote—historical or fictional—related to an event in the *parsha*.

Each of the three sections for each *parsha* is followed by a series of trigger questions, designed to encourage further reflection around the *Shabbat* table. The first question is of an intellectual nature and directly explores the section that precedes it. The second question attempts to expand on the topic being discussed. The third question is of a personal nature, affording readers the opportunity to internalize and reflect upon the topic of discussion. It reflects the belief that a person's engagement with Judaism and Torah should not be an exclusively intellectual endeavor; rather, it should involve his or her entire being.

Genesis

Bereshit

FRIDAY NIGHT MEAL: Who Am I?

The individual's search for fulfillment in life begins with the question: "Who am I?" What is the nature of a human being? What constitutes the essence of a person's uniqueness? Is it the power to think, the ability to create, the capacity of speech, the quality of decision-making and free will? Every civilization in history, consciously or subconsciously, has attempted to answer these questions and thereby construct its society. What is the Jewish answer to the question: Who am I?

The two stories of creation address this basic question, the question of all questions.

"And God created humanity in His image, in the image of God He created him, male and female He created them" (Genesis 1:27).

The human being was created in God's image. But what is God's image? Does an incorporeal, transcendent God have an image? How does this expression—God's image—help us understand our own true nature? Does the Torah ever describe qualities of God from which we can infer human qualities?

Since humanity is created in God's image, any insight gleaned from the ways of God will shed light upon the image, the true nature, of humanity. Although the Torah never defines God's image, already in the first chapter, glimpses into God's ways are revealed. First of all, God is a creator—not a random or whimsical creator but one who carefully constructs, assesses, and evaluates the final product. "And God saw everything that He had done, and it was very good . . ." (Genesis 1:31).

An examination of God's creative process reveals another insight into God's—and consequently man's—image. Why did it take God six days to create the world? All of the world could have been created in one moment; why did God separate creation into six discrete units? A closer look reveals a divine plan:

DAY:	CREATION:		DAY:	CREATION:
1	Light and Darkness	→	4	Sun, Moon, Stars
2	Sky and Waters	→	5	Birds and Fish
3	Land	→	6	Animals and Man

In fact, the six days of creation are comprised of two parallel sets of three days. During the first set of three days, God created the domains that would then become filled by their respective creations during the succeeding three days. For example, the second day was created with the awareness of, and in preparation for, the imminent creation of the fifth day. The world was not created in six days because of God's limitations, but rather to allow us another glimpse of God's image and consequently our own. The present is the basis for the future; for creation to become "very good," one must be patient and plan ahead.

The second version of the story of creation presents a different answer to the question: "Who am I?" "And the Lord God formed humanity from the dust of the ground and blew into him the breath of life, and man became a living soul" (Genesis 2:7). The human being is thus the composite of two opposite elements: dust and soul. There are two distinct and rival forces within every individual, two voices struggling to be heard, to gain control. The "dust" component represents the physical, mortal dimension: "... because you are dust and to dust you will return" (Genesis 3:19). This is the physical drive that primarily seeks self-satisfaction in the present or immediate future. The "dust" voice is expressed in the bodily needs of eating, sleeping, survival, and reproduction. This drive is interested in self-gratification and seeks "to take" from the world.

The "soul" voice, however, conveys a radically different message. The soul, the spiritual dimension of a human being, is both intangible and eternal and hence not subject to the ongoing demands of the body. Because of its independence from the daily vicissitudes of life, the "soul" voice continuously instructs the individual to strive to consider the greater picture and not that of his or her own needs. The soul encourages us not to take from, but to contribute to the greater welfare of all concerned, for all time.

Thus, according to the second account of creation, the human being's essence is inherently in conflict, two voices vying for satisfaction, operating within a set of utterly disparate concerns.

To relieve the perpetual tension between these two voices, some religions have allowed one of these components to completely overpower the other, listening to one voice alone. Yet both of these voices were created by God, and both possess the potential to be "very good." Ideally, neither voice is nullified, neither voice is crushed. Rather, the soul instructs the drives of the body as to how to best fulfill themselves, so that they will contribute positively to the continual creation of a world that will be deemed to be "very good."

According to the second account of creation, the essence of humanity is continually in conflict, forever challenged to resolve this tension in a positive manner. The escape from this tension is an escape from one's very humanness.

When these two chapters are considered together, the Torah's answer to the question of questions—who am I?—is both exceptionally optimistic and challenging. Charged with the mission of continuing the process of creation, the individual's grappling with these varied elements will determine whether this creation will ultimately merit being judged as "very good."

The process of self-fulfillment begins with the knowledge and awareness of what is self. This is where the Torah begins.

Around the *Shabbat* Table

1. Eventually, in the course of human history, someone inevitably would have eaten from the Tree of Knowledge of Good and Evil, precipitating humanity's expulsion from the Garden of Eden. Why would God have wanted us to leave paradise? What might Adam and Eve have been thinking as they left the Garden of Eden?

2. After eating from the forbidden tree, Adam and Eve hid from God. What does this tell us about humanity's natural response to sin, to failure? Why did God—who clearly knew where they were—ask them where they were, instead of punishing them immediately?

3. When you consider other cultures, past and present (e.g., ancient Greece, Renaissance Europe, Communist Russia, etc.), how do you think that they would have answered the questions: "Who am I?," "What is the essence of a human being?" and "How can the individual become fulfilled?" How would your society answer this question?

SHABBAT LUNCH: Aggression

The first story of humanity outside the Garden of Eden features the violent murder of Abel at the hand of his brother, Cain. In a painfully tragic manner, the Torah informs us of what life "in the real world" is. In this poignant story of the first generation born of man and woman, the Torah implies that beneath this brutal crime lies perhaps the most basic and dangerous model of human behavior.

Why did Cain kill his brother? What precipitated his aggression?

Cain became distraught when God accepted Abel's sacrifice while his own was rejected. A close reading of the verse reveals that whereas Abel brought from the first (*m'bchorot*) and most choice (*m'chelveihen*) animals in his sacrifice, Cain simply brought from "the fruits of the ground," neither the first nor the best fruits. God, in need of neither fruits nor animals, responded to the intention behind the offering and accepted Abel's animals but was displeased with Cain's.

When God saw Cain's anger and disappointment at his rejection, God invited him to examine his actions: "Why are you upset? . . . if you do well [improve your intentions and actions] you will be raised up, and if you will not do well, then sin will be awaiting you at your doorstep" (Genesis 4:7). What was God trying to convey to Cain through these questions? From God's response we can infer the source of Cain's despair.

What was at the root of Cain's despair? His *comparison* of himself with Abel, his brother. Comparing oneself to others lies at the root of a negative self-image and may lead to feelings of failure. God was trying to impel Cain to examine his own actions and improve them, instead of judging himself in the light of his brother.

The story of Cain and Abel is both the story of the first generation of humanity and that of every generation of humanity. As soon as there are two people in the world, the danger of destructive comparison exists. Determining one's own self-worth by means of comparison to another inevitably results in despair. There will always be someone whose talents surpass one's own. The success of others will always taste bittersweet. This frustration, left unchecked, will in due time be expressed in some form of anger and aggression.

Cain compared, became frustrated with himself, and then, unwilling to accept his own shortcomings, lashed out at the source of his frustration, his brother, Abel.

Disregarding God's admonition, Cain rises up and kills Abel. Once again, God responds with a question, imploring Cain to take responsibility for his actions. "Where is Abel your brother?" (Genesis 4:9). Once again, Cain does not look inward, does not accept his own personal accountability and admit that he has murdered his brother. Instead, he attempts to evade his culpability and utters the epic lines: "I don't know. Am I my brother's keeper?" (Genesis 4:9). At this point, perhaps realizing the futility of teaching Cain the lesson of accepting responsibility, God unleashes a fury of curses and punishments upon him. Cain is condemned to be "a fugitive and a vagabond," wandering homelessly from place to place, always dependent upon someone to care for him. He will now have to beseech others (his metaphorical brothers) to take care of him, learning, it is hoped, from their example that he needs to become "his brother's keeper."

The *tikkun* (correction) of Cain's mistake is noted much later in the Torah, when Moses' older brother, Aaron, recognizes and accepts his younger brother's leadership. This brotherly harmony is the first step in the creation of the Jewish people, signifying the first stage in the rebuilding of paradise.

Around the *Shabbat* Table

1. Is it possible to refrain from comparing ourselves to other people?

2. Maimonides wrote that "one who receives honor through the failure of another—forfeits his place in the world to come" (Laws of Repentance 3:14). When should we receive honor?

3. Have you ever been in situations/projects/groups that have precluded competition with others? How is this possible?

Seuda Shlishit: The Story of the Turkey-Prince

Rebbe Nachman of Bratslav (1772–1811) was the great-grandson of the founder of *hasidut*, the Ba'al Shem Tov. Unlike other hasidic dynasties, he had no successor, and his followers continue to regard him as their sole Rebbe. Rebbe Nachman and his followers emphasized the centrality of faith and prayer in Judaism. His works, especially his stories, are known for their layers of meaning—they can be understood on a number of levels, from the simple to the mystical. One interpretation of the following story reflects the ideas presented in the earlier section, "Bereshit: Who Am I?"

Once the King's son went mad. He thought he was a turkey. He felt compelled to sit under the table without any clothes on, pulling at bits of bread and bones like a turkey. None of the doctors could do anything to help him or cure him, and they gave up in despair. The King was very sad.

One day, a Wise Man came and said, "I can cure him."

What did the Wise Man do? He took off all *his* clothes, sat down naked under the table next to the king's son, and also began to nibble at the crumbs and bones.

The Prince asked him, "Who are you and what are you doing here?"

"And what are *you* doing here?" he replied.

"I am a turkey," said the Prince.

"Well, I'm also a turkey," said the Wise Man.

The two of them sat there together like this for some time, until they were used to one another.

Then the Wise Man gave a sign, and they threw them shirts. The Wise Man-Turkey said to the King's son, "Do you think a turkey can't wear a shirt? You can wear a shirt and still be a turkey." The two of them put on shirts.

After a while he gave another sign, and they threw them some trousers. Again the Wise Man said, "Do you think if you wear trousers you can't be a turkey?" They put on the trousers.

One by one they put on the rest of their clothes in the same way.

Afterwards, the Wise Man gave a sign, and they brought human food from the table. The Wise Man said to the Prince, "Do you think if you eat good food you can't be a turkey anymore? You can eat this food and still be a turkey." They ate.

Then he said to him, "Do you think a turkey has to sit *under* the table? You can be a turkey and sit up at the table."

This was how the Wise Man dealt with the Prince, until in the end he cured him completely.

Around the *Shabbat* Table

1. Who is the "Wise Man?" Who is the Prince?

2. What did the "Wise Man" understand that all of the King's advisers did not? Why do you think that the Prince wanted to believe that he was a turkey?

3. Is there a part of each of us that reflects "turkey-like" or "wise-man-like" behavior? (See "Bereshit: Who Am I?")

Noach

FRIDAY NIGHT MEAL: Despair and Beauty

After the destruction of the world, God promises Noah that He will never cause another flood of such proportions. God makes a covenant with Noah and all of his future descendants that henceforth, He will never destroy humanity. But, apparently, the promise alone is not enough to comfort Noah. In addition, God offers Noah a sign: the rainbow.

Why is there a need for a physical sign to affirm this covenant between God and Noah? Why is the rainbow chosen as that sign? What is special about a rainbow?

The commentaries on the Torah struggle with this question and raise a number of possibilities. Some commentators understand the uniqueness of the rainbow in its physical qualities. A rainbow occurs only if sunshine permeates the water held by a cloud. Thus, the trepidation over an impending flood is allayed by the rainbow, as it signifies that rays of sunlight are commingling with the rain. When a rainbow appears, the ominous clouds do not obscure the sun; rather, they become vessels for its regenerative light.

A different explanation is offered by Ramban (Nachmanides), a French commentator of the twelfth century. He explains that the rainbow resembles a bow used by hunters or warriors. He writes that when combating parties wanted to signal the end of a war, they would turn their bows to face themselves. Thus, the rainbow actually serves as God's bow, turned against Himself—a divine symbol of peace.

In addition to the physical attributes of a rainbow and its unique shape, there is another significant quality at its essence: its beauty.

The beauty of the rainbow is almost mystically hypnotizing in its nature. Universally, people's eyes open wider and their jaws seem to drop when they look at a rainbow. Rainbows evoke moments of serenity, moments devoted solely to the observation of their transcendent beauty. The beauty of the rainbow seems to stand apart from the timeless debate over the nature of beauty—whether beauty is objective or subjective.

Why was Noah given this sign of such otherworldly beauty?

The power of beauty, writes the Talmud (*Berakhot* 57b), is to expand one's vision of the universe, to expand one's mind. Beauty shatters the shackles of an imperfect reality and engenders dreams of optimism, dreams of abounding splendor and unconditional love. The rainbow, possessing the spectrum of all colors, serves as the basis for all beauty. All potential forms of visual beauty are simply new arrangements of the colors of the rainbow.

Noah exits the ark. He sees a world of utter desolation. Every person, every tree, every flower has been destroyed. How will he be able to continue? How will he be able to start anew? The vision of a destroyed world robs Noah of any ability to act. The fear exists that he will become enervated, empty, and overwhelmed with despair.

The rainbow is God's gift to Noah. Through its beauty, God seals the new covenant with humanity and motivates Noah to begin to create a new world. It is not only a sign precluding future destruction but is also an invitation to hope. When a person loses hope, he can only look down and await a grave. Noah is summoned to look up, to return to life, to return to hope.

Around the *Shabbat* Table

1. In 1907, at the inaugural ceremony of the Betzalel Art College in Jerusalem, Rav Kook, the future chief rabbi of Israel, said:

    Jerusalem['s history] . . . has been prolonged and stormy. . . . Many of the weak-hearted have lost hope for her life. Now she (Jerusalem) is demanding beauty and works of art. Practical men will say that perhaps this is not the proper moment—that there are priorities and more essential needs. Yes, perhaps, there are needs, but this demand comes from Jerusalem's heart . . . it is itself a sign of life, a sign of hope for salvation and comfort.

    Has any work (or works) of beauty provided you with "a sign of hope?"

2. Is it possible for a society to place too great an emphasis on art? Should any boundaries be placed on works of art?

3. What is the most beautiful thing that you have ever seen? What was its effect upon you?

SHABBAT LUNCH: Indifference

The whole world is destroyed and Noah does not utter a single word.

Perhaps Noah can be forgiven for not saving all of humanity; not everyone, after all, has the ability to influence a society. But Noah does not manage to rescue even a single individual—not a neighbor, not a friend, not one relative. Moreover, Noah expresses no signs of pain or remorse over humanity's calamity. Unlike Abraham, who beseeches God not to consume the evil cities of Sodom and

Gomorra, Noah, true to his name (in Hebrew: comfort or rest), silently acquiesces to God's plan of destruction.

The *parsha* of *Kedoshim* (Leviticus 19:16) teaches that it is forbidden "to stand on the blood of your neighbor," to remain passive while another human life is being threatened. The Talmud (*Sanhedrin* 73a) understands this "standing" to imply that it is forbidden to "withstand," or to control oneself, when the blood (life) of one's neighbor is endangered.

The Talmud offers several applications of this principle: "What is the source commanding that if one sees a person drowning in a river or being attacked by a wild animal or robbers, one is obligated to save him? The Torah states, 'One cannot stand on the blood of one's neighbor.'" The midrash adds that from this source we also learn that it is forbidden to withhold testimony and that one is legally proscribed from remaining silent. Maimonides writes that one is not only physically obligated to intervene to save another but must also financially contribute to saving another.

The question arises: "To what degree of personal danger must I subject myself in order to save someone else?" According to the Talmud Yerushalmi (*Beit Joseph, Hoshen Mishpat* 426), one is even obligated to jeopardize one's own life in order to save another. Support for this idea is the talmudic saying: "Anyone who saves one person, it is as if s/he has saved a whole world" (*Sanhedrin* 4:5). Jewish law considers the saving of another life to be Judaism's premier mitzvah. The laws of the holiest day of the year, Yom Kippur, are not only overruled in order to save a life, but even if someone is dying or on the verge of death, (in almost all cases) every effort must be made to extend the person's life. With rare exception, one additional moment of life supersedes all of Jewish law.

Even if one is not in the position to actually rescue others in need, the Talmud posits that one is not exempt from identifying with their suffering. "Anyone who is able to request mercy for the sake of another and does not, has sinned" (*Berakhot* 12b).

In this week's *parsha*, Noah only speaks up after one of his sons compromises his dignity (Genesis 9:25). When Noah is personally affronted, he does not hesitate to act. While the world was being destroyed, we find no evidence of Noah acting, talking, or praying on behalf of the rest of humanity.

This quality of indifference to the suffering of others is not present in the figure of Noah alone. Rather, Noah represents an enduring personality archetype, a "Noah-personality." The "voice of Noah," a voice of inaction in light of the pain of others, exists within each person. Sometimes we succeed in controlling this voice, and sometimes this voice controls us. The Torah presents the "voice of Noah" as an eternal challenge.

Around the *Shabbat* Table

1. The Torah refers to Noah as the "righteous man *of his generation.*" How is Noah a product of, and similar to, the people of his generation?

2. In this *parsha*, Noah does not speak up about the corruption of his society. Do you think that people are naturally indifferent or compassionate to the suffering of others? How can one educate toward concern?

3. Do you know someone who is the antithesis of a "Noah-personality?" Someone who is consistently a voice of action, seeking to improve the plight of others?

Seuda Shlishit: Bontshe the Silent

Isaac Leib Peretz (1852–1915) was one of the founders of modern Yiddish literature. He was known for his rich imagination and original ideas. "Bontshe the Silent" (1894) stands as one of his classic stories:

Here, in this world below, the death of Bontshe produced no impression whatever. In vain you will ask: "Who was Bontshe? How did he live? What did he die of? Was it his heart that burst, his strength that gave out?" No one knows.

Had a horse fallen down in the street, people would have displayed much more interest than they did in the case of this poor man.

Bontshe lived quietly, and quietly died; like a shadow he passed over the face of the earth. At the ceremony of his circumcision no wine was drunk and no clinking of glasses was heard. He lived like some dull grain of sand on the seashore, disappearing among the millions of its kind. And when the wind at last carried him off to the other side, no one noticed. In his lifetime the soil of the roads never maintained the impression of his footsteps, and after his death the wind swept away the small board over his grave. The grave-digger's wife found it at some distance from the grave and made a fire with it to boil a pot of potatoes.

He left behind neither child nor property. He lived miserably, and miserably he died.

Who knows how long he will remain undisturbed in his grave? Born quietly, he lived in silence, died in silence, and was buried in an even greater silence.

But it was not thus in the other world. There, the death of Bontshe produced a deep impression, a veritable sensation. The bugle-call of the Messiah, the sound of the *shofar*, was heard throughout the seven heavens: "Bontshe the Silent has died." Broad-winged angels flew about, announcing to each other that Bontshe had been summoned to appear before the Seat of Supreme Judgment. In Paradise, there was noise and excitement, and one could hear the joyful shout: "Bontshe the Silent! Just think of it! Bontshe the Silent!"

Very young angels, with eyes of diamonds, gold-threaded wings, wearing silver slippers, rushed out, full of joy, to meet Bontshe. The buzzing of their wings, the clatter of their slippers, and the merry laughter of their little mouths filled the heavens and reached the throne of the Most High. God Himself knew that Bontshe was coming.

Two angels were rolling an armchair of pure gold for Bontshe. Whence this luminous flash of light? It was a golden crown, set with the most precious stones, that they were carrying—for Bontshe.

"But has the Supreme Court pronounced judgment?!" asked the astonished saints, not without a tinge of jealousy.

"Bah!" replied the angels, "that will only be a formality. Against Bontshe, even the prosecution himself will not find a word to say. The case will not last five minutes. Don't you know who Bontshe is? He is of some importance, this Bontshe."

When the little angels seized Bontshe in mid-air, played a sweet tune to him, when the Patriarch Abraham shook hands with him as if he had been an old comrade, when he learned that his chair was ready for him in Paradise and that a crown was waiting for his head, that before the celestial tribunal not one superfluous word would be spoken in his case, Bontshe, as once upon earth, was frightened into silence. He was sure that it could only be a dream from which he would soon awaken, or simply a mistake.

Full of fear, he did not even hear the Head of the Court call out in a loud voice: "The case of Bontshe the Silent!" He did not hear how, after handing over a dossier to the counsel for the defense, the President had commanded: "Read, but briefly." All around Bontshe the whole hall seemed to be turning. A muffled noise reached his ears, but in the midst of the din he began to distinguish more clearly and sharply the voice of the angelic advocate—a voice as sweet as a violin:

"His name," the voice was saying, "suited him even as a gown made by an artist's hand suits a graceful body."

"What is he talking about?" Bontshe asked himself.

"Never," continued the advocate, "never has he uttered a complaint against God or men. Never has a spark of hatred flamed up in his eyes, never has he lifted his eyes with pretensions to heaven."

Again Bontshe failed to understand what it was all about.

"Job succumbed, but Bontshe has suffered more than Job. He was circumcised on the eighth day, and the clumsy doctor could not stop the blood. He was always silent, even at the age of thirteen when his mother died and a stepmother, a serpent, a wicked woman, came in her place."

"Perhaps, after all, he means me," thinks Bontshe to himself.

"She used to begrudge him a piece of bread; threw him a few three-day-old musty crusts and a mouthful of meat, while she herself drank coffee with cream. He was always miserable and alone, had no friends, no schooling, no religious instruction, no decent clothes, and not a minute of rest. He was silent even later, when his own father, the worse for drink, seized him by the hair and threw him out of the house on a bitterly cold and stormy winter night. At work, he never calculated how many pounds he was carrying for a farthing, how often he stumbled for a penny and how many errands he had to run, how many times he almost breathed his last breath when going to collect his pay. He was always silent. He was silent even when people haggled for his pay, knocked off something from it, or slipped a counterfeit coin into his hand. He was always silent!"

"Then, after all, it is me that they mean," Bontshe consoled himself.

"He was silent even when his employer became bankrupt and neglected to pay his wages. He was silent when his wife ran away from him, leaving him alone with an infant. He was silent even fifteen years later, when the same child grew up and threw his father out of his own house."

"They mean me, they mean me!" Bontshe thought joyfully.

"He was silent in his death agony, he was silent in his last hour. Never did he utter a word against God, never a word against man. I have spoken," concluded the defending angel.

Bontshe began to tremble. He knew that after the speech for the defense, it was the turn of the prosecution. "What will the prosecuting counsel say now?" Bontshe did not remember his life. Who knows what the prosecuting angel will recall?

"Gentlemen judges," began a strident, incisive, and stinging voice— but stopped short.

"Gentlemen," he began again, this time more softly, but once more he interrupted himself.

And at last, very softly, a voice issued from the throat of the accuser: "Gentlemen judges! He was silent. I, too, shall be silent."

Profound silence fell over the assembly. Then from above a new soft, sweet, and trembling voice was heard: "Bontshe, my child, Bontshe, my well-beloved child."

And Bontshe's heart began to weep for joy. He would have liked to raise his eyes, but they were dimmed by tears. Never in his life had he felt such joy in weeping.

"My child," continued the Head of the Celestial Tribunal, "you have suffered everything in silence. Down below on earth they never understand such things. You yourself were not aware of your power; you did not know that you could cry and that your cries would have caused the very walls of Jericho to tremble and tumble down. You yourself did not know what strength lay hidden in you. Down below your silence was not rewarded, but down below is the world of falsehood, while here in heaven in the world of truth, here you will reap your true reward.

"The supreme Tribunal will never pass sentence against you; it will never judge and condemn you, nor will it mete out to you such and such a reward. Everything here belongs to you; take whatever your heart desires."

For the first time Bontshe ventured to lift his eyes. Everything was sparkling, everything around him was flashing.

"Really?" he asked, still doubting and embarrassed.

"Yes, really," replied the Head of the Celestial Tribunal; "verily everything here is yours; everything in heaven belongs to you."

"Really?" Bontshe asked again, but this time his voice sounded more firm and assured.

"Certainly, certainly, certainly," he was assured on all sides.

"Then, if such is the case," said Bontshe with a happy smile, "What I'd like most of all is a warm roll with fresh butter every morning."

The judges and angels dropped their heads in shame, while Satan, the accuser, burst out into loud laughter.

Around the *Shabbat* Table

1. Why did the "accuser" laugh?

2. Why didn't Bontshe dream of asking for more? Do you think that he should have?

3. Do you think that there is a similarity between Bontshe and Noah? Is there a "Bontshe voice" in all of us? What does it ask for?

Lekh-Lekha

FRIDAY NIGHT MEAL: *Aliyah* and *Yerida*

Not long after their historic journey from their original homeland to Canaan, Abraham and Sarah leave Israel for Egypt:" ...
because the famine was very severe in the land." Perhaps the famine was great, but were they justified in leaving the land to which
God had brought them? God had already promised to give this land
to their offspring. Should Abraham and Sarah have remained in Israel?

They receive no divine guidance. The dilemma remains: how
could they decide to leave God's chosen land, yet, how could they
possibly remain in Israel during the hardship of the famine?

The commentators are divided in their appraisal of Abraham and
Sarah's actions:

The Ramban (Nachmanides) writes "know, that our patriarch
Abraham unintentionally sinned a great sin in leaving Israel, because
God would have redeemed him from the famine. Because of this act
[of leaving Israel and going down to Egypt] God decreed that his
descendants would go down to Egypt and become enslaved by

Pharaoh." According to the Ramban (and the mystical work the *Zohar*), Abraham should have exhibited a greater level of faith in God's powers to save him. Beyond the reality of the famine, there exists a greater reality, namely, God's benevolent providence, which ultimately controls and determines everything that happens on earth.

According to the Ramban, although Abraham did not receive any direction from God, he should have risen to the level in which he understood that all of existence is simply a vehicle for God's communication to humanity. In short, this experience was a test by God of Abraham, and Abraham failed.

Rashi and other commentators understand the test by God and Abraham's response to it in a completely different light. According to them (and corroborated by the language of the verse), the famine was of epic proportions. Certainly, Abraham was justified in leaving the land; God does not demand that one rely continually on miracles. Rather, the test was: after his heroic journey to Israel, would Abraham complain or resent God for not rewarding him with an easier life in Israel?

How would Abraham cope with this disappointment? Would he rail against God: "You, God, told me to leave my country and promised to give this land to me and my children, but what do we receive instead—endless suffering!!! Why do those who fulfill Your will have to undergo such misfortune and agony?!"

These commentators understand that Abraham and Sarah successfully passed God's test. Not a word of bitterness is uttered. Abraham accepts that the harshness of reality does not eclipse the truth of God's promises; momentary setbacks cannot deny God's eternal word.

Was their leaving Israel a catastrophic failure of belief in God's miracles or a profound acceptance of God's mysterious ways?

Perhaps both views are true. Perhaps the debate between these two schools of thought actually occurred in Abraham's mind. Could he possibly have acted with absolute certainty when there are apparently two diverse paths that both possess a measure of truth?

What transpires in every believing person's mind when the path of action is unclear? When there is no direct correspondence between acts and rewards in this life, when there is no definitive guidance for most of our decisions, which path should we take?

At the very outset of his life as the first Jew, Abraham is left to deliberate and struggle over what is demanded of him. Whatever decision he reached, the choice to continue despite this lack of clarity may be his greatest achievement.

Around the *Shabbat* Table

1. Which of these two interpretations of Abraham and Sarah's actions do you support more?

2. The Talmud notes three valid reasons for an extended absence from Israel:
    *   to make a living
    *   to learn Torah
    *   to marry

    Why do you think that these three reasons were singled out?

3. Do you think that Jews living outside of Israel still struggle with Abraham and Sarah's dilemma? Do you identify with their struggle?

SHABBAT LUNCH: Leadership

A leader is chosen. Abraham (presently called Abram) is selected by God to become the first patriarch of the Jewish people.

Why was Abraham chosen? What was special about Abraham?

Unlike the Torah's introduction of Noah, who was described as a "righteous man, pure, and walking with God" (Genesis 6:9), virtually no mention is made of Abraham's qualities prior to his being chosen.

Now the Lord said to Abram, "*Leck Lecka* —Leave your land, your community, and your home, and go to the land that I will show you. I will make of you a great nation, and I will bless you, and make your name great, and you will be a blessing. I will bless those that bless you, and curse whoever curses you, and in you will all the families of the earth be blessed." So Abram departed, as the Lord had spoken to him. . . . [Genesis 12:1–4].

First of all, Abraham was a visionary, an idealist. He was capable of envisioning a world totally beyond his immediate reality. When God spoke with him and commanded him to go to Canaan, Abraham was a 75-year-old man with a wife but no children. Nevertheless, he could imagine becoming the father of "a great nation" in which "all the families of the earth would be blessed." Commentaries speculate that God did not talk only with Abraham—perhaps everyone in the world heard this message. Yet, everyone else disregarded the voice they heard; everyone else discounted the call of "*lekh lekha*" (leave) and the idea of changing the world. Abraham did not know the destination of his journey, nor how God's promises would be fulfilled; nevertheless, he woke up and heeded the requests that seemingly defied rational thought.

Second, in order to fulfill God's designs, Abraham was capable of transcending normal human needs and desires. The commentators note that God's first request of Abraham is worded in seemingly inverted order. He is told to leave his land, then his community, and finally his home. The commentators explain that the Torah is not presenting a geographic movement, rather an emotional one. The progression in the verse—land to community to home—describes increasingly deep emotional attachments. To fulfill this promise of "in you will all the families of the earth be blessed," Abraham must be willing to subordinate his personal emotions and bonds.

Moreover, Abraham is willing to make these sacrifices, knowing that he will most likely not see the fruits of his labors. God promises him that he will become "a great nation." Many generations will transpire before this promise is actualized, longer than several lifetimes. Nevertheless, Abraham perseveres. He begins his journey, believing that the sacrifices he is willing to make will eventually yield invaluable worldwide results.

Although the Torah does not explicitly relate the qualities of Abraham, his essential leadership attributes can be inferred—vision, self-sacrifice, and perseverance. These qualities have become Abraham's legacy for all future generations.

Around the *Shabbat* Table

1. God not only chooses Abraham to become the leader of the Jewish people, but through these promises (of becoming a great nation for the benefit of all of the families of the earth) educates, trains, and eventually develops him into a leader. What qualities would you seek in people whom you want to develop as leaders?

2. Often, parents or grandparents find their sacrifices easier to bear when they witness the benefits that their children or grandchildren gain through their efforts. They give but also receive joy (*naches*) in return. Do you think that you would be able to sacrifice for the benefit of your distant future descendants, whom you may never see?

3. Do you know anyone with "Abraham-like" qualities? Any leaders?

Seuda Shlishit: Three Calls of the *Shofar*

Rav Abraham Isaac Kook (1865–1935) was the first chief Ashkenazic rabbi of modern Israel. A scholar, philosopher, poet, and mystic, his holistic approach to Judaism enabled him to write on such diverse subjects as art, science, athletics, music, politics, and other religions. Universally regarded for his kindness and piety, Rav Kook was one of the spiritual founders of modern religious Zionism.

In the following excerpt, one of Rav Kook's students describes the sermon delivered by Rav Kook on Rosh Hashanah in the Churvah synagogue in the Old City of Jerusalem. Delivered during difficult times, this oration left a lasting impression on all who heard it.

Toward the end of the summer of 1933, the reports from Germany of Hitler's first months in power grew more troubling from day to day. Concurrently, the *yishuv* in Israel was prospering, and immigration from all over central Europe was steadily increasing.

A week before Rosh Hashanah it was announced that Rav Kook would pray in the Churvah synagogue, in the center of the Old City of Jerusalem, and that he would expound holiday themes and current events.

Early on the first morning of Rosh Hashanah, it became apparent that a great many people wished to attend this event. At daybreak we walked the entire length of Jaffa Road. We passed through Jaffa Gate. As we approached the Jewish Quarter, we realized that a vast number of Jews would arrive in the Old City, and a constant stream of small groups poured out of the alleyways and into the main Jewish road. We were swept along by the crowd. The pressure increased in the narrow passageways and finally we burst into the synagogue, packed with people.

In a hushed voice that heightened the tension, he began to speak:

"There are three kinds of *shofars* that may be used on Rosh Hashanah. Preferably, one should blow a ram's horn. If this is impossible, one may use a *shofar* made from the horn of any kosher animal other than a cow. But if neither of these types is available, we blow the horn of an animal that is ritually impure and do so without reciting a blessing. These three classes of *shofar* parallel the three *shofars* of redemption: the great *shofar*, the medium *shofar*, and the small *shofar*.

"The awakening of the nation's desire to be redeemed and to redeem its land is a holy awakening growing out of faith in God and in the sanctity of the Jewish people. It is a response to the great *shofar*. The great and venerable of the nation heard its call and were roused to a love of Zion and a desire to rebuild it. The spiritual insight of these pious ones envisioned the heavenly Jerusalem united with the earthly Jerusalem. They longed to breathe the air of Israel, and for them every particle of dust in the Holy Land contained supreme sanctity. The sound of this great *shofar* brought Nachmanides, Rabbi Judah HaLevi, the disciples of the Vilna Gaon, and the hasidim of the Ba'al Shem Tov to Israel.

"But there is another *shofar* that also calls Jews to ascend to Israel. This is the call to the land of our ancestors, where our forefathers, our prophets, and our kings lived. Here we can live as an independent nation in our homeland; we can raise our children in a Jewish environment. This *shofar*, though smaller than the first one, is also fit for blowing. We recite a blessing when sounding this medium *shofar*."

"But" (and here the Rav burst into tears) "there is also a *shofar* taken from an unclean animal. Our enemies blow this *shofar* to warn the Jews to flee while they can, and to go to Israel. The enemy compels them to redeem themselves by sounding sirens of war and persecuting them without respite. Thus, even the *shofar* of the unclean animal becomes the *shofar* of the Messiah. Those who are deaf to the call of the first and second *shofars* are forced to listen to the sound of this small *shofar*. No blessing is recited when blowing this *shofar*, as 'We do not recite a blessing over a cup of affliction' (*Berakhot* 51b).

"We pray, 'Sound a *great shofar* for our liberation,' asking that God not liberate us by means of the calamitous sounds of the small *shofar*. Even the medium *shofar* is inappropriate for God's people. Rather, we pray for the great *shofar*, the *shofar* of true freedom, of the complete redemption originating in holiness."

Then, clear loud blasts from the great *shofar* rang through the vast hall. The entire congregation quivered and trembled, glowing in anticipation of the *Musaf* prayers. I have never experienced such a prayer since. And every Rosh Hashanah, when the *shofar* is sounded, I recall the Rav's words in the Churvah in the Old City of Jerusalem on that fateful Rosh Hashanah in 1933.

Around the *Shabbat* Table

1. In this week's *parsha*, Abraham journeys to Israel. Which one of these *shofars* do you think that he heard?

2. Rav Kook wrote that the land of Israel is not an extrinsic entity for the Jewish people but rather something essential for our very self-fulfillment, "just like a flower that will grow in many types of soil but will only fully blossom in the soil most appropriate for it, so, too, the Jewish people need the soil of Israel to fully blossom as a nation." Do you agree?

3. There were prominent rabbis who disagreed with Rav Kook's approach to the land, claiming that, by actively working toward creating a Jewish state, he was demonstrating a lack of faith in the natural arrival of the Messiah. What do you think?

Vayera

FRIDAY NIGHT MEAL: The Sin of Sodom

The cities of Sodom and Gomorra were utterly destroyed. What was their crime? What type of behavior could be so heinous as to preclude the possibility of *teshuvah*, of repentance? The Talmud relates that "the people of Sodom and Gomorra have no place in this world, nor in the world to come." What kind of people lived in Sodom and Gomorra?

The Torah does not articulate their transgression. Was it murder or incest or idolatry? Was it some form of excessive cruelty or lust?

The Sodomites' treatment of Abraham's nephew Lot, who welcomed the wayfarers/angels who entered Sodom, is graphically described: "We will deal worse with you than with them [the guests] ... and they [the residents of Sodom] approached to break down the door" (Genesis 19:9). The Talmud explains that the inhabitants of Sodom had enacted a law that no traveler was allowed to enter their city. Lot had broken this law and thus had to be appropriately punished.

The crime of Sodom was inhospitality! Their evil was not reflected in horrible crimes but rather in a rejection of mercy and kindness.

Certainly, every society is free to create its own rules and regulations, but why would a community choose to prohibit welcoming strangers? Why would this be desirable? Why would this be legislated? Why would Lot have chosen to live in such a city?

Last week's *parsha* describes Lot's motivation for choosing to live in Sodom: "And Lot lifted up his eyes and saw that the Jordan plain was utterly lush . . . like a garden of God . . ." (Genesis 13:10). Apparently, before the cities of Sodom and Gomorra were destroyed, they resembled paradise. They had everything, "like a garden of God," an echo of the garden of Eden. Sodom and Gomorra were "the lap of luxury," yet they were also evil.

The mishnah of *Pirkei Avot* (Ethics of the Fathers) denotes four categories of behavior:

> He who says "What is mine is mine, and what is yours is yours" is the average type, though some say this is a quality of Sodom;
>> He who says "What is mine is yours, and what is yours is mine" is ignorant;
>> He who says "What is mine is yours and what is yours is yours" is righteous;
>> He who says: "What is yours is mine and what is mine is mine" is wicked. [5:13]

The quality of Sodom was simply: What is mine is mine and what is yours is yours—a state of aloofness; codified indifference to the plight of the less fortunate, an addiction to a society's proper "order." The quality of *din*, of judgment, is rooted in maintaining order. The quality of *rachamim*, of mercy or kindness, is rooted in *not* simply accepting the existing order of society and thus helping those who, at first glance, may not be worthy or deserving of help.

This story of Sodom and Gomorra stands in stark contrast to the first story of this week's *parsha*, that of Abraham welcoming in three wayfaring strangers. The qualities of mercy and judgment create two vastly different societies:

ABRAHAM:	SODOM:
1. Abraham possesses practically nothing and sits by his tent.	1. The inhabitants of Sodom dwell in resplendent luxury inside their houses.
2. Abraham welcomes in the three wayfarers.	2. The inhabitants of Sodom refuse to allow the guests to lodge overnight.
3. Sarah, his wife, immediately responds to the travelers' needs.	3. Lot's wife looks back at Sodom while departing, apparently unable to separate herself from everything that it represents.
4. Sarah is informed that, despite her advanced age, she will miraculously become pregnant.	4. Lot's wife is miraculously turned into a pillar of salt.

The rabbis comment that in life there are two kinds of tests: the test of wealth and the test of poverty. The test of wealth is considered to be more difficult. Opening up one's doors to share with others signifies that one controls one's desire for possessions, that one is not enslaved to them.

On Passover, we open our doors in hopes that Elijah the prophet will summon us into the messianic age. This vision of the end of days began with Abraham's opening up his home in this week's *parsha*.

Around the *Shabbat* Table

1. Unlike almost every other human endeavor, the laws regulating the practice of welcoming guests are not standardized in Judaism. No guidelines or limitations are presented. Why?

2. How can one tell if his or her possessions do or do not "control him or her"? How does one draw the line between dangerous, self-corrupting materialism and genuine pride or care for one's hard-earned possessions?

3. What was your most memorable experience as a guest? As a host?

SHABBAT LUNCH: Healing

The *parsha* of *Vayera* begins with God's revealing Himself to Abraham. "Then God was revealed to him while he sat at the opening of his tent, in the heat of the day, amidst the trees of Mamre" (Genesis 18:1). Mysteriously, this verse, the first of the *parsha*, never mentions Abraham by name. Encouraged to look for the antecedent of the "him" of our verse, we must return to the final verses of last week's *parsha*, where Abraham is reported to have circumcised himself and the men of his house.

The Talmud sees a causative connection between these two events and suggests that God revealed Himself to Abraham as a result of his circumcision. States the Talmud, "It was the third day [the most painful] after Abraham's circumcision, and God visited him to see how he was feeling" (*Bava Metziah* 86b). Explains a second section of Talmud (*Sotah* 14a), "What is the intention of the verse: 'And you should walk in His way'? Does God have a physical way? Rather, you should imitate His qualities." At the beginning of this week's *parsha* we learn one of these qualities of God: visiting the sick.

What are the guidelines for visiting the sick?

1. The visitor should attend to the needs of the patient. When one of his students became ill, Rabbi Akiva washed and swept his floor (*Nedarim* 40a). Even if one is already assured that the patient's needs are being taken care of [by the family at home or the hospital attendants], nevertheless, one is not exempt from visiting.

The actual visit enables one to clarify what the patient may need. In some circumstances, one may fulfill the mitzvah of visiting the sick through a telephone call.

2.   The visitor should try to cheer up the patient, to distract his or her mind from the illness. Thus, one must be careful to attend at the appropriate time [not too early or late in the day] and not to overstay one's visit, so as not to become a burden on the household. However, Jewish law encourages visiting even several times in one day. It is deemed important for the patient not to remain alone, perhaps, dwelling upon his or her condition.

3.   The visitor should pray for the health of the patient and include all of the Jewish people within this prayer.

The Talmud states that the visit removes one-sixtieth of the patient's sickness (*Nedarim* 29b). This reflects the Jewish approach of the interdependence of the well-being of one's physical body and one's emotional/spiritual condition. The hasidic master Rebbe Nachman of Bratzlav remarked frequently that "joy is the great healer."

While a Jew is enjoined to heal him/herself, and the institution of doctors and medicine is advocated in the Torah (Exodus 21:19), the physical disorder may be only the external symptom of a deeper problem or situation. The Talmud (*Pesachim* 56a) writes that "King Hezkiyahu permanently hid the book of healings, and the sages praised him for this action." Commentators note that the "book of healings" was composed of ancient traditions that could heal every sickness. If so, why would someone choose to conceal it?! Was this a cruel abuse of power?

Apparently, there is a danger in being able to cure every sickness. There are also beneficial effects of temporarily undergoing a loss of health. If one simply cures an illness through the taking of pills, and so forth, then one may never seek out its underlying cause. The illness may be a message inviting the patient to fully examine his or her life, and to precipitate more comprehensive modifications.

Similarly, emotional depressions, while reflected in physiological signs, may find their source in a different context entirely. Rav Kook writes that depression is a painful communication from one's innermost being, intended to convey a lack of direction or meaning in one's life. One's innermost voice is demanding a momentary cessation of routine to reexamine one's life and purpose. Not listening to these signs may preclude the possibility of achieving true all-encompassing health.

Immediately following God's visit to Abraham, in the very next verse, Abraham runs to greet the wandering travelers and invites them into his tent. One act of kindness often generates strength and brings about more acts of giving and empathy.

Around the *Shabbat* Table

1. Despite medicine being one of the most respected professions, the Talmud (*Kiddushin* 82a) states (hyperbolically) that "the best of the doctors go to *'gehinnom'* (hell)." What quality among doctors might have motivated the rabbis to say this?

2. The midrash states that Jacob was the first person to become sick before dying. Until then, people passed away suddenly. Can a sickness, even a terminal illness, have positive side effects?

3. Have you ever become ill because of nonphysical influences?

Seuda Shlishit: Caring for the Lonely

Aryeh Levine, a rabbi in pre-state Palestine, was renowned in Jerusalem for his acts of kindness. His son related the following story:

It was my father's practice in the afternoon of every Rosh Chodesh (the first day of the Hebrew month) to place a small parcel under his arm and leave home. At home, we knew that we were not supposed to ask where or why he was going. It was a custom that he maintained for many years.

Once, though, I went with him. As we were walking, a man came over to my father and asked, "How is your relative getting along in the mental hospital?" My father answered, "The Lord be praised," and we continued on our way. "Father," I asked, "what relative do we have in the mental hospital?" Then he told me that once he visited the hospital to recommend that someone be taken in for treatment, and since he was already there he went through the wards, visiting the patients. One man there caught his attention. The poor soul was full of welts and wounds, and, needless to say, my father became interested in him at once.

The other patients explained, "After all, we are all ill, you know, and there are moments when we get wild and even out of control. Then the orderlies restrain us by force, and at times they even hit us. Now, because we all have relatives and families who come and visit us, the orderlies are always a bit afraid to injure us, lest the families complain. That poor fellow over there is the only one here with no family, no relatives at all. So the orderlies really treat him roughly. Whenever they lose their temper, he bears the brunt of it . . ."

Without a word, my father went over to the orderlies and told them that this patient was his relative. From that time on, he remained my father's "relative," and so every Rosh Chodesh he went to visit him and brought him little presents.

Around the *Shabbat* Table

1. Why are acts of kindness performed privately considered to be on a higher spiritual level than acts that are performed publicly?

2. Though a renowned scholar, Rabbi Aryeh Levine is most remembered for his acts of giving. The Kabbalah states that the *gematria* of the word *Torah*, 611, exactly equals that of *g'milut chassadim* (acts of kindness). What do you think the Kabbalah is saying about the nature of Torah?

3. What anonymous act of kindness most stands out in your mind?

Chayei Sarah

FRIDAY NIGHT MEAL: Choosing a Matriarch

How does one search for a matriarch?

Abraham and Sarah were chosen by God. Isaac was born to Abraham and Sarah.

The choice of Isaac's partner is the first human decision in the establishment of the line of the Jewish people. How will Abraham determine who this woman will be?

After Sarah's death, Abraham faces a twofold problem:

1. Who will be an appropriate partner for his son, Isaac?

2. Who will be able to direct the nascent Jewish people during its most critical and formative second and third generations?

Who will be an appropriate partner for Isaac?

In the second chapter of Genesis, the qualities of the ideal partner are described as an *ezer-k'negdo*. *Ezer* means "helper," while *k'negdo* means "corresponding to" or "against." The ideal partner is someone who helps by virtue of being "against," by virtue of being different. Ideal partners are not valued for their similarity to each other but rather for their ability to complement and complete each other. To find the ideal spouse, one must be most acutely aware not of one's strengths but, more important, of one's weaknesses. The ideal partner then supplies the qualities that are lacking.

Isaac's strength was his almost fearless spiritual power. The midrash states that by virtue of Abraham's binding him, Isaac had been transformed into a living sacrifice. He had willingly offered himself to God and then survived. A most poignant midrash states that while Isaac was bound and lying on the altar, the heavens opened up and two tears of angels fell into Isaac's eyes, dimming his vision. Isaac had great perception "into the heavens," though simultaneously, this experience began to diminish his understanding of the puzzling and often contradictory realities of this world.

Rebecca was chosen to be Isaac's wife because she could provide this insight. She had grown up in the corrupt and deceitful home of Laban. In order to survive, she had to be able to distinguish between people's external behavior and their actual intention. Unlike Isaac, who had only been exposed to the truthfulness and integrity of Abraham and Sarah, Rebecca had witnessed deception and trickery daily.

As Isaac's partner, Rebecca's "this worldliness" complemented his spiritual clarity.

Rebecca had to be more than just a partner for Isaac, more than a wife. Rebecca's destiny demanded that she become a matriarch, a leader for all future generations. Rebecca's particular role would be to shape and educate the third generation.

First-generation leaders tend to be great revolutionaries and visionaries, personalities capable of breaking with previous modes of thinking and behavior. Abraham, for example, is compared to the rising sun. Second-generation leaders stabilize these cataclysmic changes; they are predisposed to be personalities of maintenance, forces of constancy devoted to reaffirming the changes of the previous generation. This was, to a great measure, the personality of Isaac.

He repeated the actions of his father. In this *parsha*, he digs the same wells that his father dug and even calls them by the same names that Abraham called them.

In complement to Isaac's inclination toward stability, Rebecca supplies the qualities of creativity and spontaneity. In her first encounter with Abraham's servant, Eliezer, she not only gives him water as he requested but takes the initiative and offers to water his camels. When asked by her father and brother if she is willing to leave and travel to Abraham's home with Eliezer, she does not hesitate for a moment and replies, "I will go."

At the end of the *parsha*, when Rebecca sees Isaac for the first time, she immediately takes a veil and covers herself. This reflects, perhaps, her intuitive understanding that she will, in the future, need to conceal some of her actions from him.

Unlike Abraham and Jacob, who had more than one wife, Isaac has only Rebecca. Paradoxically, especially in light of what will transpire in next week's *parsha*, they are understood to be an example of an ideal couple. They complement and complete each other.

In this *parsha*, a new matriarch is chosen. In next week's *parsha*, we will see that her insight and creativity will be crucial in the raising of Jacob and the direction of the future of the Jewish people.

Around the *Shabbat* Table

1. Can you think of any other examples of historic change in which the visionaries of the first generation were followed by figures devoted to stabilizing these changes? Is there a necessary contradiction between spiritual clarity and this-worldly resourcefulness?

2. Why did the rabbis decide to model the morning service of Shacharit after Abraham and the afternoon service of Mincha after Isaac?

3. On a personal level, what do you believe your strengths and weaknesses to be? What sort of attributes would best complement them?

SHABBAT LUNCH: Mourning

And Sarah died in Kiryat Arba . . . and Abraham came to eulogize
Sarah and to cry for her. [Genesis 23:2]

In this week's *parsha*, Abraham institutes the first rituals of
mourning: delivery of a eulogy and crying for the deceased. The
midrash states that Abraham recited *Aishet Chayil* (which is now
recited every *Shabbat* evening after *Shalom Aleichem*) to recount
Sarah's life. "Who can find a woman of valor? Her worth is greater
than precious jewels" (Proverbs 31:10).

The goal of a eulogy is to open the hearts of the listeners, to
arouse them to cry for the deceased. Isaac Luria, known as the *Ari*,
one of the leading Kabbalists of Tzfat in the sixteenth century, said
that tears represent a watering of the soul, a softening of one's heart.
In the time of the Talmud, professional criers would accompany the
funeral procession, helping to stimulate tears. Lamenting for the
departed was one of the main constituents in the process of the
honoring of the dead.

Nevertheless, while trying to arouse these deep emotions, Jewish law cautions against exaggerated praise for the deceased in a
eulogy (*Shulchan Aruch, Yore Deah* 344:1). One is allowed to highlight and perhaps slightly embellish the virtuous qualities of the
deceased and certainly should not minimize his or her merits, but
an overstated eulogy may raise doubts and elicit cynicism. Ultimately,
the life that the person actually led is his or her legacy, not a fiction-
alized life that he or she might have wanted to lead or that we might
have preferred that he or she had led. The positive points of this
actual life should be emphasized in the eulogy.

Eulogies and the burial represent a turning point in the mourning process. Until then, the family and community are primarily focused on taking care of the deceased, of honoring the dead. After
the eulogies and burial, attention is directed toward the mourners,
to honoring the living. Now, the goal is to both enable the mourn-

ers to directly confront their grief and gradually return to a full active life. To effectuate this transition, two periods of mourning have been instituted: a very intense seven-day period (*shivah*), followed by a less intense thirty-day period of mourning. When one's parent dies, additional restrictions continue during the year after the death.

Jewish law looks negatively upon prolonged or excessive mourning. Though only a callous person does not shed tears and feel heartbroken over the death of a loved one, the mourning period is constructed to enable a person to both confront the loss and to gradually begin to rebuild his or her life. Excessive mourning may result in wallowing in a pessimistic state of hopelessness. After Abraham finished mourning for Sarah, he returned to his active life without delay: he began searching for a wife for his son, Isaac and, at the end of the *parsha*, married once again.

When the Ba'al Shem Tov (the founder of *Hasidut*, 1700–1760) was about to die, he gathered his students around him and said to them, "I am not worried about myself, for I know clearly that I shall go from this door and immediately I shall enter another door." In the Torah, the moment of death is expressed in the phrase: "gathered to his people." Rav Kook writes that one who lives in fear of death has already surrendered to it. Rather, the imminence of death should serve as an impetus to intensify the value and productivity of one's life.

The confrontation with death should engender a revitalized gratitude for life, an intensified dedication to fulfilling one's mission and purpose in this world.

Around the *Shabbat* Table

1. Jewish law prohibits external signs of mourning on *Shabbat*, even while the mourner may be "sitting *shiva*." Why do you think this is so?

2. According to Jewish law, the deceased should be buried in the most simple of white garments. Why?

3. What would you hope is said about you in your eulogy?

Seuda Shlishit: Precious Time

This week's *parsha* relates the death of Sarah at one hundred and twenty-seven years. Unfortunately, not all virtuous people are granted a life of so many years.

There was a legend in Europe that a child prodigy once contracted a terminal illness. The members of his community were distraught, helpless to aid the ailing young boy, whom they regarded as their future leader. They futilely sought a solution. Finally, they turned to the town rabbi to find an answer to this heartbreaking tragedy. Couldn't he do something to save the poor scholar? The whole town was depending upon him.

The rabbi struck upon a novel plan: he would approach other scholars and ask them to donate some portion of their life on this earth to the young prodigy. If each rabbi would agree to give several months or years of his life, perhaps God would listen to their prayers and allow the boy to live longer. Every gift of time would prolong the boy's life.

He came to the Chafetz Chaim, the leading rabbi of his time, and asked him if he would be willing to contribute some measure of his life. The Chafetz Chaim paused and then replied that he would consider the matter seriously. It would demand a night of study and examination. When he returned to him the next day, the Chafetz Chaim announced that he would be willing to grant a portion of his life on this earth to the young boy. Overjoyed, the rabbi asked him how much he would be willing to contribute to the young man.

The Chafetz Chaim replied, "One moment."

For some people, in a single moment lies a lifetime.

Around the *Shabbat* Table

1. What do you think of the rabbi's solution? What do you think its
    effect was upon those who were asked to contribute a portion of
    their life?

2. There is one lapse that is present in every individual, perhaps the
    most insidious transgression of all, that often goes unnoticed: the
    wasting of time. It is so subtle that often we are not even aware
    that we are doing it. What do you think enables one to live a life
    with the awareness of the preciousness of every moment? Do you
    know anyone who does?

3. During what segment of your life do you think that you most pro-
    ductively used your time? Why? Are you capable of living with that
    intensity now?

Toledot

FRIDAY NIGHT MEAL: A Question of Justice

The reactions to Jacob's deceiving of his father and stealing his brother's blessing are terrifying in the intensity of their agony: "And Isaac trembled a great trembling" (Genesis 27:33).

"Esau screamed a great scream" (Genesis 27:34).

Was Jacob morally justified in the stealing of his brother's blessing? Is there no retribution for inflicting this amount of pain?

In the beginning of this week's *parsha*, Rebecca becomes aware of something unusual about her pregnancy "and goes to inquire of God." She receives a prophecy that she is carrying two sons who will represent two future nations. These two nations will always be in conflict, will never reconcile their essential differences. Two beings wrestle in her womb, their very natures in constant conflict.

Rebecca never reveals this prophecy to her husband, Isaac. Apparently, she realizes that it is her private destiny to ensure that the correct son will become the next leader of the Jewish people. She quickly realizes that this is Jacob, "and Rebecca loved Jacob" (Genesis 25:28). He is the honest and thoughtful one, not cunning and loving to hunt like his brother Esau.

Isaac, however, perceives the situation completely differently. He sees two contrasting personalities that should ultimately share the responsibilities of this fledgling people. Jacob, described as "pure, dwelling in tents" (Genesis 25:27), will guide the spiritual aspects of the world, while his brother, Esau, the "cunning hunter," will see to its physical prosperity.

Ignorant of the prophecy given to Rebecca and aware that he is aging, Isaac calls Esau, the eldest of the twins, to receive his blessing. Rebecca then springs into action (in accordance with her spontaneity, creativity, and depth of perception noted in the *D'var Torah* on last week's *parsha*), explaining to Jacob that he must immediately act to receive this blessing instead of Esau.

Jacob seems to be a reluctant partner in this act of deception. He questions his mother as to what will happen if he is caught in his treachery. According to the commentators, he moves very slowly throughout the whole episode, fails to alter his voice, and is almost detected by his father, Isaac.

Nevertheless, Jacob eventually receives the blessing intended for his brother, a blessing bequeathing him continuous physical bounty. Coupled with his spiritual capabilities, his descendants will eventually assume responsibility for both the physical and spiritual dimensions of this world.

Let us return to our original questions: Was Jacob morally justified in his behavior? Is there no retribution for inflicting this level of pain?

Jacob's theft of his brother's blessing is an overwhelmingly complicated act. On the one hand, his act is motivated by God's prophecy to Rebecca, both sanctioned by Heaven and indispensable to the future of the Jewish people. On one level, it is simply the difficult yet correct thing to do. But, on the other hand, he is ultimately held responsible for the suffering that he directly, though unintentionally, causes to Isaac and to Esau.

Isaac suffers greatly. "And Isaac trembled a great trembling." The midrash relates that Isaac's trembling after hearing that he had been deceived by his son Jacob was in fact greater than his trembling during the *akeda* (his being bound by Abraham)! The *Zohar* states that because Jacob provoked this great trembling of his father, Jacob would in due time be made to tremble by his own sons (when they sold Joseph).

Esau also suffers greatly. "Esau screamed a great scream" (Genesis 27:34). The midrash states that God never forgets the suffering of the unfortunate: "Esau screamed a great scream. When did God respond to Esau's scream? During the time of Purim, when Haman (a direct descendant of Esau) caused the Jews to scream their great scream."

For the Jewish people, the lesson has not been to retreat from the complicated arena of action. Rather, it has been to remember, concurrently, two responsibilities: that, for the sake of the whole world, we are commanded to fulfill our destiny. Nevertheless, we are not released from the moral repercussions of our actions.

The ramifications of Jacob's stealing of his brother's blessing echo throughout the universe, throughout all of our history.

Around the *Shabbat* Table

1. Can you think of any examples in history when the necessary line of action demanded morally suspect actions?

2. Rebecca's placing of Esau's clothes and the goat's hair on Jacob has been referred to as "the binding of Jacob." Why?

3. Have you ever been in a situation in which the "right" thing to do was morally problematic?

SHABBAT LUNCH: Honoring Parents

And Rebecca spoke to Jacob her son, saying, "Behold, I heard your father speak to Esau your brother, saying, 'Bring me venison, and make some food for me to eat, so that I can bless you before God, before my death.' Now therefore, my son, obey my voice according to that which I command you." [Genesis 27:6-8]

Was Jacob obligated to obey his mother? What would the laws of honoring one's parents instruct in this situation?

Two verses in the Torah sketch the guidelines for a child's relationship to his or her parents:

"*Honor* your father and mother, that your days may be long in the land which the Lord gives you" (Exodus 20:12).	"You should be in *awe* of your mother and father, and you should keep My Sabbaths, I am the Lord your God" (Leviticus 19:3)

Honor and awe constitute the two paradigms of parent–child relationships in the Torah. While the Torah presents these relationships in the most general of terms, the Talmud and Jewish law strive to detail and concretize their respective natures. Maimonides (*Hilchot Mamrim* 6:3) writes that:

Honoring parents entails:	Being in awe of parents entails:
1. Feeding them (bringing them food or drink)	1. Not sitting or standing in their places
2. Clothing them	2. Not contradicting their words (publicly)
3. Standing to greet them and welcoming them in; escorting them out	3. Not supporting their words (if this implies that they are in need of their child's support)
4. Administering to their basic needs	4. Not calling them by their personal names

Honoring one's parents is reflected in positive actions; awe of parents is reflected in refraining from certain actions. The rabbinical formulation of "honoring parents" attempts to engender a sense of gratitude in the child, as the child reciprocates the primary actions that parents provide for their offspring. The formulation of "awe" seems to be aimed at maintaining a separation of the generations, maintaining a sense of history.

What happens when the request of a parent contravenes Jewish law? Which authority is to be obeyed? From our verse in Leviticus, an additional principle of parent-child relationships is derived: though one is in awe of one's parents, one is still commanded to observe the Sabbath. Thus, a child is not required to fulfill an illegal or immoral parental request. In addition, Jewish law regards parental demands concerning (1) where the child should live, (2) whom the child should marry, and (3) what profession the child should choose, to be beyond the scope of legitimate parental involvement.

Jacob was being asked to deceive his father; an act that was unquestionably beyond the realm of his obligation to listen to his mother. Somehow, despite the deception and the pain it generated, Jacob's relationship with his father was not permanently harmed. At the end of the *parsha*, Isaac bestows upon his son Jacob the same blessing his father, Abraham, had bestowed on him: " . . . May God bless you, and make you fruitful and multiply you, that you will become a great people, and may He give you the blessing of Abraham, to you and your descendants with you . . ." (Genesis 28:3, 4).

Around the *Shabbat* Table

1. Though "honoring one's parents" requires one to feed, clothe, and administer to their needs, one is not obligated to expend one's own finances in the fulfillment of this mitzvah. Why do you think this is so?

2. The Talmud (*Sanhedrin* 72a/b) assumes that the parents' love for the child is greater than the child's love for his or her parents. Why do you think that the Talmud makes this supposition? Is this true in your family?

3. Which of the parameters listed previously concerning *honoring* and having *awe* of parents is most significant for you? Why?

Seuda Shlishit: A *Niggun* from the Rebbe

When Rebecca could not understand what was happening to her during her pregnancy, she sought an explanation from God (Genesis 25:22, 23). When the hasidim could not understand something, they hoped to receive their answers from their Rebbe:

I remember the day that the Rebbe visited our village.

We heard that the Rebbe was coming. What excitement! You must understand, this was not an everyday occurrence. We are a small village, far from the home of the Rebbe. Once, Yossele the *mohel* (circumcisor) had gone to visit the Rebbe with a question about a sick little boy. But for the rest of us, we waited and dreamed of the day when the Rebbe would come.

The night before, none of us could sleep. We tossed and turned, urging the sun to wake up, so that we could race out to see our Rebbe. He would answer all of our questions.

We couldn't wait any longer. We lined the streets, far out of the village, even past *Moishele's* farm, looking and waiting for any sign of his arrival. Some of the children had never ventured this far from home.

Finally, a sign. Horses and a carriage. It was true, after all, the Rebbe was here. We barely dared to look. Then, as if a conductor had suddenly raised his baton, we all burst upon the Rebbe, flooding him with our questions—questions that had been held inside of us for days and months and years.

"Rebbe, why can't we have children?" "Rebbe, why is my little one so sick?" "Rebbe, just tell, when is the Mashiach coming, is it soon?" "Rebbe, oh Rebbe ... " A never-ending stream of questions. "Why did this happen and why didn't that happen?" We knew that our Rebbe would answer all of our questions.

But the Rebbe just smiled. He listened, put out his hand, and said, "Wait, wait a moment, first we must eat something."

So we waited. The horses and carriage came into our town. We all went to watch the Rebbe eat. Occasionally, the excitement was too much to bear, and one of us would begin, "Rebbe, but Rebbe, why . . . ?" But the Rebbe would just smile, wait, nod his head a bit and then in the most soft voice say, "Not yet."

Finally, the Rebbe had finished eating. The time had come. Now the Rebbe would answer all of our questions.

We opened our mouths, just to get ready. But just as we were about to ask, the Rebbe put up his hand and said, "First, we must sing a *niggun* [wordless song]. First we must sing." Well, if the Rebbe says that we must sing, then we sing. So our Rebbe began a *niggun*. It was a new *niggun* for us. Years later, legends arose of how the Rebbe had composed it on the spot. We joined in. Then the Rebbe closed his eyes, began to sway, and sang the *niggun* again and again. We closed our eyes. We all sang the Rebbe's *niggun*.

I don't know how long we sang it. In fact, nobody quite remembers how long we sang it. Some say an hour. Some say hours. Some say that we sang the same *niggun* through the whole night. Our eyes were closed as we swayed with the Rebbe. We all drifted into the world of the *niggun*, far away from our little village.

Then, our Rebbe's voice began to slow down. We opened our eyes. The Rebbe looked up. He paused and asked, "Any questions?" We sat there. No one could move. There were no questions. Our Rebbe had answered all of our questions.

Around the *Shabbat* Table

1. In the book of Deuteronomy (31:30), the Torah is called a "song." Why? Why do you think that the title of the book of love in the Bible is called, "The Song of Songs?"

2. Do you think that singing a song with words can have the same effect as singing a *niggun*? Why?

3. Did you ever have a "*niggun*-like" experience, in which your understanding was beyond cognition or rational explanation?

Vayetze

FRIDAY NIGHT MEAL: Darkness and Clarity

After stealing his brother's blessing, Jacob leaves the home of Isaac and Rebecca and begins to journey to the home of Laban in Haran. He is the first of the patriarchs ever to travel by himself.

He is utterly alone. He cannot return home out of fear of his brother Esau. He knows that his destination, the home of his uncle Laban, is filled with deceit and corruption. He has no companion. He has no physical possessions. " . . . With my stick (only) I crossed the Jordan" (Genesis 32:10).

Lacking even a pillow, he gathers rocks to make a resting place for his head. He lies down to rest and sleeps. He is alone, in the darkness, with nothing.

God told Abraham to leave his homeland and follow the signs to Canaan. God told Isaac not to leave the land. But Jacob proceeds in human and spiritual solitude, toward a strange and unknown place. His mission is unclear and filled with uncertainty.

Suddenly, he has a dream—the first time that God reveals Himself to Jacob. The dream contains two components: a visual image and a verbal message from God:

1. Jacob sees a ladder, its feet rooted in the ground, its top reaching heavenward, with the angels of God ascending and descending on it.

2. Jacob hears God tell him that He is the God of his forefathers. God promises Jacob the inheritance of the land, future progeny, and that He will guard Jacob until these promises are fulfilled.

What did God want to convey to Jacob in this nighttime revelation? How did Jacob respond?

First and foremost, Jacob realizes that he is not alone. He is not, and will never in the future be, alone. God has responded to perhaps the first existential crisis of a Jew, declaring: "I am with you, and I will guard you wherever you go . . . and I will not leave you until I have fulfilled what I told you I would do" (Genesis 28:15).

Second, the vagueness shrouding his mission has been removed by virtue of the image of the angels ascending and descending the ladder. A ladder is a means of connection that allows for movement. In Jacob's dream, the ladder unites two seemingly disparate worlds—heaven and earth. The angels symbolize the dynamism and interaction between these separate domains.

Overall, what is the meaning of God's revelation to Jacob? It affirms that God will always assist Jacob in his mission to unify the heavenly and earthly spheres, to sanctify the physical domain of human activity, and to make this world a more "Godly" realm.

Jacob's reaction parallels God's message in both his words and actions.

Jacob awakens suddenly and exclaims, "Behold, God is in this place and I did not know it!" His loneliness is dispelled. Jacob then takes the stones that he was lying upon, erects an altar, and pours oil upon it. The stones symbolize the most basic raw matter of this earthly world. Jacob uses them to build a structure through which to serve God, then anoints and sanctifies it with oil. Imitating the angels ascending the ladder, Jacob is performing an act of taking this world and "elevating it" to the heavens. Every object and place possesses the potential to be "raised up" to God.

Jacob then vows that someday he will return and transform this impromptu altar into a "house of God [Beit-El]." Jacob echoes God's promise of partnership.

Jacob then continues on his way. The journey that began in solitude and uncertainty now proceeds with resolution; Jacob has been entrusted with God's support and mission.

The commentators note that the *gematria* (numerical sum of each letter) of the word *sulam* (ladder), 130, is the same as the word *Sinai* (of Mount Sinai). This suggests that just as Jacob's ladder is a symbol for him of the connection between the earthly and heavenly worlds, so, too, Mount Sinai represents that connection for the Jewish people. Mount Sinai is also a ladder, with its feet in the ground, reaching skyward. Instead of angels going up and down, now a human being, Moses, performs that mission.

The message of Mount Sinai is the same as the message that Jacob receives through his vision of the ladder. In the book of Exodus, Jacob's ladder, the symbol connecting the earthly and heavenly domains, assumes a national, collective form. Now, not a single Jew but a whole nation will be entrusted with the mission of uniting these two worlds. And, like Jacob, the Jewish people will then understand that they will never be alone. God will always be with them in their mission to elevate everything in this world to the heavens.

Around the *Shabbat* Table

1. Although the Torah notes just five verses previously that Jacob departed from his parents (Genesis 28:5), this message is repeated at the beginning of this week's *parsha*. All of Jacob's experiences must be viewed under the title of: "And Jacob departed . . ." Do you think that leaving one's home is a necessary condition for finding oneself?

2. The commentators point out that, at first, Jacob places many rocks under his head. Yet when he rises in the morning, the Torah refers to them as "the rock," in the singular. According to the commentators, the rocks became unified during the night. What does this transformation symbolize?

3. What was the most important object or advice given to you upon your leaving home?

SHABBAT LUNCH: Romantic Love

And Jacob kissed Rachel, raised his voice, and cried. [Genesis 29:11]

Why did Jacob cry? He was overwhelmed with joy and his heart was bursting (Radak, biblical commentator, 1160–1235).

The very first time that Jacob sees Rachel, before they have exchanged a single word, he is overcome with love. " ... Rachel was beautiful and radiant. And Jacob loved Rachel and said [to her father], 'I will work seven years for Rachel, your younger daughter ...' And Jacob worked seven years for Rachel, which seemed to him like just a few days, in his love for her" (Genesis 29:17–20).

What was the nature of Jacob's love for Rachel? Should physical or intuitive attraction play a significant role in the choosing of one's partner?

The midrash relates the following story:

A Roman matron once asked Rabbi Yossi, "What has your God been doing since the completion of the Creation of the world?"

Rabbi Yossi replied, "He has been busy pairing couples."

She was astonished. "Is that His trade?! Even I can do that job. As many man servants and maid servants as I have, I can pair up as couples."

"Perhaps it is a simple matter in your eyes," answered Rabbi Yossi, "but for God, it is as difficult as the splitting of the sea."

She promptly placed one thousand man-servants opposite one

thousand maid-servants and declared, "He will marry her; she will marry him," and so forth.

The next morning, two thousand servants came marching to her door, beaten and bruised. One had lost an eye; one had a broken leg, all complaining, "I do not want her!!! I do not want him!!!"

She immediately sent for Rabbi Yossi, and conceded, "Rabbi, everything that you said was true and wise."

To which he replied, "If it were easy in your eyes, know that it is as difficult for God as the splitting of the sea."

The splitting of the sea represents the most supernatural miracle of the Torah, the division of a single, naturally united entity into two parts. Similarly, marriage represents a miracle of joining two naturally independent entities, man and woman, into one unit. According to the previous midrash, if unsuccessful, the result may be painful and scarring. How can this "miracle" be achieved?

Physical attraction, and the love inspired thereof, is one of the key ingredients in a marriage. According to the Talmud (*Sanhedrin* 105b), when a person is in love, he or she will disregard the shortcomings and emphasize the good qualities of his or her beloved. When in love, a person transcends his or her immediate existence and experiences the world in an entirely different fashion. "And Jacob worked seven years for Rachel, which seemed to him like just a few days, in his love for her." A relationship without love seems pale and lifeless.

But can love alone create a lasting relationship? Is love stable enough to withstand the possible turbulence of a lifelong relationship? Can love sustain a marriage?

Rav Kook writes that the beauty of love is its unpredictability. Love is exciting in its spontaneity, in its power to overwhelm and completely absorb the lovers. The charm of love, of passion, is its instability, and therein lies its potential weakness. Love, by its nature, is cyclical, appearing and disappearing at uncontrollable intervals. When love becomes static, controlled, and ordered at will, it loses its vital spark of unrestrained creativity; it loses its vibrancy.

What happens when love momentarily, inevitably, fades? Does the relationship simply disintegrate? How does it maintain itself?

The Bible's book of love, "The Song of Songs" (*Shir HaShirim*), refers to a couple as "loving companions" (5:1) and to the woman as "my sister, my bride" (4:9). In addition to the quality of love, requisite degrees of companionship and mutual regard are vital in the maintaining of a relationship. While love enhances, the basis and durability of a relationship are revealed in the level of its partnership, a partnership devoted to the fulfilling of mutual goals and a common purpose. When two people share dreams, dreams extending beyond the privacy and intimacy of their relationship, when their raison d'etre in life brings them together, then their relationship does not become jeopardized when their love momentarily wanes.

Rav Kook writes that all of life is cyclical; night leads to day, autumn and winter flow into spring and summer. If the relationship is based on eternal goals and dreams, then the emotions that have waned will inevitably return, yielding an even deeper and more fulfilling love.

Around the *Shabbat* Table

1. God plays the divine matchmaker in the two stories of Creation. In the first chapter, Adam and Eve's relationship is of two partners, sharing a common goal of controlling and directing the world. In the second chapter, their relationship focuses exclusively on each other, enabling them to transcend their state of loneliness. The first two chapters of the Torah reflect the aforementioned aspects of a relationship: outward, worldly goals and private, personal love. Why do you think that the Torah presented these two aspects in this order—first their goals and relationship with the world at large, and then their private relationship with each other?

2. Is "raising a family" a common purpose that can provide a lasting basis to a marital relationship? What might be its weakness?

3. What are examples of a couple's common goals or dreams, extrinsic to their relationship? What are yours?

Seuda Shlishit: A Story of Love

The *parsha Vayetze* describes the love between Jacob and Rachel. Rabbi Abraham Twerski, a contemporary rabbi and psychiatrist, author of *Living Every Day* and *Generation to Generation*, relates the following story about his parents' relationship:

> After fifty-two years of marriage, my father contracted a terminal illness. He knew that he had cancer of the pancreas, but the thought of death did not frighten him. Quite the contrary, he had been anticipating something of the sort. A few weeks before his first symptoms had appeared, my grandfather had appeared to him in a dream and had said, "You have nothing to fear. It is just like walking out of one room and into another." The only serious concern that father had was that a long and debilitating illness would be a burden on the family.
>
> My father was extremely well-versed medically. His frequent conferences with physicians and his daily visits to the hospital had kept him informed of the most recent medical advances. When the doctor suggested chemotherapy, father said, "You know as well as I do that chemotherapy for cancer of the pancreas is not effective. All it can do is produce undesirable side-effects. If it could prolong life, then I would probably be required by *halacha* to do everything humanly possible to live longer, even if it meant living with distress. However, there is certainly no requirement to subject oneself to a treatment that will cause a great deal of misery and not prolong life." The doctor had to agree that father was right.
>
> In his conversation with mother, however, the doctor indicated that chemotherapy might prolong life by perhaps three months. She was adamant. As long as there was anything that could be done, it must be done. Who knows but that during those three months, the long awaited breakthrough in a cancer cure might come about.
>
> "Foolishness," said father. But mother would not yield.
>
> One time father and I were alone, and he said, "You know, to sub-

ject myself to the misery of chemotherapy when there is nothing to be gained is ridiculous. But if it is not done, mother will not be at ease. During our marriage I have done many things for mother's happiness; if I have the opportunity to do one last thing for her, I will not turn it down."

Around the *Shabbat* Table

1. Why do you think that, in his father's eyes, it was probably impossible to persuade his wife to allow him to forgo the chemotherapy?

2. In creating a home, Jewish law stresses the centrality of *shalom bayit* (peace of the home). In your opinion, do you think that most breakdowns of *shalom bayit* are of an intellectual or of an emotional nature?

3. What examples of self-sacrifice for the sake of a relationship can you think of?

Vayishlach

FRIDAY NIGHT MEAL: Coming Home

After twenty years, Jacob returns home. Twenty years earlier he had fled, with nothing, from his brother Esau. Jacob, the "pure one who dwelled in tents," had stolen his older brother's blessing from their father, Isaac. Esau had vowed to take revenge.

For twenty years, Jacob had been plagued by lingering questions: Could he ever go home? Had his brother retained his desire for vengeance? And perhaps most tormenting of all, had he been justified in usurping his brother's blessing?

Jacob sends messengers to his brother Esau, and they return with the troubling report that Esau is approaching with 400 of his men. Jacob is distraught. Overwhelmed with fear, he divides his camp into two and prays for help. Jacob anxiously waits for the imminent encounter; he waits for tomorrow to come.

What is Jacob thinking? What is he feeling? His whole life has led up to this moment. The Torah describes this moment in the most concise terms: "And Jacob remained alone" (Genesis 32:25). Alone. His whole life passes in front of him. In the midst of his wives, his children, and his camp, Jacob is alone, alone with himself. The next day his destiny will be decided.

> And Jacob remained alone, and a man struggled with him until the rising of the dawn. And [the man] saw that he could not defeat him [Jacob] ... and he said, "Let me go ... " and he [Jacob] said, "I will not release you until you bless me." And [the man] said to him, "What is your name?" and he replied, "Jacob." And [the man] said to him, "Your name will not continue to be Jacob, rather Israel, since you have struggled with God and men and you have prevailed." [Genesis 32:25–29]

Who was this man? Or was this a man at all? Why did they struggle? Why was Jacob's name changed, and why precisely at this moment?

With whom was Jacob wrestling? Perhaps with himself. In the stark loneliness of the night, Jacob was confronting his most difficult issues—issues that, in fact, he may have repressed for the last twenty years.

The midrash states that "the man" was the ministering angel of Esau. After the confrontation, Jacob calls the place "*P'niel* ('Face of God'), because I [Jacob] have seen God face-to-face and succeeded." Jacob understands that this was a spiritual conflict; the essence of his being struggled with the spirit of Esau. The battle of their natures, originally felt in their mother's womb, has now culminated in the battle of their spirits, of their destinies.

For the first time in his life, Jacob is fighting. Twenty years earlier his mother had dressed him in the clothes of Esau and implored him to impersonate his brother, the hunter. She had conveyed to a reluctant Jacob that, in addition to his spiritual side, he must also learn to act in the often difficult and devious world. She had sent him to Laban, where for twenty years he was thrust into the depths of falseness and deceit. Rebecca, the matriarch, self-sacrificingly imparts to her son that the leadership of the world cannot be entrusted to the likes of Esau or Laban. Jacob must learn to cope with, and ultimately subdue, all of the forces that impede the perfection of this world. Jacob must learn to fight.

Jacob's wrestling with the angel reflects that he has undergone an overwhelming personality development. He confronts the angel face-to-face and refuses to relinquish control. After fleeing for twenty years, he realizes that he is now ready to confront Esau, no matter how defenseless or outnumbered he may be.

This personality change is accompanied by a change of name. No longer will he be called Jacob, "the one who has supplanted or seized." No longer will he see himself as the one who has taken his blessing in stealth. After twenty years, Jacob has come to terms with his acquisition of Esau's blessing. Jacob finally realizes what his mother had understood twenty years before: It is God's desire that he assume both the mantle of the inner, spiritual world, that of "dwelling in tents" (i.e., the tent of Torah) and also that of the outer, physical world, that of the hunter and "the field." He wrestles with Esau's angel, the essence of Esau, and wins.

Jacob's wrestling with the angel and subsequent name change are the fulfillment of the chain of events that began with Rebecca's experience of wrestling in her womb, and God's prophecy to her that she was carrying twins—twins who would always struggle and would become two nations forever in conflict. Her mission became to bequeath to Jacob the tools necessary to combat Esau. His willingness and resoluteness to confront the angel represents Rebecca's ultimate triumph.

Yet a price is paid for this victorious feat. Jacob emerges from his wrestling victorious, but not unscathed. His thigh is injured, and he continues with a limp. The Ramban writes that this is symbolic of the history of the Jewish people. Every generation of persecution recalls Jacob's wound, the limping of the Jewish people, and the price paid for continuing to wrestle and to strive to perfect the world. In the uncompromising and determined battle to overcome the forces that hinder or prevent the moral improvement of this world, we have paid terrible prices in our history. We have prevailed, though often wounded and limping.

Around the *Shabbat* Table

1. After wrestling with the angel, Jacob continues with a limp. Rav
    Kook writes that often after making a significant decision in life,
    one's will is temporarily weakened. Why do you think this is so?

2. In order to develop another dimension of his personality, Jacob
    leaves his home for twenty years. The Talmud states that even a
    prophet would not be accepted or recognized by the inhabitants
    of his native city. Why do you think this happens? Why is it some-
    times difficult to return to one's home?

3. Have you ever wrestled with yourself?

SHABBAT LUNCH: Flattery

Jacob sent messengers to Esau his brother . . . and he commanded
them saying, "Thus you should say to my master, Esau: 'This is what
your servant, Jacob, wants to tell you—I have sojourned with Laban
. . . and I have oxen, donkeys and sheep, male and female servants;
and I have sent to relate this to my master, so that I may find grace
in your eyes.'" [Genesis 32:4-6]

Jacob refers to his brother Esau as "his master." When they finally
meet, Jacob bows down seven times in front of Esau. He continually recounts to his brother Esau that the objective of all of his actions is "to be granted grace" from him.

Is Jacob being deceitful? Is Jacob, through his words and gifts,
his overall obsequiousness, attempting to manipulate Esau, to temper Esau's hostility in a disingenuous way? In short, is Jacob guilty
of flattery?

Flattery (in Hebrew, *chanupah*), the conveying of insincere,
excessive praise in order to gain the recipient's favor, is harshly condemned in Jewish sources. Earnest compliments and support are

essential for the development of a positive self-image. Positive encouragement promotes confidence and is vital for building a strong and determined will. Flattery, on the other hand, because of its insincerity and possible dishonesty, only benefits its giver. Instead of imparting true feelings, the flatterer preys on the vulnerability and insecurity of the receiver and transmits what the receiver would like to hear, rather than what he or she should or truly needs to hear. Psalms (11:9) states that the mouth [words] of a flatterer destroys his or her friend.

The Talmud (*Sotah* 41b) comments, "Rabbi Elazar stated that 'anyone who flatters, even babies in their mothers' wombs curse them.'" Why did Rabbi Elazar select this unusual image to describe the effects of flattery? The babies in their mothers' wombs symbolize the future; their "cursing" reflects their anxiety and disappointment over coming into this kind of world, a world plagued by exploitative self-interest.

The immediate danger of flattery is that the speaker is taking advantage of the listener, manipulating the listener to achieve self-serving goals. Ultimately, in a world rife with flattery, trust and confidence weakens and then eventually breaks down. Recipients regard compliments with uncertainty; every positive word of encouragement is suspected of being tainted with a personal agenda. Flattery thwarts the hope of creating a better universe, the silent prayer of all unborn children. The Talmud states that "God abhors the one who speaks words with his mouth while thinking other thoughts in his heart" (*Pesachim* 113b).

The midrash questions Jacob's behavior, asking, "How could he speak in this way to Esau, calling him his master and bowing down to him?" Isn't this a classic example of flattery? Answers Jacob in the midrash, "Master of the Universe, I am flattering the evil ones in this world, solely to escape being killed by them." Jacob recognizes the problematic nature of his behavior, that his actions are, in principle, unacceptable. Physical survival remains the sole defense for flattery.

Around the *Shabbat* Table

1. The rabbis of the Talmud disagreed over whether Jacob's attempt
    to win his brother's favor was justified. Some claimed that Jacob
    should have ignored Esau, not sent messengers, and simply entered
    Israel. Others assert that he was justified in his actions. What do
    you think?

2. What differentiates a compliment from flattery?

3. What kind of relationships or situations do you think are especially
    conducive to flattery? Have you ever struggled with the tempta-
    tion to flatter someone?

Seuda Shlishit: Learning from Thieves and Children

Jacob sojourned with his deceitful brother-in-law, Laban, for twenty
years. There, Jacob, the "pure one" (Genesis 25:27), learned how to
cope in a world filled with treachery.

The *maggid* (preacher) of Mezritch, one of the Ba'al Shem Tov's
primary disciples, noted that one could learn many lessons from a
thief. Said the *maggid*:

From a thief, one can learn many valuable principles for life:
—A thief will work even at night;
—If he does not finish what he has set out to do in one night, he
devotes the next night to it. He never gives up;
—He will work under the most difficult conditions, enduring cold,
rain, and physical hardships;
—He will risk his life for small gains;
—He and those who work with him, love and trust one another;
—He is devoted to his trade and would not give it up for any other.

The *maggid* added that one can also learn priceless lessons from the smallest, most simple, of children:

—They are often happy for no particular reason;
—They are never idle, even for a moment;
—If they want something, they demand it vigorously until they get it.

Around the *Shabbat* Table

1. The *maggid* of Mezritch wanted to stress that one can learn something from every person. *Pirkei Avot* (Ethics of the Fathers 4:1) states: "Who is wise? One who learns from everyone." What does this reflect about the Jewish approach to wisdom? What is the difference between knowledge and wisdom?

2. In light of the previous question, why do you think that the Talmud (*Eruvin* 55a) states that the primary obstacle to wisdom is arrogance? What other obstacles would you note?

3. Which one of the lessons to be learned from the thief or child do you identify with most? Why?

Vayeshev

FRIDAY NIGHT MEAL: Hatred among Brothers

"And his brothers saw that their father loved him [Joseph] more than the brothers, and they hated him and they could not talk with him in peace." [Genesis 37:4]

"Do not hate your brother in your heart, you should certainly reprove your fellow human being, and do not bear sin on his account." [Leviticus 19:17]

Are these two verses related? Is the source in Leviticus referring to Joseph and his brothers, hearkening back to an earlier fraternal struggle?

Why did the brothers hate Joseph? Is this simply another example of brotherly hatred in the line of Cain and Abel, Isaac and Ishmael, Jacob and Esau, or are other national or historical elements also involved?

Often we think of Joseph's dreams as the cause for the enmity of the brothers, but a closer look reveals that they despised him even before he related his dreams to them. Why did they hate their brother? The verse simply says: "They saw that their father loved him more" (Genesis 37:4). "More" is the key word. The brothers were loved by Jacob, their father, but Joseph was loved "more." The Talmud (*Shabbat* 10b) prohibits the favoring of one child over another. Every child must be appreciated for his or her unique qualities.

Why did Jacob love Joseph more than the other brothers? How could he have introduced such sibling rivalry into his own home? Had not Jacob himself grievously endured his own brother's hatred, fleeing to escape Esau's wrath? How could he not have learned from his own experience?! The Torah supplies the reason. Jacob loved Joseph more "because he was the son of his [Jacob's] old age" (Genesis 37:3). But was Joseph actually the son of Jacob's old age?! Joseph's younger brother, Benjamin, was the last child born to Jacob, the true son of his old age! The midrash, therefore, reinterprets the simple meaning of the verse: "Jacob loved Joseph more because Joseph was the son who would support Jacob in his old age." The midrash implies that Jacob loved Joseph more than the other brothers because he recognized that Joseph possessed leadership qualities that would eventually be fulfilled. Joseph was destined to become a leader. Wherever his fate took him, Joseph inevitably would rise to the top. He would quickly became the most powerful person in Egypt.

Because of these nascent leadership attributes, Jacob gives Joseph a special coat. What does the coat symbolize? The "coat of many colors" resembles a robe, a sign of royalty, of kingship. In effect, this symbolizes the coronation of Joseph.

Immediately after Jacob gives the coat to Joseph, the brothers begin to despise him. They realize that this is not a simple case of chosenness. The gift of the coat is the declaration of a decision— Jacob has decided that Joseph will assume the mantle of leadership in the family. Joseph, to the exclusion of the brothers, has been chosen to determine the direction of the Jewish people for the next generation and the future.

The period of Joseph and his brothers occurs at a precarious juncture in the history of the Jewish people. Until now, in each generation, whenever there had been two brothers, one had been selected to continue the line of the Jewish people and the other son had been rejected. Isaac had been chosen, Ishmael rejected; Jacob chosen; Esau rejected. These are the precedents set by the earlier generations; this is what the brothers must have assumed to be the process for the continuation of the line of Abraham. As soon as Jacob selects Joseph, they understand that they have been rejected. They perceive that their way of viewing the world and their dreams for the Jewish people have been discarded.

Why didn't the brothers talk with Joseph? Why couldn't they have approached their father? Why couldn't they have begun to discuss these issues openly, in a peaceful manner?

A closer examination of the story reveals that, in fact, the brothers did not initiate the animosity between themselves and Joseph. The second verse in our *parsha* states that, while he had been shepherding with his brothers, " . . . Joseph brought an evil report to their father" (Genesis 37:2). The air between them had been poisoned.

Why did Joseph speak against his brothers? What did Joseph say? Why did he say it? The Torah does not elaborate. Apparently, the content of his evil report is less significant than the fact that he brought it.

Perhaps Joseph's informing on his brothers is merely a symptom of his adolescence, a sign of his immaturity. Or perhaps, like his father Jacob, Joseph already intuits that he possesses exceptional leadership potential. He knows that he should and will be the one directing his brothers. The forthcoming dreams confirm this premonition of his impending sovereignty.

Joseph's challenge will be to emend these immature sensations of power, to resist their inebriating influence. Ultimately, his dilemma will be either to remove the hatred that is in his brothers' hearts or to bear sin on their account.

Around the *Shabbat* Table

1. In our opening verse, the primary caution is against maintaining hatred "in one's heart," keeping it inside. Why would it be less problematic to express one's hatred than to sustain it within?

2. Family relations may be especially prone to strong emotional reactions and hurt feelings. While sensitivity and compassion should always be encouraged, the Talmud (*Pesachim* 113b) cautions against having an "over-sensitive" personality. Great praise is offered to one who does not easily become insulted, who forgoes life's "slings and arrows." Why do you think that "over-sensitivity" is considered a personality drawback?

3. Have you ever felt intense sibling rivalry in your family? How were you able to overcome it?

SHABBAT LUNCH: *"Lashon Hara"*

. . . and Joseph brought an evil report about them [his brothers] to their father. [Genesis 37:2]

The tragic story of Joseph and his brothers begins when Joseph brings an evil report about them to their father, Jacob. The Torah does not reveal the details of this evil report, yet from the expression "evil report" (in Hebrew: *dibah ra'ah*), we can discern that Joseph's words would fall into the category of *lashon hara*, evil or destructive language.

Few human actions are condemned as harshly by the sages as *lashon hara*. Maimonides writes that it is forbidden to live in a neighborhood in which people habitually speak *lashon hara*, and that it was this crime—in the form of the evil report of the spies—that resulted in the condemnation of the Jewish people to forty years of wandering in the desert and that precluded an entire generation from entering the land of Israel.

What exactly is *lashon hara?* The Talmud set forth the general guidelines of the laws of *lashon hara,* which were then categorized by Maimonides. He lists five categories:

1. Gossip: relaying information for no essential purpose.

2. *Lashon Hara*: speaking disparagingly (though truthfully) about another.

3. Slander: speaking falsely about another.

4. A "master" of *lashon hara*: someone who habitually speaks *lashon hara.*

5. A "trace" (*avak*) of *lashon hara*: something that, though not itself *lashon hara,* will provoke *lashon hara.*

Lashon hara includes any form of communication that may negatively affect another person. Thus, joking at another's expense, using excuses like: "I wouldn't mind if he or she said that about me," or "I'd say it even if he or she were here," fall within the parameters of speech prohibited because of *lashon hara.* Furthermore, even listening to *lashon hara* is prohibited, for as the Talmud states, *lashon hara* kills three people: the person spoken about, the speaker, and the listener.

Avak lashon hara includes any form of communication that implies or is likely to generate *lashon hara.* Thus, expressions such as "he or she has really improved" (by implication: he or she was once less successful), "don't ask me about him or her; I don't want to speak *lashon hara,*" or even "What do you think of him or her?" would be proscribed. Even excessive praise of another, or commending someone in the presence of people who do not admire him or her is forbidden, out of concern that it may provoke a negative response. Thus, we are responsible not only for our own words, but also for any of their consequences.

What is the remedy for *lashon hara?* The Talmud states that there is no way to amend or rectify evil speech. Once words have been uttered, they can never be nullified; they can never be retrieved. The Talmud advises two precautionary measures that will hopefully preclude the speaking of *lashon hara*: (1) Since people are incapable of utterly refraining from talking, they should find worthy subjects for conversation. If possible, people should attempt to occupy themselves with the learning of Torah. (2) An additional preventative measure against *lashon hara* is for people to try to become more humble and sensitive. Taken together, these two suggestions indicate two of the primary causes for speaking *lashon hara*: (1) not having enough serious ideas or content to discuss, hence resorting to speaking about other people, and (2) not sufficiently recognizing or identifying with the pain inflicted upon others.

In his lifetime, the suffering that Joseph endured helped him to develop greater humility, which engendered a greater sensitivity toward his brothers. Ultimately, at the end of the book of Genesis, he accepts his role of leadership while demonstrating great compassion and love for his brothers: "And Joseph said to them [his brothers], 'Fear not, for am I in the place of God? But as for you, you thought evil against me; but God meant it for good, to bring it to pass this day that masses of people should be saved. Now therefore, fear not, I will nourish you, and your little ones.' And he comforted them, and spoke kindly to their hearts" (Genesis 50:19–21).

Around the *Shabbat* Table

1. In what circumstances would it be advisable to say negative things about another? Is there a difference between confiding in a therapist and confiding in a good friend?

2. How can one prevent listening to *lashon hara*? How can we diminish the amount of *lashon hara* spoken in our presence?

3. Do you know any people in whose presence you would never speak *lashon hara*?

Seuda Shlishit: The Torn Pillow

A man once went about his community slandering the rabbi. Wherever he went, he spoke of the rabbi's shortcomings and oversights. One day he felt remorse over his behavior and went to the rabbi to beg forgiveness. He indicated that he was willing to do anything to atone for his transgressions.

The rabbi told him to take several feather pillows from his home and go to the highest spot in the town. There, he should cut them open and watch the feathers scatter in the wind. Astonished, the man did as the rabbi had requested.

Returning to the rabbi, the man asked if there were anything else that he needed to do.

"Yes," replied the rabbi, "now go and gather all of the feathers. Despite your sincere remorse and motivation to repair your past actions," concluded the rabbi, "there is simply no way to rectify the damage caused by your words. It is as possible to retract your words as it will be to recover all of the feathers of the pillows."

Around the *Shabbat* Table

1. Why do you think that rabbis (or other public figures) are especially inviting targets for *lashon hara*?

2. What do you think are the most common character traits or circumstances that motivate the speaking of *lashon hara*?

3. What advice would you have given to the man who spoke *lashon hara*? To a friend who speaks *lashon hara*?

Mikketz

FRIDAY NIGHT MEAL: The Lesson of Dreams

And it came to pass at the end of two years, that Pharaoh dreamed
. . . [Genesis 41:1]

Where do dreams come from? Why do we dream? The rabbis asserted that dreams were the last traces of prophecy, the hints of a heavenly encounter.

Three sets of dreams cross Joseph's path. The first set he dreams in his father's house. The second set is dreamt by the butler and the baker while Joseph is confined in Pharaoh's prison. The third set is dreamt by Pharaoh himself, at the beginning of this week's *parsha*.

Why is Joseph's life continually distinguished by dreams? What is the development in this sequence of dreams and in Joseph's responses to them?

In last week's *parsha*, the first set of dreams occurs while Joseph is a 17-year-old youth, the favored son of his father, Jacob. Oblivious to the growing friction between himself and his brothers, Joseph calls to them: "Hear this dream which I have dreamt: 'Behold, we were binding sheaves in the field and, behold, my sheave arose and stood upright and, behold, your sheaves stood around mine and bowed down to my sheave'" (Genesis 37:6, 7).

The reaction of the brothers to Joseph's first dream is eminently predictable: "And the brothers hated him even more, on account of his dreams and his words" (Genesis 37:8). It is understandable that they resent him for the content of his dreams, for the dreams clearly depict Joseph's future dominance over them. But, in additional, they hate him for "his words," his untempered arrogance: "Hear this dream which I have dreamt." In an almost defiant fashion, Joseph seems self-absorbed over his impending status of greatness. In Joseph's eyes, the dreams reflect his sovereignty, which he may exploit however he so chooses.

Joseph focuses only on what the dreams portend for him. He ignores their origin as a message and gift from an unknowable source. Joseph continues to disregard the reactions of his brothers and presumptuously reports to them a second dream implying his impending superiority—eleven stars bow down to him. This time he incurs the wrath of his father as well.

There is a talmudic dictum that God responds to "all those who seek to elevate themselves in their own eyes by humbling them." Accordingly, instead of ascending to power, Joseph is continually thrust downward—down to the pit that his brothers threw him into, down to Egypt, and finally down to the dungeon.

There, in the dungeon, he is called on to interpret a second set of dreams. Now he responds differently. When approached by the butler and baker to interpret their dreams, Joseph replies: "Do not interpretations belong to God?" Joseph's suffering has diminished his pride. He now understands that God is the source of the dream. No longer absorbed with his own powers of dream interpretation, Joseph now regards himself as a medium, a person capable of providing greater insight and understanding.

Joseph correctly interprets the dreams of the butler and the baker, yet does not merit release from his state of suffering. He beseeches the chief butler to mention him to Pharaoh but to no avail—the butler forgets him. For two more years he languishes in the dungeon of Pharaoh, helplessly awaiting salvation.

Finally, "And it came to pass at the end of two years, that Pharaoh dreamed . . ."

Pharaoh dreams his dreams and summons Joseph to interpret them for him. Two years have elapsed; Joseph realizes that his release was not implemented by the butler but rather that dreams are determining his fate.

Joseph's response to Pharaoh's dreams is thoroughly unlike his reaction to his own dreams, twenty-two years earlier. When asked to interpret Pharaoh's dreams, Joseph first says: "It is not up to me" (Genesis 41:16). He no longer focuses on himself; he no longer attends exclusively to his own well-being. During his dialogue with Pharaoh, Joseph repeatedly states that the dream is what "God has shown Pharaoh to do." Joseph has finally recognized that a dream is God's transmitting of a responsibility; it is less a special privilege than a task with which one has been charged.

The series of dreams that Joseph encounters serve as his education. He is clearly graced with natural powers of leadership, and the dreams of his youth foresee a future endowed with influence and power. The danger lies in his potential conceit.

Joseph, through suffering and tragedy, learns the lesson of humility. Originally blinded by his own exceptional potential, he comes to perceive that these powers are indeed gifts and bring with them responsibility. When Joseph finally reveals himself to his brothers once he has become the vizier of Egypt, his tone bears none of his original haughtiness: "And Joseph said to his brothers, 'Please come near to me . . . I am Joseph your brother whom you sold to Egypt. Now therefore, be not grieved, nor angry with yourselves, that you sold me here, for God did send me before you to preserve our lives'" (Genesis 45:4, 5).

Around the *Shabbat* Table

1. According to Jewish law, one who takes upon himself a vow not to sleep for three days is forced by the community to annul his vow and sleep. Why is sleep so vital?

2. Exceptionally talented people often have difficulty relating to others who do not share their ability. What is the lesson of Joseph regarding the most effective way to realize extraordinary potential?

3. Rav Kook writes that "the great dreams are the foundation of the world." What is your most memorable dream—while asleep? while awake?

SHABBAT LUNCH: Giving a Name

And Pharaoh said to Joseph, "Behold, I have placed all of Egypt under your control." And Pharaoh removed his ring from his hand and placed it upon the hand of Joseph, dressed him in clothes of silk and placed a band of gold on his neck ... and Pharaoh called Joseph: "Tzafnat Paneach ..." [Genesis 41:41-45]

Why did Pharaoh change Joseph's name?

What is the significance of a name? What does it mean to change a name?

Many figures in the Torah had their names changed. Abram became Abraham. Sarai became Sarah. In both cases, the name changes were final; they were never again referred to as Abram or Sarai. Jacob's name was changed to Israel, though he continued to be called Jacob as well. Later on in the Torah, Moses' disciple and successor, Hoshea Bin Nun, will have his name changed to Yehoshua (Joshua). Of all the personalities of the Torah, however, perhaps Joseph was the recipient of the greatest number and variety of names.

Rachel, Joseph's mother, gave him a name reflecting two diverse qualities. "She became pregnant and bore a son, saying 'God has taken away [*asaf*] my shame.' And she called him Joseph, saying 'God will add [*Yosef*] another son to me'" (Genesis 30:23, 24). Rachel's first expression—*asaf*—implies a concluding (*sof*) of her misery, while her second expression—*Yosef*—reflects hope and the yearning for a second son. Joseph will both bring an end to suffering (via supplying Jacob and the other sons with food during the famine) and serve as a springboard for a succeeding stage (eventually yielding his leadership to that of Judah).

Joseph's brothers, while plotting to slay him, apparently cannot bear to call him by his given name and refer to him pejoratively as "that dreamer" (Genesis 37:19). While he is in the dungeon, the Egyptian butler refers to him as "the Hebrew slave" (*eved ivri*) (*Bereshit* 41:12). Pharaoh calls him *Tzafnat Paneach* (the revealer of the hidden). In the Talmud (*Yoma* 25b) and throughout Jewish history he is referred to as *Joseph HaTzaddik* (Joseph the righteous).

What is the meaning of a name?

A name is the primary social device of human interaction, the meeting place between the individual and society. First of all, the name should reveal some of the individual's essential character to others. Thus, the name bestowed should ideally provide some insight into the true nature of the individual. In the Garden of Eden, Adam's first task was to name the animals, to give them external labels that reflect their innermost beings. In the Talmud, Rabbi Meir attempted to detect some aspect of a person's nature from his or her name; he presumed that a name served as an invaluable guide, reflecting the person's hidden nature (*Yoma* 83b). For parents, the choice of a name is one of the first crucial moments in child-raising.

Every human being possesses a unique and ultimately unknowable essence. In the eyes of Judaism, the greatest challenge in life is to acquire greater insight into what this unique gift is and then to understand how to channel and direct these qualities to create a better society. One's name, if properly bestowed, is the first clue in understanding what this character or gift may entail. The name changes of Abraham, Sarah, and Jacob/Israel were God's most poignant messages to them that they must begin to regard themselves differently; they have undergone qualitative changes and must now begin developing and presenting to the world heretofore untapped aspects of their personalities.

Second, a society confers a name to every individual, an appellation reflecting how others regard the most essential aspects of his or her identity. In the Mishnah in *Pirkei Avot*, Rabbi Shimon Bar Yochai states that "a good name" is more valuable than wisdom, holiness, or power. Rabbi Shimon said: There are three crowns: the crown of Torah, the crown of priesthood, and the crown of royalty;

but the *crown of a good name* exceeds them all (*Avot* 4:17). Ultimately, the name that the world gives to a person, that is, his or her reputation, reflects his or her most significant and lasting contribution.

The many names of Joseph reflect his process of growth and transformation. His special gift of experiencing and understanding dreams undergoes a metamorphosis; once perceived negatively as "that dreamer," he is ultimately exalted by Pharaoh as "the revealer of the hidden." Eventually, Jewish history will bequeath upon Joseph the most valued of all names: Joseph *HaTzaddik*.

Around the *Shabbat* Table

1. The protagonist of Franz Kafka's classic, *The Trial*, was never given a name. He was referred to simply as "K." Conversely, commentators write that God has an infinite number of names. What do you think these two ideas represent?

2. What is the significance of having, or not having, a Hebrew name? What "name" would you like, ideally, for others to give to you?

3. What names would you like to give to your children? Why?

Seuda Shlishit: The Holy Goat

This week's *parsha* spoke of thin and fat cows. Other animals have also played a role in Jewish history and thought.

The following is a story told by Rabbi Mendel of Kotsk (1787–1859), known as the "Kotsker Rebbe." The "Kotsker" was renowned for his unqualified passion for truth, his unyielding resoluteness to serve God without any personal concern or gain. "Everything in the world can be imitated except truth. For truth that is imitated is no longer truth." Unlike other hasidic leaders who were known for their unconditional love for all Jews and who attracted wide followings, the Rebbe of Kotsk's zealous fury terrified the few hasidim who dared to enter his circle. His presence served as a continual reminder for the Jewish people of the ability to strive, without compromise, toward a more sanctified life. During the last years of his life he retreated into seclusion, unable to face the shallowness and hypocrisy endemic to a human world. The following story reflects how he perceived his role amidst his hasidic followers:

Rabbi Isaac of Vorke was one of the very few who were admitted to Rabbi Mendel during this period. Once he visited Kotzk after a long absence, knocked, entered Rabbi Mendel's room, and said in greeting: "Peace be with you, Rabbi."

"I am no rabbi! Don't you recognize me! I am the goat! I'm the sacred goat. Don't you remember the story?

"An old Jew once lost his snuffbox made of horn, on his way to the *Beit Midrash* (house of study). He wailed, 'Just as if the dreadful exile weren't enough, this must happen to me! Oh my, I've lost my snuffbox made of horn!' And then he came upon the sacred goat. The sacred goat was pacing the earth, and the tips of his black horns touched the stars. Whenever the goat moved its horns, the most heavenly music resonated from the moving of the stars. When he heard the old Jew lamenting, he leaned down to him, and said, 'Cut a piece from my horns, whatever you need to make a new snuffbox.' The old Jew did this, made a new snuffbox, and filled it with tobacco. Then he went to the *Beit Midrash* and offered everyone a pinch of snuff. They snuffed and snuffed, and everyone who snuffed it cried, 'Oh, what wonderful tobacco! It must be because of the box. Oh, what a wonderful box! Wherever did you get it?' So the old man told them about the sacred goat. And then one after another they went out and looked for the goat.

"The holy goat was pacing the earth and the tips of his horns were touching the stars, conducting the celestial symphony. One after another they went up to him and begged permission to cut off a bit of his horns. Time after time the sacred goat leaned down to grant their request. Box after box was made and filled with snuff. The fame of the boxes spread far and wide. At every step he took, the sacred goat met someone who asked for a piece of his horns.

"Now all the Jews have special snuffboxes to fill their noses with snuff. And the holy goat still paces the earth. But there is no more heavenly music. His horns no longer reach the stars.'"

Around the *Shabbat* Table

1. What does this story say about the awareness or priorities of people who were solely concerned with their snuffboxes? Why do you think the goat was willing to sacrifice its horns? Should the goat have consented to sacrifice its horns?

2. The Talmud states that one who purifies those who are impure becomes impure in the process. Those who heal others may often pay a price for their efforts. Why do you think this is so?

3. According to the Kabbalah (Jewish mysticism), to enable someone else to grow, one must contract (*tzimtzum*) him- or herself to create space for the other to expand. Have you ever "contracted" yourself in order to create or maintain a relationship?

Vayigash

FRIDAY NIGHT: Reconciliation

And Joseph could not control himself . . . and he raised his voice in crying that was heard in all of Egypt and the house of Pharaoh. And Joseph said to his brothers, "I am Joseph. Is my father still alive?" But his brothers were not able to answer him because of their shock. [Genesis 45:1–3]

For twenty-two years, Joseph had not revealed his identity to his brothers and father. For twenty-two years, Jacob had inconsolably mourned his favorite son, while the brothers bore witness to their father's grief and suppressed their guilt over selling Joseph to Egypt. For twenty-two years Joseph had controlled himself, never sending word of his fate, never seeking to relieve his family's pain.

But now, finally, in one earth-shattering moment, he can no longer control himself. "I am Joseph."

We have to try to understand two questions: What motivated Joseph to conceal himself, and what finally prompted him to reveal his identity to his brothers?

One clue to Joseph's secrecy appeared in last week's *parsha*. "And Joseph saw his brothers and recognized them, but he made himself unrecognizable to them and spoke harshly with them. . . . and Joseph remembered the dreams which he had dreamt about them, and said to them, 'You are spies . . .'" (Genesis 42:8, 9). Joseph does not remember "his dreams," rather "the dreams." As Joseph had already told the baker, the butler, and Pharaoh, Joseph understood that dreams came as messages from God. He identifies them as traces of prophecy, which he is forbidden to ignore. Joseph's dream of the stars bowing down to him was finally being realized; the brothers had just bowed down to him. Yet something was missing—here there were only ten brothers, while he had envisioned eleven stars bowing down to him. To completely bring the dreams to fruition, Joseph must devise a family intrigue that will ultimately bring his brother Benjamin, the eleventh star, down to Egypt.

Yet despite the fulfillment of the dreams, Joseph still does not reveal himself to his brothers. Apparently, an additional factor contributes to Joseph's hiding of his true identity.

What finally brings Joseph to reveal his identity? Judah's speech. Immediately after Judah's dramatic monologue at the opening of this week's *parsha*, Joseph realizes that he no longer needs to disguise himself. With a screaming cry that is heard throughout Egypt, Joseph releases twenty-two years of isolated suffering. His superhuman control no longer necessary, Joseph breaks down in an outpouring of love and compassion for his brothers. They are stunned. How could the one who has tormented them, ridiculed them, and compelled them to jeopardize their youngest sibling Benjamin, now proclaim his love for them? What could have motivated him?

What would have happened if Joseph had immediately revealed himself to his brothers upon their arrival in Egypt? They would forever have berated themselves over their mistreatment of him. They would never have been able to absolve themselves of their sin; they could never have redeemed themselves. Their guilt would have precluded any possible family reconciliation.

Joseph, the original cause of the family dissension, will ultimately become the force enabling their reunion. Joseph carefully engineers the scenario through which Judah is able to atone for the sin of the brothers. Judah, the very brother who proposed to sell Joseph to the Ishmaelites, now emerges as Benjamin's defender and savior. Judah is now willing "to sell himself into slavery" in order to save Rachel's second and only other son, Benjamin. His emotional plea to Joseph to take him into slavery, and release Benjamin, confirms his complete turnaround. Joseph, having enabled Judah and the brothers to exonerate themselves, has nothing left to prove. He collapses with a cry of release, a cry of joy, a cry of freedom.

The confrontation between Joseph and Judah is understood by the rabbis to have eschatological implications. This is not only a struggle between two individuals but between two forces in history. The "end of days" will be ushered in by the succession of two messiahs: *Mashiach ben Yosef* (Messiah as the son of Joseph) and *Mashiach ben David* (Messiah as the son of David, a descendant of Judah). Like Joseph, who provided food during the famine, *Mashiach ben Yosef* will foster the physical prosperity of the Jewish people. *Mashiach ben Yosef* will ultimately yield to *Mashiach ben David*, who will lead the Jewish people into an epoch of internal, spiritual fulfillment.

The rabbis state that the final Messiah will be a descendant of Judah because of Judah's ability to change, to atone for his prior mistake, to recognize his faults and amend his ways.

Around the *Shabbat* Table

1. Following Joseph's revelation of his identity, the Torah states that "And afterward his brothers spoke with him [Joseph]" (Genesis 45:15), though it does not detail the content of their conversation. Why are the details of their conversation less significant than the mere fact that they were communicating? Why is this a fitting end to their crisis?

2. In his eulogy at the funeral of Theodor Herzl, Rav Kook referred
    to Herzl as a spark in the line of "Mashiach ben Joseph." Why do
    you think that he said this?

3. What do you think usually prevents family members from recon-
    ciling conflicts?

SHABBAT LUNCH: Giving and Taking Advice

"And Judah drew near to him [Joseph] and said: My master, please
let your servant speak a word in my master's ears, and do not be
angry at your servant, because you are just like Pharaoh." [Gen-
esis 44:18]

At the end of last week's *parsha*, *Mikketz*, after the stolen silver
goblet had been found in Benjamin's belongings, Judah offered to
indenture himself and all of the brothers to Joseph. Joseph refused
his proposition, stating, " . . . the man in whose hand the goblet was
found shall become my servant, and the rest of you may peacefully
return to your father" (Genesis 44:17). Judah then changes his tone,
takes the liberty of approaching Joseph, and courageously admon-
ishes Joseph, presently the second most powerful figure in Egypt.
In one of the longest speeches in the Torah (seventeen verses), Judah
attempts to convince Joseph to change his mind and not subject
Benjamin to servitude.
     Was Judah obligated to intervene on behalf of his brother, Ben-
jamin?
     One of the most crucial, difficult, and hazardous mitzvot in the
Torah is the obligation of *tochacha*, understood either as rebuking
or giving advice. A Jew is not allowed to idly observe another's behavior; we are actors on the world stage, not spectators. Rabbi
Yochanan states in the Talmud, "Anyone who could possibly have
prevented another from transgressing and does not prevent it, will
eventually receive the punishment for that sin" (*Shabbat* 54b). In

his epic work, the *Mishneh Torah* (Laws of Knowledge, Chapter 6:6, 7), Maimonides codifies and extends this principle:

1. When a person hates another person—he should not despise him in silence . . . rather it is incumbent upon him [the hater] to talk to the one he hates and say: "Why did you do this to me? Why did you transgress against me in this matter?"

2. Someone who notices that his friend has sinned, or is not going on a beneficial path, is obligated to return his friend to a better way and to inform him that he is sinning against himself through his actions.

We are obligated not only to prevent someone from sinning but also to prevent one from straying from "a beneficial path." What is this beneficial path? Who is to decide exactly what it is?

Maimonides, always precise in his language, alters the relationship in question in these two laws. The first law, pertaining to the more objective act of "transgressing," concerns "another person," whereas the second law, describing this "beneficial path," deals in the context of a "friend." Precisely because of the depth and trust of the relationship, one bears a special responsibility toward one's friends. This responsibility means not only to be the voice of love and support but also to counsel and, on occasion, to criticize a friend's behavior. To refrain from involvement is regarded as being negligent in the duty and true concern of friendship. It is virtually impossible for one to objectively assess one's own life; one's friends fulfill the critical role of providing greater clarity and insight.

Yet isn't there a great risk involved here? Can't the most well-intended advice sometimes backfire and endanger the strength or very existence of a relationship? Is every piece of advice worth articulating?

Rabbi Ellah said, "Just as a person is commanded to say something which will be heard, so too he or she is commanded *not* to say something which will *not* be heard" (*Yevamot* 65a). The goal is not for the friend to offer advice but to improve the situation. Over 2,000 years ago, the midrash lamented the precariousness of this endeavor:

> Rabbi Tarfon said: "I swear that there is no one in this generation who is worthy of giving someone else advice."
> Rabbi Elazar . . . said: "I swear that there is no one in this generation who is capable of receiving advice ."
> Rabbi Akiva said: "I swear that there is no one in this generation who knows how to offer advice."

Prior to delivering words of advice, the individual must examine three elements of the procedure: (1) Am I worthy of offering advice? Is the advice sincere and not stemming from any anger or conceit; could I be accused of being hypocritical? (2) Is my friend capable of accepting the advice? Will he or she become defensive; is he or she feeling secure enough at this time? (3) Is the style and method of giving advice appropriate? If one cannot respond positively to these questions, then one is obligated to remain silent.

Judah's reproof of Joseph serves as a classic example of successfully fulfilling the three components of giving advice. His brave act precipitates the family's ultimate reconciliation.

Around the *Shabbat* Table

1. What are the major obstacles or qualities that preclude the receiving of advice? What eventually happens to a person who is incapable of accepting advice?

2. What usually happens to a relationship when appropriate advice is offered and accepted? How might one overcome the hesitancy of giving advice?

3. Have you ever given or received advice that ultimately deepened the relationship? When?

Seuda Shlishit: A Scratch on the Crown

In our *parsha,* Judah acknowledges and repents for his past mistakes. Twenty-two years after he had suggested selling Joseph into slavery, he defends Joseph's brother Benjamin and offers to take his place as a servant to the Pharaoh of Egypt. His awareness of his previous failings enables him to grow, confront Joseph, and ultimately emerge victorious.

The *Maggid* of Dovno (1741–1804) was renowned for his moralistic stories. The following story echoes the theme of this week's *parsha:*

Once, a king owned a great diamond. It was his prize possession, as it had no equal in the world. But one day, he noticed that the diamond had become chipped. Stretching from this chip was a scratch on the diamond—a very deep and jagged scratch. The diamond was no longer perfect. The king despaired.

He consulted all of his experts, diamond-cutters, and artists. They told him that it was impossible to repair the diamond. One offered to cut off the section that was damaged, but the king did not wish to shrink his precious diamond. One said that the king would simply have to look for a new diamond—for this one was irreparably flawed, but the king did not want to part with his diamond.

Then, one day, a new diamond-cutter came to the kingdom. He had heard about the king's problem and offered to fix the diamond. He said that he could make it look even more beautiful than before.

So the king entrusted him with the diamond, and the new diamond-cutter secluded himself in his workroom. For days he did not emerge, his light remaining on all night. How could he repair the chipped and scratched diamond?

Finally, he appeared. With a triumphant expression upon his face, he approached the king and presented the diamond, resting upon a scarlet cushion. The king looked, and then smiled. He saw what the diamond-cutter had done. There sat the diamond, the most beautiful diamond in the world.

In the place of the chip, the diamond-cutter had engraved a rose;

out of the long and jagged scratch the diamond-cutter had carved the stem of the rose.

Around the *Shabbat* Table

1. What light might this story shed on dealing with moments of despair?

2. Moses requested to see the "face of God." God responded by saying that Moses could see "His back." Rav Soloveitchik explains that this enigmatic section of the Torah refers to God's role in history. We cannot understand the "face of God," how God functions in the present, though sometimes when we look "back" in history, hundreds of years later, we can begin to fathom why certain events occurred. Can this idea be connected to the Maggid of Dovno's story?

3 Have you ever profited from a difficult experience?

Vayechi

FRIDAY NIGHT MEAL: Dying Words

The *parsha* of *Vayechi* concludes the book of Genesis. Twenty-three generations after the creation of the world, the human race seems immeasurably removed from its original state. We have moved from the paradise of the Garden of Eden to the spiritual abyss of Egypt. Irrevocably distant from the original world of endless life, the book of Genesis now closes with the embalming of Joseph. Even his physical body is prevented from returning to the cycle of life, "from dust to dust," and now exists in a state of continuous, ceaseless, perpetual death.

The hope of either regaining or recreating paradise has become increasingly remote. The visions and sacrifices of the forefathers have seemingly disappeared as internecine strife plagues the family of Jacob. In the depths of Egypt, amid the impending emergence of a wicked Pharaoh and generations of enslavement, the *parsha* of *Vayechi* renews the hope and vision of the Jewish people.

The centerpiece of the *parsha* of *Vayechi* is Jacob's blessing of his twelve sons. On his deathbed, Jacob gathers all of his sons to hear his final words. Each son receives his own individual blessing, without competition, without comparison. Yet it is not clear what Jacob's motivation is for this last dramatic act. What is the nature and purpose of these blessings? Why does Jacob feel a need to bless each of his sons? What is Jacob's intention?

Several questions must be addressed:

1. In the beginning of this *parsha*, Jacob blesses Joseph's children, Efraim and Menashe. Why does Jacob bless his grandchildren before he blesses his own children?! Joseph's children receive a blessing from their grandfather before Joseph receives his own blessing from his father! Why?

2. Jacob begins his blessings with a unique preamble: "Gather yourselves together, that I may tell you that which will befall you in the end of days" (Genesis 49:1). Why does Jacob mention "the end of days?"

3. Why does Jacob first entreat Joseph (Genesis 47:30) and then again command the rest of his sons (Genesis 49:29) to bury him in Israel? Both before and then immediately after the blessings, Jacob returns to this theme of not burying him in Egypt. Why the emphasis and repetition?

Jacob's actions indicate a penetrating awareness of the fragility and potential crisis that the nascent Jewish people may undergo at the moment of his death. First of all, it is critical that he, the last of the forefathers, unite his sons in a bond of mutual cooperation and dependence. There must be an immediate halt to internal dispute; otherwise, the Jewish people is liable to fracture into contentious, vying sects, determined to destroy each other. In order to rectify this problem, Jacob not only gives each of his sons his own unique blessing, but does so *in the presence of all of the other sons*. Each son hears the others' blessings. Each son now realizes that everyone has received a special blessing, that none are competing with or threatening the others' portions. Moreover, the destinies of the brothers are all now interlinked, their futures all mutually dependent.

Unity, however, is not enough. The sons must also be reminded of their ultimate responsibility and purpose.

The next generations of Jews who will be raised in Egypt will be completely different from that of Abraham, Isaac, Jacob, and his sons. These first four generations all lived in Israel. They all benefited from Abraham's historic journey and viscerally experienced the spiritual power of living and walking in Israel. Now, for the first time in its history, the Jewish people faces the predicament of assimilation into a foreign culture, in a foreign land. The next generations of Jews will live and die outside of the Promised Land, never having tasted what the Talmud refers to as "the air of Israel, the air that makes one wise."

Thus, Jacob directs his sons toward the future. Jacob's first goal is to remind them not to forget that they have a mission extending far beyond themselves, that they are essential links in a chain that must continue well after their demise. They must not become consumed with their present life; they must not become enamored of the luxury and modernity of Goshen (their place of abode within Egypt).

To this end, Jacob begins by blessing the grandchildren, Ephraim and Menashe. First and foremost, Joseph (and all of the sons through him) must become future-oriented. The blessing for the present only has meaning insofar as it will be sustained in future generations. Similarly, when Jacob gathers together his sons, he does not simply offer them his blessing. Rather, he instructs them to reflect upon "the end of days." He wrests them away from the present, engaging them with visions of hope and of their greater, ultimate destiny.

Similarly, Jacob emphasizes and repeats his wish to be buried in Israel. One last time, before they sink into the quagmire of Egypt, the sons must again walk in Israel. Jacob's dying wish is to be buried "with his fathers ... [in the burial site] which Abraham bought." One last time, he reminds them of their past, of their history. Jacob uses the blessings to eternalize his mission and that of his sons, to cogently convey to his sons their role in the fulfilling of this dream.

In Jacob's mind, the memory of the past and the sustained claim on the future are inherently intertwined.

In the depths of Egypt, on the brink of cruel and wearying slavery, the *parsha* of *Vayechi* bears the seeds of a better future.

Around the *Shabbat* Table

1. When Jacob sees his grandchildren, Efraim and Menashe, he asks their father, Joseph, "Who are these?" (Genesis 48:8). Yet Jacob had already been with them in Egypt for almost twenty years. What was Jacob really asking Joseph?

2. To what degree are our actions functions of our personal, present needs or of our considerations for the needs of the future generations?

3. What advice would you give to your children?

SHABBAT LUNCH: Raising Children

In his final words, Jacob blesses his sons. He speaks to each of his children differently—each child receives a unique message. For the first time in Jewish history, the line of inheritance, the acceptance of the mission first transmitted to Abraham, is bestowed upon each and all of the sons.

Is there a Jewish approach to raising children? What characterizes Jewish parenting?

"Educate a child according to its way, even when he grows old he will not depart from it" (Proverbs 22:6). What does "its way" refer to? Are children born with a natural "way" of their own, or are children born with a *tabula rasa* (blank slate) and then nurtured or socialized into their behavioral patterns? In contemporary parlance, are we products of "nature" or "nurture"?

While never underestimating the influence of environment or experiences, the Talmud relates that a person is born with natural qualities and inclinations. A child's "way" begins at conception. This "way" is then expressed through character traits, for example, being artistic or musical, introverted or extroverted, cerebral or experiential, and so on. These traits serve as the raw material of the child and are, in and of themselves, value-free, reflecting neither "good" nor "bad" behavior.

Thus, the first challenge for parents is to observe carefully their child's behavior and to attempt to discern his or her natural tendencies. Their conclusions should become the basis for the parents' expectations of the child. Expectations stemming from the parents' own desires, rather than from the child's innate qualities, will inevitably yield distress and frustration for both parent and child. The Talmud (*Shabbat* 156a) relates that if a child is born with an "affinity for blood" (i.e., aggressive tendencies), it is incumbent upon the parents to perceive this quality and to direct it positively. If the parents are unsuccessful, the child may become a violent criminal; if the parents are moderately successful, the child may become a *shochet* (ritual slaughterer of animals), and if the parents direct this tendency productively, the child may become a *mohel* (circumcisor).

Hence, the primary role of parents is to help the child understand, fulfill, and productively channel his or her "way." For this reason, the Talmud (*Bava Batra* 21b) reports that only with great reluctance did the rabbis accept and introduce public elementary school education. Prior to this, home education allowed the parent to mold the educational process according to the unique traits of their child, to the child's being, the child's "way"; in contrast, formal group education focuses more on transmitting objective content and maintaining social discipline, frequently inhibiting the child's creative potential.

The ultimate test of the parents' success will be the child's direction of his or her natural qualities toward the common benefit, toward something beyond him- or herself, toward the improvement of the world. The self-awareness that the child develops will eventually yield an independent personality and maximize the child's potential contribution to society. Independent thinking does not simply manifest itself when the child has reached adulthood. Rather, its roots are present from the very first moments of a child's life, as the parents endeavor to understand that the child already possesses, and must strive to fulfill, its own "way."

The midrash states that on his deathbed, Jacob was worried that not all of his sons would continue his struggle to establish monotheism in the world. When he asked them, they replied, "*Shema Yisrael* (Jacob's other name), the Lord is our God, the Lord is one." They affirmed Jacob's primary tenet of belief; each, in his own way, would be devoted to Jacob's mission.

Around the *Shabbat* Table

1. *Pirkei Avot* 5:21 (Ethics of the Fathers) states that the decade of one's twenties should be dedicated to "pursuit" (dreams, exploration, etc.). How might this be connected to the discovery of one's own way?

2. Do you know any parents who, in your opinion, successfully raised their children each in his or her own "way?" What was the key to their success?

3. What do you think characterizes your "way"?

Seuda Shlishit: Friendship beyond Words

Jacob blessed each of his sons with a different blessing. The tribe of Zebulun, for example, was destined to grow wealthy through trade and commerce. The tribe of Yissachar was gifted with intellectual skills, excelling in the learning of Torah. The midrash (*Bamidbar Rabbah* 13:17) relates that together, these two brothers created an ideal friendship and partnership. Zebulun shared his financial wealth with Yissachar; Yissachar shared his wealth in learning with Zebulun.

The hasidim tell the story of another ideal friendship:

> The Rebbe of Vorke and the Rebbe of Trisk were childhood friends. They went to school together; they were inseparable. As time passed, they both became leaders of hasidic dynasties.
>
> They made a promise to each other that every week, they would write letters to each other. A hasid was chosen and given the honor of delivering the letters between the Rebbes.
>
> Every Friday morning the Vorker Rebbe would hand an envelope to the hasid, who would carry it through the woods till he reached Trisk and give it to the Trisker Rebbe. Usually within just a few minutes, the Trisker Rebbe would give him a letter in response, and he would carry it back to Vorke. Each time the Rebbes would open the letter, huge smiles would appear on their faces.
>
> This continued for week after week, year after year, for over fifteen years.
>
> Then, one time, while the hasid was carrying the letter to the Trisker Rebbe, a thought suddenly passed through his mind. "I have been carrying these letters for over fifteen years, and I have never once dared to open up the letters of the Rebbes. I wonder what they are saying to each other?"
>
> The thought nagged at him ceaselessly, until he could no longer control himself. With trembling fingers he opened the Rebbe's letter. Inside—was only a blank piece of paper. The hasid was overcome with astonishment and confusion. "Can it be that for fifteen years I have been delivering blank letters?"
>
> He delivered the letter to the Trisker Rebbe and received another one in return. As on his way to Trisk, he could no longer control himself. This time he tore open the envelope only to find—another blank piece of paper!
>
> The hasid delivered the letter to the Vorker Rebbe, but later on that night he was ridden with guilt and curiosity. He could not sleep.

Early the next morning he rushed to the Rebbe, confessing. "Rebbe, I have to talk to you. After all these years, I couldn't resist. I opened your letter. But all I found was a blank piece of paper. Rebbe, I'm ashamed that I opened your letter, but Rebbe, please explain to me—have I been carrying blank letters for fifteen years?"

The Rebbe comforted the hasid with a kind look, and then began to explain. "You have to understand. The Rebbe from Trisk and I have a very special relationship. A relationship that goes well beyond what words can express. Sometimes, we do send actual letters to each other. But sometimes, the letters are blank. You see, sometimes we don't have the words to express how we feel about each other. What we want to communicate can only be done on a blank piece of paper."

Around the *Shabbat* Table

1. Why do you think the two Rebbes made this agreement of sending weekly letters? Do you think that it was for the giver or the receiver of the letter?

2. Often partnerships, like that of Yissachar and Zebulun, develop into deep and lasting relationships. Why do you think this is so?

3. Did you ever send or receive a "blank letter"?

Exodus

Shemot

FRIDAY NIGHT MEAL: Slavery and Freedom

In the first five chapters of the book of Shemot, two themes are woven together: the beginning of the subjugation of the Jewish people and the emergence of Moses as their leader.

First, a new king (Pharaoh) reigns over Egypt, issuing decree after decree enslaving the nascent Jewish people and afflicting them with increasingly hard labor. Year after year, generation after generation, the Jewish people toil in servitude. Finally, Pharaoh ordains that all of their newborn sons shall be cast into the river. "And it came to pass in the course of those many days, that the king of Egypt died, and the children of Israel sighed from their bondage, and they cried out . . . " (Exodus 2:23). There are no signs of rebellion, no clandestine plotting. Denied of all control over their plight, they are left to lament and bewail their pitiful situation.

In the midst of this travail, their future leader, Moses, is born. Separated from his family at infancy, he grows up in the palace of Pharaoh. His reality is diametrically opposed to that of his people. He never works for Pharaoh's taskmasters, never dreads their cruel beatings. The midrash states that Pharaoh would hug and kiss young Moses and place his crown upon the child's head. While the Jewish people were being enslaved, their future leader was being adorned with Pharaoh's crown.

Why does the Torah weave together two utterly distinct and seemingly opposing themes—the slavery of the Jewish people versus the luxury of Moses?

Why couldn't a leader emerge from within the people? Why didn't a Jew who had endured the bitter suffering of slavery foment the rebellion? Why was it necessary that he who brings the Jewish people to freedom be raised apart from his people, on Pharaoh's lap?

One of the tragic effects of slavery is the incremental submission to and acceptance of its reality, until the slave cannot imagine a different existence. Imperceptibly, the slave begins to see him- or herself as a slave, incapable of imagining a different life. The slave's loss of control over his or her time and actions eventually leads to the loss of control over one's own persona. Almost involuntarily, the slave begins to believe that—"just as my condition is unchangeable, so, too, am I." When Moses spoke God's words of the hope of redemption to the Jewish people, they could not hear him, "because of the smallness of [their] spirit and [their] hard labor" (Exodus 6:9). The hardness of their labor eventually debilitated and enslaved not only their bodies but their spirit and their self-image as well.

Concomitant with this self-perception comes a similar attitude toward others. Burdened by the hopeless drudgery of their predicament, slaves cannot imagine that any other slave might have the power to transform or transcend circumstances. Their collective slavery diminishes their individual self-value and consequently affects how they view each other.

Individually and collectively, the oppressive reality of slavery crushes the dreams and yearnings of the people. The not-too-distant memories of their ancestors in the Promised Land, or of Joseph and his pivotal role in Egypt, are obliterated through the daily harshness of their labors. Pharaoh succeeds in his objective of disabling the Jewish people, weakening them in both body and spirit.

The future leader must be wholly detached from this inescapable dilemma. Moses grows up as the heir apparent to the leader of the most powerful country of his time. His whole childhood is directed toward taking responsibility for a people. Growing up in the palace of Pharaoh, Moses undergoes an apprenticeship to power. According to several commentaries, Moses' initial reluctance to accept God's mission for him to help emancipate the Jewish people does not stem from his lack of self-confidence but rather from his concern that, because he has not shared their experience of slavery, they will not listen to him.

These two themes—(1) a nation trying to sever its bonds of physical and psychological enslavement, and (2) Moses' attempt to assert his leadership and have it accepted by the people—will continue to be woven together throughout the entire book of Exodus.

Around the *Shabbat* Table

1. Moses remonstrates with God that he cannot talk to the Jewish people because of the "heaviness" of his speech (Exodus 4:10). God then appoints his brother Aaron to be Moses' mouthpiece. Yet the entire book of Deuteronomy is a single speech of Moses. Why do you think that Moses thought that he could not speak to the people, and what happened to change that perception?

2. At the beginning of the Siddur (prayerbook) is a blessing thanking God for not making one a slave. During the Holocaust, in the ghetto of Kovno, the question was asked if it was still appropriate to utter this blessing. The rabbi of Kovno responded that, then of all times, it was essential to recite it. Why do you think he gave that answer?

3. The redeeming leader, Moses, did not emerge from amid the people. The Talmud states that "a person cannot become a prophet in his home city." Why? Do you think that friends and relatives promote or hinder a person from making changes in his or her life? Why?

SHABBAT LUNCH: Having Children

The first chapter of *Shemot* describes the afflictions that Pharaoh decrees upon the Jewish people, culminating with "Every son that is born you shall cast into the river ... " (Exodus 1:22). How do the Jewish people respond to their increasing hardship? There are no signs of rebellion or clandestine plotting, but are there any subtle indications that the Jewish people somehow defy their adversity?

The beginning of the account of the response of the Jews, the opening verse of the second chapter of this *parsha*, is remarkable only in its vagueness. "And a man from the house of Levi went and betrothed a woman from the tribe of Levi" (Exodus 2:1). This man and woman would subsequently give birth to Moses, "And the woman conceived, and bore a son." Yet the Torah would not reveal the names of these two figures until the sixth chapter of Exodus, five chapters later, when we learn that "Amram betrothed Yocheved ... and she gave birth to Aaron and Moses ... " (Exodus 6:20).

Why does the Torah present Moses' mother and father as nameless figures? Why did Amram decide to marry Yocheved precisely at this juncture in history? And most important, what does this event, the advent of the Jewish resistance to Pharaoh's decrees, signify?

From the juxtaposition of events in the Torah it is known that Yocheved had given birth to their first two children, Aaron and Miriam, prior to this betrothal. If Yocheved and Amram already were husband and wife, why was there a need here for a second betrothal? The Talmud (*Sotah* 21a) explains that immediately after Pharaoh decreed that Jewish males must be cast into the river, Amram publicly announced that it was now futile to bring children into this world and set a precedent for the community by divorcing his wife. His daughter, Miriam, then castigated him, claiming that his decree was harsher than that of Pharaoh, since Pharaoh had only dictated that sons were to be thrown into the river, while Amram's decision included daughters as well. Persuaded by his daughter, Amram remarried his former wife, Yocheved. It is this betrothal that this week's *parsha* refers to. Thus, the first defiance of Pharaoh's decrees was the decision to continue to have children.

Since Amram and Yocheved already have a son and a daughter, do they have any responsibility to have more children? What are the criteria by which to decide the number of children to have?

The Mishnah (*Yevamot* 61b) states that a man should not refrain from the mitzvah to "be fruitful and multiply" (Genesis 1:28) unless he has had two children. The Talmud then comments that the school of Shammai defined this parameter in terms of two males, based either upon the example of Moses (who had two sons, Gershom and Eliezer), or Adam (who had two sons, Cain and Abel). The ruling (*Shulchan Aruch, Even HaEzer* 1:5) eventually sided with the school of Hillel who posited that one has fulfilled the mitzvah to "be fruitful and multiply" by having one daughter and one son, based upon God's creation of the world with one male and one female, Adam and Eve.

The Talmud further states that a person who has had children in his youth should, nevertheless, continue to have children in his "old age." Maimonides writes that "even if one has fulfilled this mitzvah, one should not refrain from bearing children while he still has vigor, as any Jew who brings another being into this world has, in effect, built a whole world" (Laws of Marriage 15:16).

Amram and Yocheved were introduced anonymously, known simply as "a man from the house of Levi . . . and a woman from the tribe of Levi" (Exodus 2:1). At this crossroads in history, their individual identities are not significant. Instead, the Torah are portrays them as the prototypes of a man and woman who chose, despite the inherent dangers, to continue to have children. Since they already have two children, their decision to remarry and have another child serves as an inspiration for the whole community. This act of courage and leadership resulted in the birth of Moses, the next leader of the Jewish people.

Around the *Shabbat* Table

1. According to Jewish law, one only fulfills the mitzvah of "be fruit-
    ful and multiply" through having grandchildren. Why might this
    be so?

2. Yocheved and Amram chose to have another child, Moses, who
    eventually led the Jewish people out of their bondage in Egypt.
    The Talmud (*Shabbat* 119b) states that the verse, "Do not touch
    my anointed ones [messiahs]" (Psalms 105:15) refers to children
    who are studying Torah, and that the world only continues to ex-
    ist because of their learning. Furthermore, it adds that one should
    not interrupt the learning of children even to rebuild the Temple
    and that any city that does not have a school for children should
    be either destroyed or excommunicated. Why do you think that
    the rabbis chose these ways to convey the centrality of the edu-
    cation of children? Do you think that this emphasis is reflected in
    your society today?

3   How many children would you like to have? Why?

Seuda Shlishit: Removing A Holocaust Number

This week's *parsha* describes the first persecution of the Jewish
people. "And Pharaoh charged all his people, saying, 'Every son that
is born you shall cast into the river . . .'" (Exodus 1:22). In the twentieth century, during the Holocaust, the Jewish people were once
again forced to suffer from the decrees of an evil ruler. The memory
of these tragic experiences did not vanish with the conclusion of
the war. After the Holocaust, Rabbi Oshry, the former rabbi of the
Kovno ghetto, wrote a book of responsa, including questions he was
asked both during and after the Holocaust period. One such question dealt with removing numbers branded by the Germans on their
Jewish victims. Rabbi Oshry writes:

After the liberation, a young woman from a respected family asked me the following question. Since the Germans had branded her with a number in accord with their system of assigning numbers to every prisoner in the concentration camp, she wanted to have plastic surgery performed to remove the mark that constantly reminded her of the horror of those years. According to Jewish law, was it permissible to remove the number?

Response:

The Germans branded these numbers on the arms of Jews as a sign of shame, as though to say that the bearers of these branded numbers are not human beings, but cattle to be brutally beaten, tortured, and slaughtered at will.

Not only should these numbers not denigrate us but, on the contrary, such a number should be viewed as a sign of honor and glory, as a monument to the unforgivable bestiality of those vile murderers. As part of the plot to exterminate the Jewish people ... the branded numbers guaranteed that if a Jew ever escaped from a camp, the imprint on his arm would reveal to everyone who found him that he was a Jew and fair game to be put to death.

The obligation to recall the entire scope of the Holocaust, not taking our minds off it for even a moment, is today a redoubled obligation, [to prevent] the world from forgetting the evils that the Germans perpetrated.

I feel that this woman should under no circumstances remove the branded number from her arm, for by doing so she is fulfilling the wishes of the German evildoers and abetting their effort to have the Holocaust forgotten, as if we Jews had created a fiction against them. Let her wear the sign with pride.

Around the *Shabbat* Table

1. The memories of persecution and evil continue long after the events have passed. How do you think that the experience of slavery in Egypt continued to affect the Jewish people after their

exodus? In what ways do you think the Holocaust continues to affect the Jewish people today?

2. What do you think is the purpose of remembering and commemorating tragedies that have befallen the Jewish people? Do you agree that there is an obligation to remember the Holocaust? Why?

3. Have you ever experienced anti-Semitism in your life? How did you respond? Does its memory still affect you?

Vayera

FRIDAY NIGHT MEAL: The Hardened Heart of Addiction

And the Lord said to Moses, " . . . You will speak all that I have commanded you, and Aaron your brother will speak to Pharaoh, that he send the children of Israel from his land. . . . But Pharaoh will not listen to you, and I will place my hand on Egypt, and I will bring . . . my people, the children of Israel, out from Egypt in great miracles." [Exodus 7:2-4]

And Pharaoh hardened his heart at this time also, and would not let the people go. [Exodus 8: 28]

The *parsha* of *Vayera* describes the first seven of the ten plagues that afflict Egypt. With ascending vehemence, the supremely powerful people of Egypt is rendered utterly helpless, the most fertile of countries becomes a wasteland. Over the span of more than a year, the people of Egypt live in psychological terror of the visitation of the plagues. All this transpires because "Pharaoh will not listen to you."

During the first five plagues, despite Pharaoh's witnessing of the continual ravaging of his land, despite the warnings and their fulfillment, he refuses to accede to Moses' request to let the Jewish people go. (During the last five plagues, God "hardens" Pharaoh's heart, removing his free will.)

Why didn't Pharaoh listen to the warnings of Moses and Aaron? Why didn't Pharaoh change his mind? What does it mean "to harden one's heart"? What prevented Pharaoh from seeing the folly of his decisions and led him to bring about the devastation of his own people and land?

Pharaoh imprisoned himself in a reality from which he could not escape. Despite the drastic consequences, Pharaoh was unable to change. He had become addicted. To what? To himself. He singlehandedly ruled Egypt, acquiring for himself the status of a god, neither respecting nor considering any contrary opinions. He rejected the advice of those closest to him (Exodus 10:7), and having convinced himself of his mythical powers and exaggerated position, he sought absolute control.

Paradoxically, in the end, Pharaoh loses all control—over his nation, his people, and even himself. The one who attempts to enslave an entire people, ironically, becomes the epitome of a slave, bereft of any power to alter his life. He becomes addicted to his set of principles, his vision of himself, his power. This addiction precludes any change. Despite the clear and disastrous consequences, Pharaoh refuses to adjust his convictions. How does this happen?

The Talmud (*Yoma* 87a) affirms that someone who says, "I will sin and [afterward] repent, I will sin and [afterward] repent," will not be able to actualize his repentance. Why not? The Talmud's repetition of the declaration implies that the declaration is not an isolated remark; rather, it represents a habit, a syndrome. The sinner continues to perform the same actions, while simultaneously thinking that it will be possible to change these actions or to disassociate from them. Eventually, this dissonance will be resolved in favor of the action, as the habit will become part of the person's normative behavior. The Talmud contends that *the action will control the person more than the person will shape the action.* Despite the expressed desire to abandon the behavior, eventually, we will somehow rationalize our actions and convince ourselves that the actions were justified.

Pharaoh, having convinced himself for so long that he possessed complete and supreme control over his nation, fell victim to his own self-perception. He could not listen to others and eventually imprisoned himself in his own conceptions. His worldview became petrified, his heart became hardened, he himself became a slave.

Around the *Shabbat* Table

1. The quintessential conflict in Egypt is reflected in the personalities of the respective leaders, Moses and Pharaoh. In what way is Moses the antithesis of Pharaoh? Who do you think is a more typical prototype of leadership?

2. Why do you think that some people are more able to listen than others? At what times are you more ready to listen and change your mind than at others? Why?

3. How is it possible to "soften" someone's hardened heart?

SHABBAT LUNCH: Getting Closer

And God spoke to Moses, and said to him, "I am the Lord; and I appeared to Abraham, to Isaac, and to Jacob by the name of God Almighty [*El Shaddai*], but my name, the Lord [*Ado-nai*], I did not make known to them." [Exodus 6:2,3]

The beginning of this week's *parsha* involves a breakthrough in the relationship between God and Moses. Though there have already been numerous prophetic revelations in the Torah in which God's words are communicated to the patriarchs and matriarchs, nevertheless, the beginning of this *parsha* manifests a qualitatively new and deeper stage in the relationship between God and humanity. A new name of God—*Ado-nai*—is revealed.

The revelation of this name indicates that Moses achieves a closeness with God that eludes all of the previous figures in the Torah. The mystics considered the name *Ado-nai* to be the most intimate and holy name of God. Whereas other names of God may express qualities of power, mercy, or creation, this name is comprised of the past, present, and future constructs of the verb "to be" in Hebrew, indicating God's eternality and transcendence.

Why did God disclose this special name only to Moses? Furthermore, why did this breakthrough occur precisely at this moment in their relationship?

There is one fundamental change that transforms God's relationship with Moses: the emergence of the Jewish people. Moses has now become the spokesman for the Jewish people, not only to Pharaoh but also to God. He does not speak to God from the vantage point of an individual Jew but rather as the representative of an entire people. At the end of last week's *parsha*, after Pharaoh refused to allow the Jewish people to leave Egypt and increased the intensity of their labors, Moses challenged the effectiveness of God's actions. "And Moses returned to the Lord and said, 'Lord, why have you dealt badly with this *people* . . . You have not saved Your *people* at all'" (Exodus 5:22, 23). God does not reveal this new name to Moses—the individual prophet—but rather to Moses, the spiritual/political leader of his people.

Moses speaks, not as an individual, but rather as a representative of the Jewish people. It is on this national level that God now relates to him and thus enables their relationship to reach more profound depths. All of the previous figures in the Torah had related to God either as individuals or as forerunners of a future people. For each of them, the existence of the Jewish people possessed a dreamlike quality, a hope or an abstract vision. For Moses, however, the vision becomes reality. This aspect of the relationship, the impending destiny of the Jewish people, becomes the focus between God and Moses and several verses later will culminate with "And I will take you to me for a people" (Exodus 6:7).

This model of the growth and deepening of a relationship between God and Moses is also applicable to the human realm. While two individuals may develop a serious attachment to each other, if it is limited to the scope of their particular worlds and personalities, part of their beings will never be shared, names will not be disclosed. The sharing of dreams, goals, or concerns that are beyond personal well-being, will afford insight and understanding into each other that their purely personal, individual bonds would most likely not generate. In Moses' case, God revealed a new name, reflecting a new level in their relationship.

When Rabbi Akiva, one of the most romantic personalities of the Talmud, proposed to his wife, he promised her a bracelet engraved with "Jerusalem of Gold." Their love for each other transcended their individual personalities and bonded them with the Jewish people and Jerusalem.

Around the *Shabbat* Table

1. Moses achieved a deeper relationship with God because he represented the Jewish community. One of the rationales for the requirement of a *minyan* for prayer is to indicate that each Jew needs a community to fulfill his spiritual self. Why is it preferable to develop one's spiritual self in the context of a community? Do you think that there is a potential danger in developing one's spiritual self alone?

2. In the blessing after eating, Birkat Hamazon, additional names of God are inserted if there are more than ten men. An opinion in the Mishnah (Berakhot 7:3) suggests inserting additional names of God if 100, 1,000, or 10,000 men are present. Were you ever in

a setting of thousands or tens of thousands of Jews? Did this affect your Jewish identity or your relationship with God? In what ways? Why?

3. Did you ever experience a moment in which you were functioning not only as an individual, but as a representative of the Jewish people?

Seuda Shlishit: Courage and a Modern Pharaoh

And the Lord spoke to Moses, saying, "Go in, speak to Pharaoh, king of Egypt, that he may let the children of Israel go out of his land." [Exodus 6:10,11]

Moses' courageous example of confronting Pharaoh and demanding freedom for the Jewish people has been replicated countless times in Jewish history. Natan Sharansky resolutely defied the totalitarian regime of the Soviet Union and campaigned for the right of Soviet Jews to emigrate to Israel. For his beliefs, he was sentenced to thirteen years' imprisonment, including long stretches of solitary confinement. Following is his statement to his accusers prior to his verdict:

Five years ago I applied for an exit visa to emigrate from the USSR to Israel. Today I am further than ever from my goal. This would seem to be a cause for regret, but that is not the case. These five years were the best of my life. I am happy that I have been able to live them honestly and at peace with my conscience. I have said only what I believed, and have not violated my conscience even when my life was in danger.

I feel part of a marvelous historical process—the process of the national revival of Soviet Jewry and its return to the homeland, to Israel. I hope that the false and absurd but terribly serious charges made today against me—and the entire Jewish people—will not impede the process of the national revival of the Jews of Russia, as the KGB has assured me they would, but will actually provide a new impulse, as has often happened in our history.

My relatives and friends know how strong was my desire to join my wife in Israel . . . For two thousand years the Jewish people, my people, have been dispersed all over the world and seemingly deprived of any hope of returning. But still, each year Jews have stubbornly, and apparently without reason, said to each other, *Leshana haba'a b'Yerushalayim* (Next year in Jerusalem)! And today, when I am further than ever from my dream, from my people, and from my Avital, and when many difficult years of prisons and camps lie ahead of me, I say to my wife and to my people, *Leshana haba'a b'Yerushalayim.* [*Fear No Evil*, p. 224]

Almost ten years later, Natan Sharansky saw the fulfillment of these words, as he was reunited with his wife, Avital, and his people, in Jerusalem.

Around the *Shabbat* Table

1.   It is stated in the Ethics of the Fathers (Mishnah, *Pirkei Avot* 4:1) that a "hero" is one who controls his or her own desires. Why do you think that the rabbis thought of heroism as a private, internal process?

2.   Who is the most courageous person you know? Why?

3.   Which Jewish value would you most adamantly defend?

Bo

FRIDAY NIGHT MEAL: A Battle of Futures

This week's *parsha*, *Bo*, culminates with the final three plagues. With intensifying frenzy, Egypt is plunged into darkness. First, hordes of locusts swarm like a black cloud over the land, then the plague of darkness grows successively more palpable, and finally, in the middle of the night, death strikes the firstborn. The year-long drama of plagues has brought about the collapse and ultimate demise of Egypt. The Jewish people are on the verge of their exodus to freedom.

Why was the plague of the firstborn, the most ghastly of them all, chosen to be the decisive and culminating plague? Nine other plagues had attacked the land and animals of Egypt; now the angel of death was unleashed upon the Egyptian people themselves. But why did this angel of death strike only at the *children* of Egypt?! The adults of Egypt had enslaved the Jewish people; were they not responsible? Why were the adults not killed? Why, instead, were their children punished?

The *parsha* alternates between two themes: the present exodus and its future commemoration. At the very beginning of the *parsha*, God tells Moses: "Go to Pharaoh, for I have hardened his heart, and the heart of his servants, that I might show them My signs before him; and that you may tell in the ears of your children, and your child's children, what things I have done in Egypt . . ." (Exodus 10:2).

The celebration of Passover is detailed not only for the present generation that is about to observe it but also for all future generations:

> And this day will be a memorial for you . . throughout your generations you will keep it a feast by ordinance, forever. [Exodus 12:14]

> And you will observe this thing for an ordinance to you and to your children, forever. [Exodus 12:24]

Why does this *parsha* continually juxtapose the future observance of the children and grandchildren of the Jewish people with the impending plague that will strike the sons of the Egyptian people? Until this tenth plague, the conflict of the Jewish people in Egypt existed primarily between the two peoples and their respective leaders. At this juncture, the focus of the conflict shifts from the present to future. The plagues no longer destroy the *land* of Egypt and its inhabitants; now the thrust of the tenth plague is the destruction of the *future* of Egypt, its children. Pharaoh had ordered that the sons of the Jewish people be thrown into the Nile, hoping to obliterate their future; now, with Divine justice, the screams in Egypt announce that *its* future has been destroyed.

Passover celebrates the birth of the Jewish people. The Passover seder centers on the children of each Jewish home. When a Jewish child is born, a song of joy is sung, "*Siman tov u'mazel tov* (it is a good sign and good luck) *y'heh lanu, u'l'chal Yisrael* (for us and for all of the Jewish people)." The birth of a child is the cause for both individual and collective rejoicing. As in this week's *parsha*, individual and collective futures are seamlessly interwoven.

Around the *Shabbat* Table

1. The rabbis of the *Zohar* ask, "It is written, 'And it came to pass
    that at *midnight* the Lord smote all of the firstborn in the land of
    Egypt' (Exodus 12:29), but it is also written, 'And it came to pass
    on the *middle of that day* that the Lord did bring the children of
    Israel out of the land of Egypt . . .' (Exodus 12:51). Why did the
    Jewish people wait till the middle of the day, and not leave at night
    after the striking of the firstborn?" The *Zohar* answers that the
    Jewish people waited in order to create the stark contrast of one
    people going to freedom while the other people was burying its
    dead. For what other reasons might the Jewish people have waited
    for the middle of the day to leave?

2. On Passover we are supposed to simulate the exodus of the Jew-
    ish people from Egypt. What do you think that the Jewish people
    were thinking and/or feeling as they left Egypt?

3. Can a moment of epic proportions ever truly be remembered ac-
    curately? What are the inherent difficulties in eternalizing an ex-
    perience? Are there any moments in your life that you have
    struggled to perpetuate?

SHABBAT LUNCH: When Enemies Fall

Pharaoh, the greatest enemy the Jewish people had ever known, has
been defeated. "And Pharaoh rose up in the night, he, and all his servants, and all of Egypt; and there was a great cry in Egypt; for there
was not a house where there was not one dead. And he called for
Moses and Aaron by night, and said, 'Rise up, and leave my people,
both you and your children of Israel, and go, serve the Lord, as you
have said'" (Exodus 12:30, 31).

How should the Jewish people respond to the downfall of Pharaoh and his people? How should they look upon the decimation

of the very forces that tortured and enslaved them? Egypt had been their home for several generations. It had provided the food for their survival during the great famine in Israel. It had also reduced them to pathetic beings, bereft of spiritual, emotional, or intellectual vitality. Should they now rejoice? Or should they pity the Egyptians?

In next week's *parsha*, *Beshallach*, after the Egyptians drown in the sea, the Jews rejoice and sing, "I will sing to the Lord, for He has triumphed gloriously; the horse and his rider He has thrown into the sea" (Exodus 15:1). In his commentary on the verse " . . . when the wicked perish there is jubilation" (Proverbs 11:10), the Vilna Gaon writes, "When God takes revenge on their [the Jewish people's] enemies, then there is jubilation, as during [the drowning of the Egyptians] in the sea and as in Purim." These sources and historical realities indicate that the removal of dangers to the Jewish people and the destruction of evil is grounds for jubilation. An absence of rejoicing may reflect an inadequate grasp of the peril and oppression that the Jewish people underwent during these times.

A different approach is expressed in the Mishnah: "Samuel, 'the small one' [*hakatan*] would say: 'When your enemy falls, do not rejoice, and his stumbling should not gladden your heart, for the Lord may see it and find displeasure in it and He will remove His wrath from him'" (Ethics of the Fathers, 4:24). Here, one is instructed not to rejoice.

This rabbinic figure, Samuel, was referred to as "the small one" because of his modest and unassuming nature. The Talmud notes several occasions on which he chose to accept public humiliation rather than have someone else suffer embarrassment. Nevertheless, one incident in his life, during the times of Roman persecution shortly after the destruction of the Second Temple, seems at first glance to be quite out of character. The leader of the Jewish people, Rabban Gamliel of Yavne, requested that the rabbis compose a prayer asking for the breakdown and eradication of the enemy forces that sought to destroy the Jewish people, both physically and spiritually. None of the rabbis complied until Samuel, "the small one," the one who had instructed that one should not rejoice when your enemy falls, stood up and singlehandedly created the prayer calling for the destruction of the enemies of Israel!

Many commentators understand that, in fact, only Samuel *hakatan* possessed the moral stature to pen this prayer. Only a person whose self-nullification would preclude the seeking of personal gratification over the downfall of his enemy could objectively pursue the eradication of evil. Only a person who had demonstrated that he sought no individual satisfaction could ask for the dissolution of the opponents of the Jewish people.

The resolution of the seeming contradiction between these two sources, " . . . when the wicked perish there is jubilation" and "when your enemies fall, do not rejoice," may be resolved in a similar manner. One is instructed not to rejoice in the case of *"your* enemies." If one is personally involved and regards the adversaries as his or her own, then this subjectivity may impede an impartial understanding of the situation and we are cautioned against this potentially vindictive, retaliatory rejoicing. However, if one is able to remain objective, to realize that these enemies are not personal ones but rather adversaries of the entire Jewish people, then his or her rejoicing reflects communal joy of enabling the Jewish people to advance and flourish.

Around the *Shabbat* Table

1. The Talmud relates that whenever there was a drought, the rabbis would go to Abba Chilkiya and urge him to pray for rain. One time, upon being asked, he went up to his roof and prayed in one corner while his wife prayed in the other corner. The rain clouds gathered over her corner. Abba Chilkiya remarked that this was because of her exceptional merit. One time, there were some troublemakers in his neighborhood and Abba Chilkiya prayed that they should die, while his wife prayed that they would reform their

ways (*Taanit* 23b). With whom do you naturally identify more—
Abba Chilkiya or his wife?

2. Do you know anyone who reminds you of Samuel *hakatan*?

3. Did you ever defeat an adversary? How did you feel afterward?

Seuda Shlishit: On Meeting a King

This week's *parsha* describes the culmination of the confrontation
between Moses and Pharaoh, the king of Egypt. Shmuel Yosef (Shai)
Agnon (1888–1970), was one of the central figures in Hebrew literature in the twentieth century. His works deal with the philosophical and psychological problems of his generation and include nov-
els, folk-tales, and stories. On December 10, 1966, Agnon, upon
receiving the Nobel Prize for Literature, also met with a non-Jewish
king, the king of Sweden. The following is an excerpt from his acceptance speech.

Your Majesty, Your Royal Highnesses, Your Excellencies, Members of
the Swedish Academy, Ladies and Gentlemen:
   Our Sages of blessed memory have said that we must not enjoy
any pleasure in this world without reciting a blessing. If we eat any
food, or drink any beverage, we must recite a blessing over them before and after. If we breathe the scent of goodly grass, the fragrance of
spices, the aroma of goodly fruits, we pronounce a blessing over the
pleasure. The same applies to the pleasures of sight: when we see . . .
the trees first bursting into blossom in the spring, or any fine, sturdy
and beautiful trees, we pronounce a blessing. And the same applies to
the pleasures of the ear.
   It is through you, dear sirs, that one of the blessings concerned
with hearing has come my way.
   It happened when the Swedish Chargé d'Affaires came and
brought me the tidings that the Swedish Academy had bestowed the
Nobel Prize upon me. Then I recited in full the blessing that is enjoined

upon one who hears good tidings for himself or others ... And now that I have come so far, I will recite one blessing more, as enjoined upon he who beholds a monarch: "Blessed are You, Lord, our God, King of the Universe, Who has given of Your glory to a king of flesh and blood."

Around the *Shabbat* Table

1. Why do you think that a special blessing was created to say upon seeing a king? What effect do you think that the hearing of this blessing might have upon a king?

2. Rav Kook, the first chief rabbi of Israel, wrote that a president or prime minister elected democratically acquires the status of a king, and should be honored accordingly. Is there anyone to whom you would afford this level of honor today?

3. Have you ever, upon meeting someone for the first time, been inspired to recite a blessing or other words commemorating the event? Who inspired such a reaction?

Beshallach

FRIDAY NIGHT MEAL: Growing Pains

The *parsha Beshallach* bridges the two historic events of the book of Exodus: the departure of the Jewish people from Egypt and their experience at Mount Sinai. Within the span of seven weeks, the Jewish people will metamorphose from an enslaved mass of individuals to a united people embracing holiness and divine purpose. *Beshallach* recounts their journey out of Egypt into the wilderness of the desert, their fears, their joys, and the travails of their nascent independence.

The journey out of Egypt climaxes with the miraculous parting of the sea, which saves the Jewish people from the advancing Egyptian army. The Jews spontaneously respond with a poetic explosion of song, replete with musical instruments and dancing. Yet seemingly only moments after celebrating their supernatural deliverance, the Jewish people begin to bemoan their pitiful state, complaining about the bitterness of the available water. This complaint is followed by further murmuring over the lack of food and then once again over the lack of water. Only days removed from their house of bondage, the Jewish people have already began to wax nostalgic for their preferable conditions in Egypt:"Would that we had died by the hand of the Lord in the land of Egypt, when we sat by the flesh pots, and when we ate our fill of bread . . . " (Exodus 16:3).

How could the Jewish people have become so ungrateful? How could they complain about mundane realities such as food and water in light of their miraculous experiences? How could a people who had endured the slavery of Egypt and who would soon stand at Mount Sinai rapidly become so preoccupied and distressed over food and water?

The journey from Egypt to the Promised Land was much more than a trek across the desert. It was a period of transformation and maturation of a people who had assumed a slave mentality.

The Torah describes the journey of the Jews through the desert as follows:"And the Lord went before them by day in a pillar of a cloud, to lead them the way; and by night in a pillar of fire to give them light; that they might go by day and night"(Exodus 13:21).They traveled according to divine guidance.Their nourishment was supplied for them without their laboring: "and the Lord spoke to Moses saying,'At evening you shall eat meat, and in the morning you shall be filled with bread' (Exodus 16:11, 12) . . . and the children of Israel ate the manna for forty years, until they came to inhabited land" (Exodus 16:35). Even their wars were fought miraculously. "And it came to pass, that when Moses held up his hand, Israel prevailed; and when he let down his hand, Amalek [the enemy] prevailed" (Exodus 17:11).The Midrash adds that not only did their garments never wear out during their forty years in the desert, but that they even expanded with them so that no one ever lacked for clothing.

What visual image of the Jewish people is being created through all of these dimensions of their life in the desert? A nation of children, a nation undergoing the childhood of its development.What characterizes childhood? While traveling or walking, children hold their parents' hands (symbolized by God's nocturnal fire and daily cloud). In the eyes of children, food is never lacking; it miraculously and effortlessly appears, like the manna in the desert. In times of conflict, parents providentially arrive to rescue their children from any peril, as God rescued the Jews in their victory over Amalek. Even their clothes, from the vantage point of young children, are purchased and cleaned by an invisible source.

The exodus from Egypt represents the birth of the Jewish people. It marks the beginning of the childhood of their national existence. Subsequently, the stage of adolescence will be reflected through their struggle with the prophets' instructions during the First Temple period (approximately 996-586 B.C.E.). Adulthood will be simulated during the Second Temple period (516-70 C.E.), epitomized by the hiddenness of God and the emergence of rabbinic authority. Seen in this historical perspective, the limited scope and brazen impatience of the Jewish people at this time, while perhaps disappointing, may be construed as natural growing pains in the long journey to adulthood.

Around the *Shabbat* Table

1. In the *parsha* of *Beshallach*, the Jewish people are given a new mitzvah. In the midst of their complaining, they are told to collect manna for six days but to refrain from collecting it on *Shabbat*. Instead they should prepare a double portion of food on the sixth day, because on *Shabbat* no manna will fall. One of the messages of *Shabbat* is patience—that whatever work consumes us during the week can wait. Why is this an appropriate lesson for the Jewish people at this stage of their development? What else do you think that the idea of *Shabbat* might convey to them?

2. The two momentous events of the last two *parshiyot* (portions), the exodus from Egypt and the splitting of the sea, impart different messages. Of the two, the exodus is considered to be the essential moment, whereas the splitting of the sea has been referred to by commentators as "God's superfluous miracle, the miracle that comes to reflect God's love for the Jewish people." Why?

3. What qualities of childhood, adolescence, or adulthood do you see in the Jewish people today?

SHABBAT LUNCH: Overcoming Fear

The Jewish people leave Egypt and after six days reach the unbridgeable sea. The Egyptian soldiers and chariots are pounding on their heels. They cannot return to Egypt, nor can they advance, as the sea is in front of them. "And Egypt pursued after them, all the horses and chariots of Pharaoh, and his horsemen, and his army, and overtook them encamping by the sea . . . and the children of Israel lifted up their eyes, and behold, Egypt marched after them; and they were very much afraid" (Exodus 14:9, 10). Panic rages throughout the camp. Frenzied questions abound. The people attack Moses, ". . . have you taken us out to die in the wilderness? Why did you do this to us, to take us out of Egypt?" (Exodus 14:11).

How will the Jewish people overcome their fear? How does anyone overcome fear?

Moses' attempt to allay the fears of the Jews is rejected by God. "And Moses said to the people, 'Fear not, stand still, and see the salvation of the Lord, which He will show you today . . . the Lord will fight for you, and you will hold your peace" (Exodus 14: 3, 14). The Talmud (*Sotah* 36b) states that Moses' plea to the people infuriated God: "'My beloved people are on the verge of drowning in the sea, and you are spinning out lengthy prayers before Me?!' Moses said to God, 'But what else can I do?' God replied, 'Speak to the children of Israel that they go forward!'"

The same section of the Talmud describes the pandemonium besieging the camp. "Rabbi Yehuda said, 'One tribe said, "I will not be the first to go into the sea"; and another tribe also said, "I will not be the first to go into the sea." While they were standing there deliberating, Nachshon ben Aminadav sprang forward and jumped into the sea. As he entered it, the sea parted.'" Nachshon's courage and willingness to walk into the unparted sea saved the Jewish people.

How did Nachshon have the courage to jump in?

Rabbi Eliyahu Dessler (a leading rabbi of England and Israel in the twentieth century), offers an insight into how one can strive to overcome feelings of anxiety. He writes that one of the underlying psychological causes of worry is often a sense of guilt, a subconscious feeling that one actually deserves punishment. A person's inner notion of unworthiness, of fault, or of insecurity over his or her actions may result in the incessant agonizing over the consequences of his or her decisions. One feels that one is simply not worthy of receiving benevolence. Thus, writes Rabbi Dessler, the focus of one's concern, one's fear, should always be focused on improving oneself, on improving one's self-image and fulfilling one's moral potential. All moments of fear are likely to be external manifestations of this problem of lack of self-esteem.

Through his feat, Nachshon became an eternal symbol of courageous action for the Jewish people: he transcended fear and worry and generated positive results. The Talmud states that, following his example, future leaders of Israel would continually emerge from Judah, his tribe.

Around the *Shabbat* Table

1. Why did God delay the parting of the sea? What was achieved by causing such stress to the Jewish people? Apparently, God did not want to fight for the Jewish people while they waited passively. The Jewish people needed to learn how to transcend their worries and fear, how to move beyond their present trauma, and especially, they had to learn not to rely exclusively on God to perform miracles for them. Do you think that one can learn to transcend fear and worry?

2. The Ba'al Shem Tov, the founder of Hasidism, once said that life is like climbing a ladder. If one wants to climb to the next rung in life, one must be willing to endure a moment of instability, when only one foot is on the ladder and the other is in the air, between the rungs. Have you ever experienced this feeling? How did you cope with the period of uncertainty?

3. Have you ever felt paralyzed by worry or fear? Why? Do you know any people who seldom worry? Why do you think they seem so calm?   .

Seuda Shlishit: Poet Parachutist

While the Jewish people trembled with fear, waiting for the sea to part, Nachshon ben Aminadav bravely dove in to the sea (see *"Beshallach:* Overcoming Fear"). Nachshon's courageous act established a historic precedent of being daring and taking risks to ensure Jewish survival. Over 3,000 years later, a young woman would follow in his path and became a modern symbol of hope and heroism.

Hannah Senesh, born in 1921 in Budapest, Hungary, settled on a kibbutz in Israel in 1939. At an early age she revealed exceptional intellectual and literary talent. In 1943, Hannah joined thirty-one volunteers in a dangerous rescue mission. Their plan was to parachute into enemy territory and attempt to liberate Allied pilots who had been shot down behind Nazi lines. After completing their mission, they intended to make contact with underground partisan fighters and to rescue Jews trapped in Romania, Hungary, and Czechoslovakia. Hannah parachuted on March 13, 1944. After completing the first stage of her task, she was captured by the Hungarian police and brutally interrogated for months.

A well-known poet, Hannah wrote several poems while in her prison cell, including:

> One—two—three . . .
>   eight feet long,
> Two strides across, the rest is dark . . .
> Life hangs over me like a question mark.
>
> One—two—three . . .
>   maybe another week,
> Or next month may still find me here,
> But death, I feel, is very near.
>
> I could have been
>   twenty-three next July;

I gambled on what mattered most,
The dice were cast. I lost.

Days before her execution she pressed a small piece of paper into the hand of another member of her mission. It contained the poem that would become known by heart by virtually every Israeli school child.

Blessed is the match consumed
    in kindling flame.
Blessed is the flame that burns
    in the secret fastness of the heart.
Blessed is the heart with strength to stop
    its beating for honor's sake.
Blessed is the match consumed
    in kindling flame.

Shortly after her period of interrogation, Hannah Senesh was executed by a Nazi firing squad. She is buried at the Israeli military cemetery of Mount Herzl in Jerusalem.

Around the *Shabbat* Table

1. What do you think that Hannah Senesh was trying to express in her poem "Blessed Is the Match"?

2. Hannah Senesh's act of bravery was not an isolated moment in her life; rather, it reflected her entire approach and passion for life. At the age of 17, she wrote in her diary that "one needs something to believe in, something for which one can have wholehearted enthusiasm. One needs to feel that one's life has meaning, that one is needed in this world." What is this "something" for you?

3. What is the most courageous or giving act that you have ever witnessed? That you have ever done?

Yitro

FRIDAY NIGHT MEAL: Wonder and Mystery

Fifty days after their exodus from Egypt, the Jewish people stood at Mount Sinai, ready to receive the Ten Commandments. For Moses, this moment represents the return to the spot where God had originally chosen him to lead the Jews out of slavery. The diminutive burning bush has now become a mountain, where the course of human history would, in a single moment, be indelibly changed. God's promise to Moses at the beginning of this book has been fulfilled; Moses' mission has been completed: "And God said to Moses, 'I will be with you . . . in your bringing the people out of Egypt to serve God *on this mountain*" (Exodus 3:12).

Yet the minute after the Jewish people depart from Mount Sinai, it reverts to being merely another mountain in the howling wilderness of the desert. The exact location of Mount Sinai is not known. It does not acquire eternal sanctity; eternal words were spoken at a *transitory site*.

In this week's *parsha*, however, the words of the Ten Commandments (Exodus 20:1–14) seem to be very much dependent upon the events occurring at Mount Sinai. The preceding chapter (Exodus 19) struggles to find the words and images to describe the setting of Mount Sinai. "And it came to pass on the third day in the morning, that there were *voices* [thunder?] and lightning, and a thick cloud upon the mountain, and the voice of a *shofar* was *exceedingly strong*, and all the people in the camp trembled . . . and Mount Sinai was enveloped in smoke . . . and the *whole mountain trembled* . . . and the voice of the *shofar* became *stronger and stronger"* (Exodus 19:16-18). After the Ten Commandments are given, the Torah states that "the people *saw the voices* (!) and the fires and the voice of the *shofar* and the mountain of smoke and the people saw it and were shaken and stood at a distance" (Exodus 20:15).

What is this otherworldly description attempting to convey? Could the content of the Ten Commandments have been given without the dramatic setting of voices, lightning, and blasting of the *shofar*?

When the Jewish people arrived at Mount Sinai, they knew very little about themselves. Most likely, they were aware of their ancestors, their patriarchs and matriarchs. They knew that they were different from the Egyptians and that they were headed toward the Promised Land. But what did they know of their collective identity or responsibility? Did they have any idea how they would begin to fulfill the prophecy to Abraham of "being a blessing" and that "through him [them] all the families of the world would be blessed?" Their collective identity remained unknown.

The relationship between God and the Jewish people is created through both articulate and inexpressible domains. The Ten Commandments represent the revelation of the *content* of this relationship. Beyond the "letter of the law" of this relationship, however, lies an infinite dimension of the relationship that can never be communicated through speech. The description of the events at Sinai before the giving of the Ten Commandments struggles to convey that which is beyond conveying, that which is beyond all sensory reception, the indescribable, the mysterious. The images of the primal sound of a *shofar* becoming louder and louder, the "seeing" of the voices, a mountain trembling on fire, all strive to transmit a sense of wonder and awe.

In Chapter 19, before the Jewish people receive the Ten Commandments, they are told that their collective destiny is to become a "nation of priests, a holy people." To achieve this goal, they must acquire a sense of living for "something beyond" their material reality. The midrash states that the Torah is "black fire written on white fire." The black fire is represented by the letters, the white fire by the spaces between the letters, that which could not be limited to words. There is much more white fire than black fire. This moment of grandeur and mystery then becomes the foundation for the collective Jewish attempt to see the sublime in all of existence.

Abraham Joshua Heschel writes:

> Awareness of the divine begins with wonder. It is the result of what man does with his higher incomprehension. The surest way to suppress our ability to understand the meaning of God and the importance of worship is to take things for granted. Wonder or radical amazement is the chief characteristic of the religious man's attitude toward history and nature. The profound and perpetual awareness of the wonder of being has become a part of the religious consciousness of the Jew. [*God in Search of Man*, p. 46]

Mount Sinai was a moment in history. This moment has continued to reverberate through time, throughout the universe. The establishment of the national Jewish identity begins with a sense of wonder.

Around the *Shabbat* Table

1.   In the song that we sing at the Pesach seder, "*Dayenu*," it says that "if God had brought us near to Mount Sinai and had not given us the Torah—*Dayenu* (it would have been enough)." How could one understand this?

2. What moments have engendered a sense of wonder and/or awe in your life? Do you know people whose lives are generally filled with a greater sense of wonder? Why do you think that this is so?

3. How might the idea of "white fire and black fire" shed light on human relationships? What is the potential hazard of only seeing the black fire or only the white fire?

SHABBAT LUNCH: Studying Torah—"Means" or "End"?

This week's *parsha*, *Yitro*, records the giving of Torah at Mount Sinai. For countless generations, the Jewish people have bonded together through the learning of Torah. Throughout history, and most recently during the Holocaust, Jews risked their lives to learn Torah.

What is the purpose of this learning? Is the learning of Torah an "end" in and of itself, or is it the "means" to achieve a further goal?

Approximately two hundred years ago, Rabbi Chaim of Volozhin, the foremost student of the Vilna Gaon, wrote his epic work *Nefesh HaChaim*. There he states that the goal of studying Torah is the learning of Torah itself. "The truthful understanding is that one should learn Torah 'for its own sake'" (Section 4, Chapter 3). No other ulterior motive should be involved. Rabbi Chaim further explains that studying Torah is tantamount to coming closer to God, and through learning Torah a countless number of mystical worlds are created and redeemed. While learning Torah, one is allowed to break for several minutes daily to strive to purify one's thoughts and to strengthen one's fear of Heaven, but the primary focus of one's studies should be exclusively the learning at hand. This represents the highest endeavor possible for humanity.

A different approach was adopted by the Maharal of Prague, almost four hundred years ago. In his sermon on Rosh Hashanah, the Maharal decried the deplorable quality of learning in his community. Although the members of his community faithfully spent their time learning, the Maharal lamented that their approach to the learning of Torah was flawed. He wrote that their love of learning Torah was so strong that it had eclipsed the purpose of their learning, namely, to bond with the Giver of Torah, God. The learning of Torah is the path through which one is able to receive and express one's love for God. His community's love for learning had, ironically, become an obstacle in their relationship with the transcendent. The studying of Torah should serve as the "means" through which one advances one's relationship with God.

A third approach is reflected in a discussion that took place almost 2,000 years ago. The Talmud (*Kiddushin* 40b) relates that the rabbis raised the question: "Which is greater—learning or doing?" Rabbi Tarfon asserted that practice is more important, while Rabbi Akiva advocated learning. The rabbis deliberated on these responses for a period of time and finally concluded enigmatically that "learning is greater, because it brings one to action." From their answer, it is not clear whether the rabbis sided with Rabbi Akiva or Rabbi Tarfon, because while they stated that learning is "greater," they emphasized it as a means to an end—action. Later commentators clarify that the intention of the rabbis was not to endorse either of the two perspectives, but to establish a comprehensive approach to the learning of Torah. The process of learning Torah, when performed correctly, should necessarily result in action. According to this approach, one's behavior should stem from the learning of Torah, and, conversely, the true purpose of learning Torah is to affect one's course of action.

Around the *Shabbat* Table

1. In his book *Nefesh HaChaim*, Rabbi Chaim points out a number of dangers when the study of Torah is understood as a "means" and not as an "end." Can you think of any? Can you think of any dangers when it is understood as an "end?"

2. With which of these three approaches—learning for its own sake, learning to bond with God, or learning to affect one's actions— do you most agree? What argument could you make for the other two points of view?

3. In the blessing recited before the learning of Torah, we ask that our learning always be sweet. Have you ever had any moments of learning that you would consider to have been "sweet?"

Seuda Shlishit: Learning in Danger

The value of learning Torah has been essential to the Jewish people since their inception. The Talmud (Berakhot 61b) recounts a famous parable depicting the centrality of this learning.

One time the evil rulers decreed that the Jewish people were prohibited from engaging in the learning of Torah. Papus ben Yehuda found Rabbi Akiva publicly convening large groups of people to study Torah.
He said to him, "Akiva, aren't you afraid of the rulers?"
He replied, "I will tell you a parable—what is our situation comparable to? To a fox that was walking by the side of the river, and saw fish scurrying from place to place. The fox asked them, 'Why are you fleeing?' They told him, 'We are escaping from the nets of the fishermen.' He said to the fish, 'Would you like to come up to the dry land, and we will live together, just like our ancestors lived together?' They replied, 'Are you the one that they say is the most clever of the animals?! You are not smart at all. If, in the place that gives us life [water] we are afraid, all the more so will we be afraid in the place of our death [dry land].'"
Continued Rabbi Akiva, "So too it is with us. Now that we are engaging in the learning of Torah, which is our sustenance, and our situation is so dire, if we desist from this learning, all the more so will our situation deteriorate."

It was said that not many days passed until Rabbi Akiva was caught and imprisoned. The rulers also placed Papus ben Yehuda in jail with him. Rabbi Akiva said to him, "Papus, what brings you to this place?" He replied, "Fortunate are you, Rabbi Akiva, that they arrested you on account of your learning Torah; woe to Papus, who was caught because of petty offenses."

Around the *Shabbat* Table

1. Why are the images of fish and water used as symbols of the Jewish people and Torah?

2. During the Holocaust the question was often asked, "Is one obligated to endanger one's life to try and continue learning Torah?" The rabbis ruled that one was not required to risk one's life in order to learn. Does this judgment contradict the example set by Rabbi Akiva?

3. Do you know of anyone who has gone to considerable lengths or sacrifice to further his or her learning of Torah?

Mishpatim

FRIDAY NIGHT MEAL: Enslaving Love

What could possibly have followed the moment of sublime inspiration of voices, lightning, and *shofar* at Mount Sinai?

Seemingly anticlimactic, the *parsha* of *Mishpatim* begins abruptly with a list of over fifty new laws, ranging from various degrees of murder and stealing to accidental damages and negligence. Still standing at Mount Sinai, the Jewish people no longer are "seeing the voices and the lightning" (Exodus 20:15). The sound of the *shofar* reverberates only in their memories. Now their lives and reality are about to be transformed through this-worldly laws and judgments. Almost 100 verses will elaborate the particular rules that will govern their nascent society.

What could the Jewish people have been thinking during this lengthy enumeration of regulations? Until this time, most of the laws that they had received had dealt with the Passover sacrifice and the departure from Egypt. A moment earlier, they had encountered the Ten Commandments, general in content and inspiring in message. But this list is much different. The details of their marketplace and community, the basic fabric of their daily lives, must now reflect this

Sinai experience. No longer the slaves of Pharaoh, the Jewish people cannot for a moment refrain from their mission of becoming a "nation of priests and a holy people" (Exodus 19:6).

Is there an order to the listing of laws in *Mishpatim*? Does the arrangement of the laws reflect subtle priorities? Rav Kook wrote that just as there are laws in poetry, so, too, there exists poetry in laws. What message is underlying the sequence and system of these laws?

The laws in this *parsha* progress in descending order of severity. Intentional manslaughter is followed by accidental homicide, then kidnapping, then injuring another. Then come the laws of reparations when a person's animals or indirect actions kill or harm another. Eventually, one is held responsible for neglecting to return a lost object to one's enemy (Exodus 23:4) and even for helping one's enemy to unload his or her animal. In this progression from the most severe transgression to the lesser ones, what stands out in bewildering fashion is the placement of the first law of this list: the buying and keeping of a Jewish servant (slave). Apparently, there is a quality or situation concerning the Jewish servant that, in the eyes of the Torah, supersedes even manslaughter!

The system of slavery in Judaism, no longer practiced, was actually a form of social rehabilitation. The Torah does not mention the institution of prisons. Incarceration was not considered to be a viable solution. The Torah does not regard a criminal as a deviant but as one in need of help. It is the responsibility of the community to assist the criminal to alter his or her behavioral patterns. The goal is not to remove the criminal from society but rather to enable him or her to return and productively contribute to society. To achieve this goal, a criminal was "adopted" by a family for six years, hopefully to learn from its example how to better conduct his or her life, and then be "let free," to return to society as a completely independent member.

The family that chose to "adopt" this criminal assumed the position of "foster parents" and was responsible for educating and helping the servant amend erring habits. The family members were obligated to call a servant by his or her name and not employ derogatory labels. If this servant had a profession in his or her former life, the family was not allowed to demand work in a different field. The family was required to maintain the servant's honor; the midrash proscribes requesting that the servant do any menial or self-degrading acts (Leviticus 25:43). Throughout the Torah (the *parshiyot* of *Behar*, Leviticus 25, and *Re'eh*, Deuteronomy 15) this servant is continually referred to as "your brother."

The Talmud explains that the case of slavery in this week's *parsha* is of a man who had not managed his finances correctly, had ended up irretrievably in debt, and consequently had been apprenticed to another family. This process should ideally give him a second chance to learn how to successfully manage his income and return to society. It is hoped that he will mature and learn to live with greater foresight, so that ultimately he will be able to accept full responsibility for his actions.

The chance of tragic failure of this system is reflected in the beginning of this week's *parsha*. What happens if, after six years of "second childhood," the servant chooses to remain a servant? "And if the servant will continually say, 'I love my master, my wife, and my children; I will not go out free,' then his master shall bring him ... to the doorposts [*mezuzot*], and his master shall bore his ear through with an awl; and he will serve him forever" (Exodus 21:5-7).

The servant chose to remain a servant, "a slave." The first of the Ten Commandments states that "I am the Lord your God Who brought you out ... of the house of bondage" (Exodus 20:2). Now this servant says, "I love my master," which is a denial of freedom, a denial of the lesson of the exodus. In response, the servant is brought to the doorposts of the house. In Egypt, the Jews placed the blood of the *paschal* sacrifice on the doorposts of their homes, symbolizing their freedom from human masters, from Pharaoh. The servant has his ear branded with an awl at this doorpost. "Rabbi Yochanon Ben Zakkai said, '...Why was the ear singled out from all of the other bodily parts?' Said God: 'The ear which heard my voice on Mount Sinai when I said, "that the Jewish people are my servant unto me," and then went and acquired for himself another master, let it be branded'" (*Kiddushin* 22b).

Apparently, in the eyes of this week's *parsha*, even more serious than the physical damages that one may inflict upon another is the crime that one can do to oneself: the rejection of freedom, the denial of independence, the choosing to remain a slave.

Around the *Shabbat* Table

1. Why might the "slave" have chosen to remain a slave? What do you imagine that the slave thought as he was being led to the doorpost?

2. After this period of adoption, this "second childhood," the servant chose to remain a child. The servant's adopting family did not inculcate in the servant a desire for freedom and independence. What do you think the mistake of the family might have been?

3. What advice would you suggest today for someone afraid to face the freedom and adversity of adulthood?

SHABBAT LUNCH: Overcoming Hatred

On occasion, the Torah presents two verses that appear to be remarkably similar, yet, upon a closer reading, significant differences emerge. Two such verses, one in this week's *parsha* and one in *Ki Tetze* (Deuteronomy 22:4), seem to invite examination and comparison.

Exodus 23:5	Deuteronomy 22:4
If one sees a donkey of one that hates you (or you hate him) collapsing under its burden, and you consider resisting to assist him, then you must surely assist him.	You should not see the donkey or ox of your brother fall and ignore them [the donkey and ox], you should surely raise them up with him.

Though the examples are similar, as both involve the distress of someone else's animals, there are at least two clear differences. In the first case (Exodus), the relationship with the owner of the animal is one of hatred, whereas in the second case (Deuteronomy) it is one of closeness. Second, the situation of the two animals is not identical. In Exodus, the animal has been overburdened and is presently suffering under this load; in Deuteronomy, commentators explain that the verse refers to the owner's belongings, which were on the animal and have fallen, and now the owner is in need of help to load the animal again. The case in Exodus emphasizes the suffering of the animal, while that in Deuteronomy accents the misfortune of the owner of the animal.

The Talmud (*Bava Metziah* 32b) raises a third hypothetical situation and poses the following question: "If one were to encounter two situations at exactly the same time: (1) someone he *hated*, who needed assistance in *loading* his animal, and (2) someone he *liked* whose animal needed to be *unloaded* from its burden—who should one help first?"

At first glance, the question may seem simple, since one is required to remove unnecessary pain from animals, and only the animal who is overburdened is in need of immediate help. Nevertheless, the Talmud answers, "It is a mitzvah to help the one he hates first, in order to curb his desire [of hatred]!" Although a person's natural inclination might be to help the animal in distress and to assist his or her friend, the first priority in the eyes of the Talmud is to restrain and emend his or her current feelings of hatred. The power of hatred may eventually intensify and become uncontrollable. Slowly, it grows to be virulent and destructive and may ultimately become self-consuming, affecting not only the particular relationship involved but also influencing all of a person's actions and general frame of mind. The effort to reduce this hatred supersedes other rightful concerns, even the suffering of an animal.

How does the act of assisting an enemy reduce the enmity between the two people?

The act of working together shifts the focus of the two parties from the tension between them to their shared objective of loading the animal. The Talmud adopts the principle that a person's emotions are influenced by his or her actions. The act of kindness, even when performed in the context of an unfriendly relationship, impels the doer to lessen feelings of anger, to "curb his desire." Then, once one of the parties involved has changed the status quo and created a positive environment, a window of potential reconciliation has been opened.

The Book of Knowledge (Sefer HaChinuch, written anonymously in the eleventh century) generalizes this principle into an all-embracing approach to human relationships. "More than a person's thoughts direct his actions, one's deeds ultimately shape one's heart." A person's behavior will eventually greatly influence his or her emotional composition.

In an antagonistic relationship, it is precisely the witnessing of the misfortune of a hated person, that may afford an opportunity to overcome hatred, for one's own sake as well as for the sake of the relationship.

Around the *Shabbat* Table

1. The Torah and Talmud propose a number of methods for sublimating and overcoming hatred, but they never instruct a person to eradicate the power to hate. Why might this be so? Could there be a worthy dimension to the capacity to hate?

2. Have you ever felt such hatred or anger that it influenced your other relationships or impeded your functioning? How did you resolve it?

3. Has your emotional state ever been shaped by your actions? How so?

Seuda Shlishit: A Corrected Judgment

This week's *parsha* lists many of the laws that the judges of the
Jewish people are required to enforce. Yet judgments are not only
made by legal authorities and do not occur exclusively in courts of
law. Every day, individuals form opinions and evaluate the actions
and attitudes of those around them. The following is a story of mistaken judgment related by Rabbi Shlomo Carlebach.

An orphan had been taken captive and was being ransomed for five
thousand rubles. The townspeople did not have enough money to pay
the ransom, so they turned to the rabbi of the town, Rabbi Shneur
Zalman, the founder of Chabad Hasidism. When the townspeople came
to Rabbi Shneur Zalman, he was sitting with two other rabbis, Rabbi
Menachem Mendel of Vitemsk and Rabbi Levi Yitzchak from
Berditchev. After hearing the townspeople, he told them not to worry,
he would ask "Moishele the miser" for money. The two rabbis were
shocked. "Don't you know that Moishele hasn't given money to anyone in twenty years!" "Do not worry," replied Rabbi Shneur Zalman.

The three rabbis went to see Moishele the miser. Rabbi Shneur
Zalman knocked on his door. Moishele was surprised to see the three
rabbis. He allowed them to enter and the three rabbis sat down.

Rabbi Shneur Zalman began to explain the grave situation of the
child, how they needed to pay the ransom of five thousand rubles.
Moishele listened intently and then said, "I am sorry but I cannot help
you." Rabbi Shneur Zalman accepted Moishele's words, stood up, and
gave Moishele a blessing. The three rabbis prepared to leave, but as
they were closing the outside gate, Moishele opened the door to the
house and ran after them, calling out, "Wait, wait. Come back. I have
changed my mind." The rabbis returned to the front door.

"Rabbi, I have changed my mind." Moishele opened his hand and
gave Rabbi Shneur Zalman one kopeck (one penny). It was an old and
dirty kopeck. But Rabbi Shneur Zalman put his hand over Moishele's
and thanked him effusively for his gift. The two other rabbis remained
silent, baffled by the depth of appreciation shown by Rabbi Shneur
Zalman.

As the rabbis were leaving for a second time, Moishele again summoned them back, calling out, "'Wait, wait. Come back. I have changed my mind.' Again the rabbis returned, and again Moishele gave Rabbi Shneur Zalman one kopeck.

Again and again, the rabbis would leave and Moishele would call them back. First it was another dirty kopeck, then a new one. Soon he began to give five kopecks, then ten, then five rubles, then ten rubles, then one hundred, then five hundred, until Moishele had given Rabbi Shneur Zalman all five thousand rubles. Each time he gave something, Rabbi Shneur Zalman would thank him profusely for his gift.

Later that night, the two rabbis turned to Rabbi Shneur Zalman and asked him if he knew all along that Moishele would give them the five thousand rubles so desperately needed. Rabbi Shneur Zalman replied, "Do you remember anything special about the first kopeck that Moishele gave us?"

"Yes, it was old and dirty, almost black."

"Yes," answered Rabbi Shneur Zalman, "you see, Moishele had the potential to become one of the most generous people, but someone had to be willing to take that first kopeck. Every time that someone asked him for money, he would open his hand and show them the old and dirty kopeck, and no one would take it from him. That was all that he was able to give at that moment, but everyone expected him to give more. No one let him give what he was able to at that moment. I saw that if I just accepted what he was able to give then, that would gradually open him up and enable him to give more. And so it was."

Around the *Shabbat* Table

1. What do you think that Moishele was thinking or feeling when he gave that first "dirty kopeck"?

2. The previous story is a paradigm for all human interaction. Can you think of other (nonfinancial) examples of miserliness and, according to this model, how they might be overcome?

3. Have you ever had the wisdom and perception to accept "a dirty kopeck" from someone, somehow knowing that that was all they could give at that time? How did you know? Did someone ever accept "a dirty kopeck" from you?

Terumah

FRIDAY NIGHT MEAL: The Unknowable

The *parshiyot* (portions) of the Torah often come in pairs, the second *parsha* expanding and deepening themes introduced in the first. The two *parshiyot* dealing with the laws given at Mount Sinai, *Yitro* and *Mishpatim*, are now succeeded by two *parshiyot* detailing the construction of the Tabernacle (in Hebrew, *Mishkan*, dwelling place), *Terumah* and *Tetzaveh*. *Terumah* primarily elucidates the building of the *Mishkan* and its components, while *Tetzaveh* describes the clothes and consecration of the priests who worked in the *Mishkan*.

The *Mishkan* structure, approximately twenty meters long, was located at the center of the Jewish encampment. It was divided into two rooms. The larger room, referred to as the "Holy Chamber," housed the menorah, the table, and the golden altar; the smaller room, known as the "Holy of Holies," housed the ark that contained the tablets of the Ten Commandments. The daily work of the priests (*kohanim*) occurred in the larger room, while the "Holy of Holies" was restricted solely to the service of the High Priest (*Kohen HaGadol*) once a year, on Yom Kippur.

Though the idea of the *Mishkan* seems very far removed from

141

today's reality, in the world of the Torah it represents the completion of a process that has extended for over a book and a half (Genesis and half the book of Exodus) and lasts twenty-six generations. In paradise, the Garden of Eden, humanity could hear the voice of God. Since the loss of paradise, however, the spiritual harmony between God and humanity had been broken. Finally, at Mount Sinai, this relationship is restored. Heaven and earth touch. But the Jewish people cannot remain at Mount Sinai forever.

What would eventually happen to this Sinai experience with the passing of time? Would it simply vanish once the Jewish people began to journey, fading with the weakening of its memory? How could the Jewish people preserve this life-changing, world-changing moment?

The ultimate purpose of the *Mishkan* was to create a physical space that would sustain the spiritual bond between God and the Jewish people, which reached a peak at Mount Sinai. "And there I [God] will meet with you, and I will speak with you from above the covering [of the ark]" (Exodus 25:22). Nachmanides, a medieval Torah commentator, refers to the *Mishkan* as a portable Mount Sinai. Every relationship requires renewing, rekindling, and, sometimes, repairing. The *Mishkan* was the vehicle that served these purposes for the relationship between God and the Jewish people.

The symbolism of the structure and components of the *Mishkan* convey the secret to preserving the relationship between God and the Jewish people. This week's *parsha* details the two principal utensils in the "holy chamber," the table and the menorah. The table, located on the northern side of the *Mishkan*, held twelve breads that were eaten by the priests working in the *Mishkan*. The breads symbolized the physical and material nourishing of the Jewish people. The Talmud (*Bava Batra* 25b) writes that one who wanted to prosper financially should look at the table and draw inspiration from it.

The menorah, a seven-branch candelabrum lit daily by the *kohanim*, was located on the southern side of the *Mishkan*. Its light symbolized human enlightenment and understanding. The Talmud relates that one who wanted to become wise would look at the menorah (*Bava Batra* 25b). Similarly, the women of Tekoa (village south of Jerusalem) were known to have been wise because of their meticulous use of olive oil in lighting their *Shabbat* candles (*Menachot* 85b). These sources gave birth to the customs on Friday night of gazing at the *Shabbat* candles after lighting them and during the making of *Kiddush*.

The holy chamber, exemplifying the material and intellectual achievements of humanity, was not, however, the final destination. It was the antechamber, the room that led to the essence of the *Mishkan*, the "Holy of Holies" (*Kodesh HaKodashim*). Therein rested the ark that held the tablets of the Ten Commandments, the physical reminder of humanity's connection to the transcendent.

Yet this chamber, the heart of the *Mishkan* and the Jewish camp, was off limits to virtually all of the Jewish people. More than anything else, the "Holy of Holies" symbolized that which was unapproachable, inaccessible, beyond the human domain. Unlike today's synagogues, which are intended to be places of gathering and prayer, the *Mishkan* was primarily the house of mystery.

The presence of this unapproachable, unknowable reality, this hidden room, would preserve the memory of the moment of Mount Sinai. The primary obstacle to sustaining the spiritual harmony between humanity and God is the lack of awareness that there is something beyond this physical world. The failure to hear God's voice is often simply a result of not listening. The hiddenness of the "Holy of Holies" continually reminded the Jewish people of the "unknowable" reality in this world, inviting them to listen and be influenced by that which lies beyond.

Around the *Shabbat* Table

1.   Do you think that simply looking at the table or the menorah could actually change someone's behavior? Why?

2. If you were to construct your own *Mishkan*, what would you put into the "Holy of Holies"?

3. In your own life, what places or moments, experiences or coincidences, have made you more aware of "the unknowable?"

SHABBAT LUNCH: *Tzedakah*—Giving or Taking?

The Jewish people are about to create their first national sanctuary, the *Mishkan*. Where will the resources come from? "And the Lord spoke to Moses, saying, 'Speak to the children of Israel that they bring a contribution for Me; every person according to the generosity of his heart will bring something'" (Exodus 25:1, 2). Only months ago, the lives of the Jews had been drastically overturned, and they had left Egypt with only their most portable possessions. Now they were being asked to willingly donate some of their belongings for the building of their sanctuary. Will they give enough? "And all the wise men, that carried out all the work of the sanctuary ... spoke to Moses saying, 'the people bring much more than enough for the task' ... and Moses commanded and proclaimed throughout the camp, saying, 'Let neither man nor woman do any more work of contributing to the building of the sanctuary.' So the people were restrained from bringing" (Exodus 36:4–6). Thus, the people responded overwhelmingly with "the generosity of their hearts."

But what would have happened if the Jewish people had been less amenable to Moses' request, if their hearts had been reluctant to contribute to the building of the sanctuary? Would Moses have compelled them to donate to the collective cause? Should one be forced to give *tzedakah* (charity)?

Almost one thousand years ago, Maimonides wrote, "we have never seen or heard of a Jewish community that does not have a *tzedakah* fund. ... We must observe the precept of *tzedakah* more carefully than any other positive commandment. ... No one ever becomes poor from giving *tzedakah*" (Laws of Gifts for the Poor, Chapters 9, 10).

Maimonides also delineated guidelines for giving, clarifying eight degrees of charity, each one higher than the other:

First Level—The giver enables the recipient to become self-supporting.

Second Level—Neither the giver nor the recipient is aware of the other's identity.

Third Level—The giver knows the recipient, but the recipient does not know the giver.

Fourth Level—The recipient knows the giver, but the giver does not know the recipient.

Fifth Level—The giver gives directly to the recipient without being solicited.

Sixth Level—The giver gives directly to the recipient after being solicited.

Seventh Level—The giver gives less than she or he should, but cheerfully.

Eighth Level—The giver gives begrudgingly.

The highest degree (first level) is to aid a Jew in need by offering him a gift or loan, by entering into a partnership with him, or by providing work for him, so that he may become self-supporting, without having to ask people for anything.

What is special about the "second level" of giving, being unaware of the other's identity, making it superior to the remaining levels?

Maimonides refers to this level, which has the highest degree of anonymity, as "doing a mitzvah for its own sake." Rabbi Eliyahu Dessler writes that every act can be classified as either an act of "giving" or of "receiving." Either the person is motivated to act for the sake of a greater cause, independent of personal reward and satisfaction ("giving"), or else she or he is driven by a personal need of self-gratification ("taking"). Similarly, each particular act can have varying degrees of the qualities of "giving" and "taking."

When an individual gives *tzedakah*, how does he or she truly know whether this is a purely giving act or if it is mixed with certain elements of self-gratification? According to the eight levels of Maimonides, when the giver does not require personal accolades or even a moment of recognition, then he or she knows that the money has been given for the sake of giving, of "doing a mitzvah for its own sake." Though a person has fulfilled the mitzvah of *tzedakah* if he or she has given according to any of these eight levels, nevertheless, this highest stage represents an ideal. Furthermore, this act of sincere giving should then become a paradigm for all of one's behavior in the future.

Around the *Shabbat* Table

1. According to Jewish law, it is preferable to give small amounts many times than to give a single large amount. Why should this be so?

2. Why do you think that Judaism turned *tzedakah* into a commandment that a person must do regardless of how he or she feels at the present moment and does not leave the decision of giving to the impulses of one's heart?

3. What act of *tzedakah* stands out most in your mind? By others? By yourself?

Seuda Shlishit: Fund-Raising

Since their very inception, the Jewish people have been noted for their giving *tzedakah*. In January of 1948, Golda Meir was sent on a crucial fundraising mission for the soon-to-be declared Jewish state. She writes in her autobiography:

> We were, of course, totally unprepared for war. That we had managed for so long to hold the local Arabs at bay, more or less, didn't mean that we could cope with regular armies. We needed weapons urgently, if we could find anyone willing to sell them to us; but before we could

buy anything, we needed money—millions of dollars. And there was only one group of people in the whole world that we had any chance of getting these dollars from: the Jews of America. There was simply nowhere else to go and no one else to go to.

Who would go? At one of these [governmental] meetings, I looked around the table at my colleagues, so tired and harassed, and wondered for the first time whether I ought not to volunteer for the mission. After all, I had done some fund raising in the States before, and I spoke English fluently. . . . I began to feel that I should suggest this to Ben-Gurion. At first, he wouldn't hear of it. . . . "Then let's put it to a vote," I said. He looked at me for a second, then nodded. The vote was in favor of my going.

"But at once," Ben-Gurion said. "Don't even try to get back to Jerusalem." So I flew to the States that day—without any luggage, wearing the dress I had worn to the meeting with a winter coat over it.

The first appearance I made in 1948 before American Jewry was unscheduled, unrehearsed and, of course, unannounced. . . I didn't speak for long, but I said everything that was in my heart. I described the situation as it had been the day I left Palestine, and then I said:

"The Jewish community in Palestine is going to fight to the very end. If we have arms to fight with, we will fight with them. If not, we will fight with stones in our hands. . . . My friends, we are at war. There is no Jew in Palestine who does not believe that finally we will be victorious. That is the spirit of the country . . . but this valiant spirit alone cannot face rifles and machine guns.

"You cannot decide whether we should fight or not. We will. The Jewish community in Palestine will raise no white flag for the mufti. That decision is taken, nobody can change it. You can only decide one thing: whether we shall be victorious in this fight or whether the mufti will be victorious. That decision American Jews can make. It has to be made quickly, within hours, within days. And I beg of you—don't be too late. Don't be bitterly sorry three months from now for what you failed to do today. The time is now."

They listened, and they wept, and they pledged money in amounts that no community had ever given before. . . . by the time I came back to Palestine in March I had raised $50,000,000, which was turned over at once for the Haganah's secret purchase of arms in Europe. . . . Ben-

Gurion said to me, "Someday when history will be written, it will be said that there was a Jewish woman who got the money which made the state possible." But I always knew that these dollars were given not to me, but to Israel. [*My Life*, pp. 213, 214]

Around the *Shabbat* Table

1. The Talmud (*Bava Batra* 9a) states in the name of Rabbi Elazar that one who causes others to give *tzedakah* has greater merit than those who actually give the *tzedakah*. Why do you think that this is so?

2. What would you have said if you had been in Golda Meir's place? Have you ever been in the position of asking others to contribute to a cause? Were you successful?

3. What cause(s) do you most believe in supporting?

Tetzaveh

FRIDAY NIGHT MEAL: Clothes of Humility

This week's *parsha* concludes the two *parshiyot* (portions) that describe the building of the Tabernacle and the sacred service. The first *parsha*, *Terumah*, described the external nature and physical construction of the Tabernacle. The second, *Tetzaveh*, concentrates on human responsibility within the Tabernacle and focuses on the primary caretakers of the Tabernacle: the *kohanim* (priests). *Tetzaveh* begins with the daily lighting of the menorah by the *kohanim* and concludes with their offering of the daily sacrifice and burning of the incense. From the beginning of the book of Exodus until the conclusion of the Torah, this will be the only *parsha* in which the name Moses does not occur, focusing exclusively upon the role of Aaron, his brother, and Aaron's descendants, the *kohanim*.

The book of Genesis relates that Jacob had twelve sons, each of whom became the founder of his respective tribe. Each tribe ultimately had its own location within Israel, its own special attributes, and its own particular responsibilities to perform for the sake of the Jewish people. The tribe of Levi, Jacob's third son, was eventually

149

divided into two groups: the *kohanim*, who were responsible for the service of the Tabernacle, and the Levites, who assisted them in their duties. *Tetzaveh* recounts the consecrating of the *kohanim*. "And you [Moses] should select Aaron and his sons from out of the Jewish people to administer to Me ..." (Exodus 28:1) " ... And Aaron and his sons I will sanctify to minister to Me in the Priest's capacity" (Exodus 29:44).

From birth, the *kohanim* were different from the other tribes. They were trained for holiness. Their whole lives were dedicated to the performance of their holy work in the Tabernacle in the desert and, ultimately, in the Temple in Jerusalem. Particular laws and practices separated them from all of the other tribes of Israel. They did not own land or engage in practical trades. They were allowed to eat specially ordained foods that possessed higher spiritual qualities (tithes). To this day, *kohanim* are limited in whom they are permitted to marry and are not allowed to come into contact with dead bodies. The Talmud states that the *kohanim* were both God's spiritual messengers to the Jewish people and the Jewish people's spiritual messengers to God (*Yoma* 19a).

In light of all this, the thrust of *Tetzaveh* is surprising. The major concern of this week's *parsha* is the specification of the special clothes that the *kohanim* were obligated to wear while working in the Tabernacle. Almost fifty verses, half of the whole *parsha*, describe the garments of the priests in great detail. None of the other tribes were obligated to wear particular clothes. Moreover, the work of the *kohen* was utterly dependent upon his wearing these clothes; a *kohen* performing holy service in the Tabernacle without any piece of his clothes was subject to the death penalty.

Why were the *kohanim* singled out to wear a special uniform? Were they simply clothes of identification?

Doesn't the emphasis on these external symbols contradict the spiritual, internal thrust of the *kohanim's* lives? The more elevated and spiritual the role of the *kohen*, the greater the emphasis the Torah placed on his clothes—four for the other priests and eight for the High Priest. Why?

One effect of wearing the priestly clothes cited by the Talmud (*Zevachim* 88b) is that each particular garment possessed special atoning qualities that influenced the behavior of its wearer. For example, the special pants worn by the priests atoned for sexual promiscuity and the tiny ringing bells at the bottom of the coat reminded the wearer not to speak gossip.

The Talmud relates that the continual work in the Tabernacle and the Temple transformed the nature of the *kohanim*. They became the most zealous tribe, purified in thought, meticulous in detail. Their role utterly separated them from the rest of the Jewish people and perpetually reminded them of their special stature and holy occupation. And, perhaps, therein lay the single greatest danger to the successful functioning of the Tabernacle—the danger of the *kohanim*'s gradual feelings of spiritual superiority, of self-righteous conceit. Will their automatic hereditary status engender a vain pompousness, an elitist disdain for those whose lives do not center around the Holy of Holies?

The clothes of the *kohanim* were the primary vehicle that served to keep them humble. The clothes were contributed by the people of Israel and did not become the private possessions of their wearers. The wearing of these clothes was limited to the service of the Tabernacle; the Talmud states that the *kohanim* were not allowed to sleep in these special clothes and questions whether they were even allowed to walk in them while not involved in the actual services. Without these clothes, the *kohanim* could not take part in any of the holy ceremonies; only after donning the clothes that were bestowed upon them by the rest of the Jewish people were the *kohanim* able to function.

How can the Jewish people raise a select group dedicated to a life of holiness, yet prevent them from becoming a holy aristocracy? By perpetually reminding them that they are indebted to all those whom they are presently serving, that their privileged function is solely a result of the contributions of all of the Jewish people. Every time the *kohanim* prepared themselves for their work, they had to dress themselves in the gifts from their people. They were continually reminded that not only do they represent the entire people but, as was told to the entire Jewish people at Mount Sinai, the whole nation is, in fact, a *memlechet kohanim*, a nation of priests (Exodus 19:6).

Around the *Shabbat* Table

1. What do you think are the positive and negative messages of clothes today? Does the example of the clothes of the *kohanim* have any relevance for contemporary society?

2. How might one raise children to a life of holiness today?

3. What safeguards would you suggest today to prevent self-righteousness among spiritual leaders?

SHABBAT LUNCH: Worn-Out Clothes and Empty Synagogues

This week's *parsha*, *Tetzaveh*, focuses on the significance and centrality of the clothes of the *kohanim*. These clothes were essential to the *kohen's* role of caring for all matters of holiness in the Temple and even acquired a level of sanctity of their own. The Torah states that these clothes were to be holy garments, "for honor and for beauty" (Exodus 28:2), and Maimonides writes that because of their special stature, the clothes of the *kohanim* would always have to appear clean and new. They were never to be bleached or washed. Eventually, like all clothes, they would wear out. What would happen to them then?

What happens to an object of sanctity after it has fulfilled its purpose? Is it simply discarded, or is its memory somehow sustained and hallowed? Is it still held in regard for the service that it once performed, or is it deemed dispensable?

The Talmud (*Sukkah* 41a) states that the *kohanim* would re-move the hems of their worn-out pants and belts and then use them for wicks to light torches to illuminate the courtyard of the Temple during the celebrations of Sukkot, known as *Simchat Beit HaShoevah*. During the seven days of Sukkot, it was customary in Jerusalem to rejoice in communal singing and dancing. Though the clothes were no longer fit to be worn by the *kohanim*, they were not simply abandoned; they were appropriated to perform an addi-tional function within the domain of the Temple—to light the holi-day torches.

Other tasks may be found for the worn-out clothes of the *kohanim*, but what happens to a synagogue that is no longer needed by its community? Can a building that was once dedicated to the spiritual lives of its constituents, that housed sacred articles and books, now be sold? Can it be used for commercial or secular pur-poses? Among the many opinions mentioned in the Talmud, the rab-bis stated that a synagogue may be sold with the stipulation that the new owners not turn it into a bathhouse, a tannery, a *mikveh*, or a laundry. These four possibilities all involve a more physical and less sacred level than the synagogue's former status.

The Mishnah further states in the name of Rabbi Yehuda that a synagogue that has been destroyed cannot be used for any other purpose; one may not even walk through it as a shortcut. If weeds grow inside it, they should not be pulled out, in order to intensify the anguish of those who see them. He explicates the verse "And I [God] have made desolate your holy places" (Leviticus 26:31) as meaning that "they are still holy places, despite having become deso-late."

Around the *Shabbat* Table

1. The Talmud (*Berakhot* 8b) relates that while in the desert, the Jewish people carried the shards of the first set of the Ten Com-mandment tablets with them for all forty years. Though broken,

the original sanctity of the tablets merited their safeguarding. From this example, the Talmud learns that one should continue to give respect to an elderly person even after he or she has forgotten his or her learning. To what other examples would this principle apply?

2. Have you ever seen a synagogue now in disuse or being occupied for other purposes? How did it make you feel?

3. Do you have any possessions that you would not discard even after they have served their purpose? Why?

Seuda Shlishit: The Rabbi's Boots

Rav Chaim Soloveitchek (1853-1918), known as the "Brisker Rav," was one of the premier rabbinical figures of his time. Possessing outstanding analytical powers, he created a new approach to the study of Talmud, "the Brisker system," whose categories and terminology would influence the next century of talmudic study. He was one of the leading rabbis and teachers of the famous Volozhin Yeshiva.

This week's *parsha, Tetzaveh,* describes the many clothes of the priests and High Priest. The priests, know for their eagerness and zeal, always performed their sacrificial duties barefoot. Rav Chaim, though, had a pair of special boots.

Rav Chaim always kept these high coarse farmer's boots in the corner of his private study. Such boots were out of character with Rav Chaim's normal manner of impeccable dress. Out of respect for their rabbi and teacher, his students never asked him why he kept such boots in his study.

At the Volozhin Yeshiva, the students' dormitories were approximately one hundred yards from their central study hall, the *Beit midrash.* One morning, after a particularly heavy snowfall, Rav Chaim put on his heavy boots and walked from the dormitory to the *Beit midrash*. To the astonishment of his students, upon reaching the *Beit midrash*, he turned around and walked back to the dormitory. He continued to walk back and forth from the dormitory to the *Beit midrash* until he had cleared a path in the snow for his students to walk.

Around the *Shabbat* Table

1. Did you ever have a teacher express such concern, or perform acts of kindness, for you? For others?

2. What might this act of the "Brisker Rav" reflect about his approach or philosophy of education?

3. Have you ever performed an act of kindness with any of your clothes? What is your most special article of clothing?

Ki Tissa

FRIDAY NIGHT MEAL: Leadership of the Heart and the Mind

Forty days after arriving at Mount Sinai, forty days after seeing the voices and hearing the *shofar*, the Jewish people danced around a golden calf. They could not wait for Moses to descend from the mountain; they could not bear to remain without a leader. "And when the people saw that Moses did not come down from the mountain, the people congregated around Aaron and said to him, 'Get up, make us gods which shall go before us; for this man Moses that brought us up out of the land of Egypt, we do not know what has become of him'" (Exodus 32:1).

This failing, tragic and grievous as it was, is not altogether surprising. Once again, the Jewish people fell victim to the impatience of their childhood (see: "*Beshallach*"). Amid their many crises, a momentary lapse and return to the practices of idolatry that were part of their experience in Egypt is not entirely shocking and is, perhaps, even inevitable.

The more pressing question is—what is the correct response to the demand of "make us gods"? How should their leaders have responded not only to the flagrant betrayal of loyalty to God, but also to the violation of the Second Commandment, heard so recently, "You should have no other gods beside Me"?

Aaron and Moses provide two very different models of response. Moses' brother, Aaron, is thrust directly into the dilemma of responding to the demand to "make us gods." Seemingly without a moment of hesitation or a word of protest, Aaron directs the Jews to "break off the golden earrings which are in the ears of your wives and sons and daughters and bring them to me" (Exodus 32:2). Aaron subsequently fashions the gold that he receives into a calf. After the people see the calf and proclaim, "These are your gods, Israel, which brought you up out of the land of Egypt" (Exodus 32:4), Aaron builds an altar and announces that "tomorrow is a holiday for God" (Exodus 32:5).

Why did Aaron, the High Priest, acquiesce so readily to the egregious demands of the people?!

Unlike Moses, Aaron had always coexisted with his brethren. He had been a slave with them during their affliction in Egypt and he remained with them while Moses ascended Mount Sinai. He realized that the people, having been led into the desert by Moses only to see him disappear several weeks later, were filled with apprehension and terror. The people did not know how long Moses would be on Mount Sinai; from their vantage point, he had simply disappeared: ". . . We do not know what has become of him." Aaron understood what they had endured and recognized the limits of their newly found freedom. The people were much too vulnerable to grapple with this uncertainty. For years, as slaves, their lives had been determined for them; now they were prematurely thrust into the unknown, expected to cope with the void of leadership and security.

The commentators explain that Aaron's plan was not to acquiesce to their demands; rather, he sought to delay an impending rebellion of the people. First, assuming a natural reluctance of people to part with their precious possessions, he instructed them to bring their gold and that of their families. To further deter them, he declared that they could only worship the golden calf "tomorrow." Of course, Aaron understood the gravity of their actions and consequently bore a measure of culpability for assisting them: as we find later in the Torah, God punished Aaron for his behavior. "... And the Lord was very angry with Aaron" (Deuteronomy 9:20). Nevertheless, Aaron was aware of the overall context of the situation of the Jewish people; his caring for his people was so great that he was even willing to sacrifice a degree of his own innocence to try to help them. The Mishnah states that one should strive to be like "the students of Aaron, loving and pursuing peace." Aaron is regarded as the prototype of love and compassion for others.

Moses, however, had not shared this experience of subjugation with his people. Separated at childhood, he grew up as a prince in Pharaoh's palace and grew to manhood as a shepherd in the desert (see: "*Shemot*: Slavery and Freedom"). Now, after forty days of exalted solitude on Mount Sinai, at the very moment of the giving of the tablets, he is told by God, "Go down, because your people have become corrupt ... " (Exodus 32:7). Moses descends, breaks the tablets, burns and grinds the golden calf, and then forces the people to drink the ashes of the idol that they had made. He unceremoniously rebukes Aaron and calls out, "Who is on the side of God?" (Exodus 32:26). The Levites respond to the challenge and proceed to kill three thousand men who instigated the idol-worship.

Moses does not tolerate a moment of concession to the needs of the people. Moments later, Moses will plead with God not to destroy the whole people, but his first response is that those directly responsible must be unequivocally punished. There is no room to consider extenuating circumstances. He is unwilling to become reconciled to the limits of this slave people.

In the *parsha*, we see two responses: Aaron responds within the context of the present reality, he accepts human limitations and expresses his love for the people; Moses acts apart from their reality, he demands the transcending of present constraints and teaches truth to the people. Aaron responds from his heart; Moses, from his mind.

The midrash asks: "Where is wisdom found? Rabbi Eliezer says: 'in one's head,' Rabbi Joshua says: 'in one's heart.'" The mind and the heart—two centers of life, two centers of wisdom, both indispensable.

Around the *Shabbat* Table

1. Why did Aaron mold the gold into the shape of a calf? Rabbi Samson Raphael Hirsch speculated that Aaron wanted to choose a symbol of childishness and weakness. What do you think?

2. Which contemporary leaders do you think are more similar to Aaron's form of leadership? To Moses' leadership? What happens when only one approach exists?

3. With which style of leadership do you most identify? Why?

SHABBAT LUNCH: Persistence

Tragedy strikes the Jewish people. After forty days atop Mount Sinai, Moses descends from the mountain, sees the people dancing around the golden calf, and casts down the tablets of the Ten Commandments. The tablets, symbolizing an engagement ring, have been broken; the relationship between God and the Jewish people has been jeopardized. Moses will have to plead for forgiveness for the people and then once again ascend Mount Sinai, eventually to return with a second set of tablets.

The Jewish people did not know how long Moses intended to remain on Mount Sinai. They did not know, originally, that he was ascending for forty days. He had simply disappeared, without food and provisions. Barely seven weeks out of Egypt and suddenly leaderless, the Jewish people eventually suffered a loss of nerve, a collapse of faith and hope in Moses' return.

Apparently, God kept Moses up on Mount Sinai until the Jewish people faltered and resorted to idolatry. Why? Why couldn't God have had Moses descend with the first set of tablets just a bit earlier, before the Jewish people lost their will and fashioned the golden calf? What was accomplished by having Moses ascend Mount Sinai a second time, to return with the second set of tablets?

There is a critical difference between the first and second experiences of Moses on Mount Sinai. The Torah states that the first set of tablets "were the *work of God*." Miraculous in nature. For the second set, however, God told Moses to carve the two tablets of stone *himself*. The first set of tablets was a gift; the second set required Moses to do the work himself.

Furthermore, the first time Moses ascended Mount Sinai, every step was new, every moment a new experience of exhilaration. But what about the second time? A repeated experience never carries with it the thrill and excitement of the first time. What was the second climbing of Mount Sinai like for Moses? Every step he had already traveled, every sight he had already seen. It was a climb of mission and purpose but, perhaps, bereft of the spiritual euphoria that had accompanied the first ascent.

But therein lies the greatness of Moses and, consequently, of the Jewish people: the strength to climb the mountain a second time. Moses discovered the wherewithal not to give up, not to despair, even after crisis and tragedy, to somehow locate the resources to climb the mountain a second time. The first set of tablets was a gift. It is very difficult to fully appreciate a gift. The second set of tablets was the product of difficult but sincere human labor and persistence. Only *these tablets* would remain intact.

Around the *Shabbat* Table

1. It is written in the Talmud that Moses ascended the mountain for a second time forty days before Yom Kippur and then descended with the second tablets on Yom Kippur. What might this symbolize?

2. What other figures or historical examples exemplify the quality of persistence? Do you think that one can develop this attribute in oneself or in others?

3. The breaking of the first tablets and the hewing of the second tablets are a symbol for all of life's endeavors. Have you ever persisted in "climbing the mountain a second time?" When? Why?

Seuda Shlishit: Defender of the People

When the Jewish people sinned in making the golden calf, God threatened to destroy them completely. "And the Lord said to Moses, 'I have seen this people, and, behold, it is a stiff-necked people: now therefore let Me alone, that My wrath may burn against them, and that I may consume them: and I will make of you a great nation'" (Exodus 32:9, 10). Moses does not accede to God's request; instead, he defends the people and fights on their behalf. "And Moses besought the Lord his God, and said, 'Lord, why does Your wrath burn against Your people, whom You brought forth out of the land of Egypt with great power, and with a mighty hand? . . . Turn from Your fierce anger, and relent of this evil against Your people'" (Exodus 32:11, 12).

Three thousand years later, another major figure would appear who was known for his unrelenting defense of the righteousness of the Jewish people. Rabbi Levi Yitzchak of Berditchev, one of the major hasidic leaders of Polish Jewry, was known for his great and unconditional love for all Jews. He epitomized the hasidic trait of always finding a "spark of goodness" in all people, despite their outward behavior. He was noted for saying, "No one has the right to say anything evil about the Jewish people, only to intercede for them." The following stories are told about him:

Once Rabbi Levi Yitzchak encountered two Jews, smoking publicly on the Sabbath. He approached them and, in a gentle tone, remarked that they had obviously forgotten that it was the Sabbath. "No," they replied, "we are perfectly aware that today is the Sabbath." "Then you must not know that it is prohibited to smoke on the Sabbath," continued Rabbi Levi Yitzchak. Again they replied, "No, we are perfectly aware that it is forbidden to smoke on the Sabbath." Thereupon, Rabbi Levi Yitzchak raised his hands toward the heavens and called out, "Master of the Universe, see what an honorable and virtuous people you have! Twice these Jews could have falsely replied to me, but You see, your people are only capable of telling the truth."

Even while confronting God, Rabbi Levi Yitzchak would not desist in his defense of the Jewish people. In the middle of his prayer, Rabbi Levi Yitzchak once exclaimed, "Lord of all the world! There was a time when You went around the world with that Torah of Yours, and were willing to sell it at a bargain, like apples that have gone bad, yet no one would buy it from You. No one would even look at You! And then we took it! Because of this I want to propose a deal. We have many sins and misdeeds, and You have an abundance of forgiveness and atonement. Let us exchange! But perhaps You might agree only to an even exchange? In that case, my answer is, 'Had we no sins, what would You do with Your forgiveness?! So you must balance the deal by giving us life and children and food in addition!'" [*Tales of the Chassidim*, p. 209]

Around the *Shabbat* Table

1. After the sin of the golden calf, God offered to Moses to make a new nation from him. "And the Lord said to Moses, 'I have seen this people, and, behold, it is a stiff-necked people, now therefore let Me alone, that my wrath may burn against them, and that I may consume them, and I will make of you a great nation" (Exodus 32:9, 10). Why do you think that Moses did not accept God's offer to make a new nation from him? Do you think that God would actually have destroyed the Jewish people, or was this only a test to see how Moses would respond?

2. Rav Kook wrote that "hate stems from an overabundance of self-love." Do you agree? What prevents people from focusing on the "sparks of goodness" in others?

3. Do you know anyone who always seeks to find something positive in others? What effect does this person's attitude have upon others? Upon him- or herself?

Vayakhel/Pekudei

FRIDAY NIGHT MEAL: Details of Creation

The book of Exodus ends with two *parshiyot* that focus on a similar theme and are often read together. The *parshiyot Vayakhel/Pekudei* recount the actual construction and sanctification of the Tabernacle.

Major sections of these *parshiyot* closely resemble the content and style of two previous *parshiyot, Terumah* and *Tetzaveh.* Once again, each utensil of the Tabernacle is described; once again, the clothes of the priests are specified in great detail. All that God told Moses to do in the two previous *parshiyot,* Moses now directs the Jewish people to carry out. Moses appoints Betzalel to be the primary architect of the Tabernacle, and he oversees this national endeavor through to its conclusion. Notwithstanding the significance and centrality of the Tabernacle (see:"*Terumah*: the Unknowable"), the tedious repetition of so many details creates an almost burdensome monotony.

Why does the Torah repeat the instructions for erecting the Tabernacle in such detail? Since we are already familiar with all of the details of the Tabernacle from the previous *parshiyot*, why doesn't the Torah simply state:"And all that God told Moses to do, so he did"?

The book of Exodus begins with the Hebrew letter "vav" ("and"), signifying its connection to the first book of the Torah, Genesis. Exodus completes and fulfills the processes begun in Genesis. Genesis begins with the creation of the world, the paradise of the Garden of Eden and then chronicles the history of the world through the events of the flood, the tower of Babel, and the choosing of Abraham. It culminates several generations later with the descent of the sons of Jacob to Egypt, who are about to become enslaved. This continuing descent, from paradise to Egypt, is reversed in the book of Exodus. The birth of the Jewish people, the giving of Torah, and the return to Israel are the building blocks for the restoration of the harmony that is lost with the exile from the Garden of Eden.

Yet this harmony, this return to paradise, will not be achieved effortlessly. Unlike God's creation of the world, accomplished through eternal, all-embracing utterances, the human process of creating a world of harmony will be realized only through a gradual and painstaking course, necessitating a countless number of minute and detailed actions. For the success of this process, there can be no grandiose illusions of power or fantasies of miraculous feats. National and universal harmony will not simply come to pass; human beings must struggle to bring it about incrementally, improving the world through small, modest steps of transformation.

Only a rare individual is able to perceive both the beauty of the overall project as well as the significance of each detail. The Torah writes that Betzalel, who was chosen to direct the building of the Tabernacle, was "filled with the spirit of God, in wisdom, understanding, and in knowledge, and in all matter of workmanship" (Exodus 31:3). His wisdom devolved to each element of workmanship. Metaphorically, the Talmud states that Betzalel had the power to see the value of individual letters as well as the value of words. Not only is harmony restored to the world through a process of countless details, but the truly wise are able to see the building of this harmony in each minute aspect of the process.

Around the *Shabbat* Table

1. In the *parsha* of *Vayakhel*, the description of the construction of the Tabernacle is preceded by the statute to observe *Shabbat* (Exodus 35:1–3). From this juxtaposition, the rabbis conclude that the work from which we must abstain on *Shabbat* includes only those creative acts that were involved in the building of the Tabernacle. What additional lessons can be drawn from the juxtaposition of these two ideas?

2. Have you ever had the experience of seeing the "big picture" in a tiny moment? Have you ever engaged in a seemingly minor endeavor that you thought possessed national significance?

3. Do you know people who have great ideas yet falter when it comes to details? Have the frustrating details of a project ever prevented you from completing it?

SHABBAT LUNCH: Healthy Growth

The book of Exodus closes with Moses calling together the Jewish people:"And Moses gathered together all of the congregation of the people of Israel" (Exodus 35:1). Instead of proceeding directly to the task at hand, the building of the Tabernacle, the entire people first have to be convened together. Then, after they have finished their work of building the Tabernacle, Moses proceeds to bless them:"And Moses saw all the work ... and Moses blessed them" (Exodus 39:43).

Apparently, their receiving of this blessing, which advanced them to a new level of spirituality, was contingent upon their coming together as one. Why was this so?

This theme of unity preceding growth echoes throughout the whole Torah. At the close of the book of Genesis, before Jacob blesses his twelve sons, he summons them: "Gather yourselves together" (Genesis 49:1). Before the giving of the Torah at Mount Sinai, the Midrash comments that the Jewish people achieved an unprecedented cognizance of their oneness. Similarly, the final mitzvah mentioned in the Torah, the commandment for everyone to write their own Torah, is immediately preceded by the mitzvah of *hakhel,* the gathering of all of the Jewish people together in Jerusalem.

Why is spiritual growth dependent upon this prior condition of harmony and unity? Why is it necessary to gather everyone together before the giving of a blessing?

The rabbis chose to conclude their monumental work, the Mishnah, with the following statement: "God did not find any channel through which a blessing could be bestowed upon Israel other than *shalom* (peace)." Without *shalom,* without a harmonizing of all of the various parts of the whole, there can be no blessing, no spiritual growth. The commentators indicate that any blessing that is received without the requisite equilibrium of *shalom* is not destined to be maintained. The founder of Hasidism, the Ba'al Shem Tov, compares spiritual growth to the climbing of a ladder. One must have a stable footing on each rung before climbing higher. Spiritual growth is a precarious stage of development, and, if it does not occur in a stable and healthy environment, it will most likely collapse amid calamitous consequences.

Similarly, the Talmud states that God's presence only dwells in a home that is characterized by *shalom bayit* (peace at home), and it will not dwell in a home in which there exists internal strife. A home characterized by dissension reflects the insistence and collision of particular concerns and an inability to reconcile these conflicting viewpoints through a higher unifying principle. Such a condition of dissension is antithetical to developing a more elevated spiritual state, to receiving a blessing. *Shalom,* peace, does not entail a negation of differences; rather, it entails the harmonizing of divergent perspectives through understanding the opinions and needs of others. Awareness of a greater picture and striving for *shalom* is the foundation and catalyst for lifelong growth.

Moses wants to give a blessing not to a countless number of individuals, but to the Jewish people as one. As a prerequisite for this blessing the Jewish people must be assembled together, so that it is clear that they understand the unique role that every member of the Jewish people plays in this national undertaking. Without national shalom there can be no national blessing.

Around the *Shabbat* Table

1. The Talmud includes innumerable arguments among the rabbis. Why do you think that these are not considered to be examples of dissension?

2. The importance of achieving peace between all of the individual parts as a prerequisite for receiving a blessing is true both on a collective and individual level. Have you ever known someone who tried to grow and change before harmonizing the disparate elements of his or her personality? What happened? Could this have been avoided?

3. Rav Kook wrote that a person suffers greatly and experiences profound anguish when his internal life is not "harmonized." Conversely, achieving unity and clarity of purpose accords the exhilaration of almost unlimited powers and potential. Have you ever felt either of these two experiences?

Seuda Shlishit: Building Dreams

The book of Exodus concludes with the building of the Tabernacle, which includes the construction of the menorah, the bronze and gold altars, the golden table, and the ark. For the Jewish people, who began the book of Exodus afflicted with the slavery of Egypt, the reality of their liberation and collective building must have seemed almost dreamlike. Their suffering in Egypt had once caused them to lose even the capacity to fantasize about a better world, "and they did not listen to Moses because of the anguish of spirit and the cruel bondage" (Exodus 6:9). Once, they were forced to build monuments for Pharaoh. Now, they are engaged in physical building again, but as a free people, exploring the untapped potential within.

Almost a century ago, a lone figure managed to transcend the manifest reality of his world and to dream of building, together with others Jews, a model society. Theodor Herzl (1860–1904), an assimilated journalist from Vienna, sought to overcome the virulent anti-Semitism of his time through the creation of a Jewish homeland. For several years his efforts met with general disdain and ridicule by the Jewish community of Europe, typified in an episode in his fictional work *Altneuland* (*Old-New Land*):

> Dr. Weiss, a simple rabbi from a provincial town in Moravia, did not know exactly in what company he found himself, and ventured a few shy remarks. "A new movement has arisen within the last few years, which is called Zionism. Its aim is to solve the Jewish problem through colonization on a large scale. All who can no longer bear their present lot will return to our old home, to Palestine." He spoke very quietly, unaware that the people about him were getting ready for an outburst of laughter . . . The laughter ran every gamut. The ladies giggled, the gentlemen smirked and roared.

Nevertheless, Herzl continued to toil ceaselessly for his vision. In 1897, Herzl convened the First Zionist Conference in Basel. A delegate later recounted that "For us, the first congress was a crisis that changed our fate. It revolutionized our entire world and divided the history of our exile into two parts, the first before the congress and the second the part that came after." Herzl himself wrote in his diary:

> Were I to sum up the Basel congress in a few words—which I must guard against uttering publicly—it would be this: In Basel I founded the Jewish state. If I said this aloud today, I would be answered by universal laughter. *Perhaps in five years, and certainly in fifty, everyone will agree.* The state is already founded, in essence, in the will of the people to be a state; yes, even in the will of a sufficiently powerful individual.

At the conclusion of his book Herzl wrote, "Dreams are not so different from deeds as some may think. All the deeds of men are only dreams at first."

Around the *Shabbat* Table

1. Why do people of vision often provoke reactions of scoffing and sarcasm? Do you know anyone who has overcome the skepticism or derision of others to pursue a dream?

2. What do you think is the difference between a visionary and an eccentric or insane person?

3. What dream would you like to see fulfilled for the Jewish people fifty years from now?

Leviticus

Vayikra

FRIDAY NIGHT MEAL: A Call of Forgiveness

The third book of the Torah begins with the words, "And [God] called to Moses." The book of Genesis described the creation of the world, the patriarchs and the matriarchs, and the development of the twelve tribes of Israel. The book of Exodus recounted the birth of the Jewish people, the giving of the Ten Commandments at Mount Sinai, and the building of the Tabernacle. The book of Leviticus is referred to in Hebrew as *Vayikra*, "and He called." It reveals God's "calling" to the Jewish people—a call of affection, according to Rashi, summoning them to affirm their relationship with God and to live as a holy people.

Eventually, however, every relationship may suffer temporary breakdowns. In a moment of oversight, a thoughtless act may be committed, a date may be forgotten. Unintentionally, a strong bond may be weakened or even endangered. The Jewish people's relationship with God, both individually and collectively, undergoes times of crisis and strain. Then what? After a moment of broken trust, of carelessness and disappointment, how can the relationship be restored?

The first *parsha* of the book of *Vayikra*, which is also called *Vayikra*, describes several of the types of sacrifices that the Jewish people brought in the desert. Though far removed from our contemporary reality, these sacrifices represented an archetype for mending a broken relationship. Among these offerings were several sacrifices that were brought by individuals to repair their relationship with God after incidents of breakdown." ... And it will be forgiven him for anything of all that he has done wherein to incur guilt" (Leviticus 5:26). Each sacrifice was accompanied by a personal admission of guilt and contrition for previous actions.

How can the process of bringing an offering be able to heal an injured relationship? How does this act serve as a paradigm for the restoration of harmony and trust?

The commentators explain that the *olah* sacrifice of this week's *parsha* atones for an act of omission, a missed opportunity to strengthen a relationship, and the Torah explicitly states that the *chattat* offering yields forgiveness for an accidental transgression. Intentional acts of malice, of course, severely damage a relationship. An act of hostility clearly reflects the desire to inflict pain upon the other person. But what does an act of forgetting or an accidental oversight express? What does a simple act of overlooking imply about the relationship? Relationships may be weakened and even destroyed through unintentional acts of carelessness. What should the response to such acts be?

The mystical book of the *Zohar* explains that sacrificing an animal is meant to convey a poignant message—that a person who has been careless, who has forgotten to perform an expected act, has, in a certain way, diminished his humanity and behaved like an animal. The ability to exercise free will and make productive decisions separates humans from the animal kingdom. Mindlessness is a symptom of an unhealthy relationship that must be set back on course. The bringing of a sacrifice serves as a powerful reminder that one must struggle to ensure that all of one's thoughts and actions reflect a conscious decision-making process and do not simply occur instinctively.

Yet there is another obstacle impeding the resumption of the relationship. Even after recognizing a mistake, it is difficult to ask for forgiveness. The person who intends to apologize may fear that the attempt to heal the relationship will be met with frustration and anger and that his "peace offering" may be rejected. In addition, the combination of guilt about having damaged the relationship and the fear that positive overtures may be repulsed may preclude someone from reaching out for forgiveness.

To alleviate these concerns, the *parsha* of *Vayikra* both begins and ends with God's calling out and offering forgiveness to man. God initiates the healing process; the Hebrew word for sacrifice is *korban*, meaning literally "a coming closer." The *parsha Vayikra* begins with God's call to come closer, to resume and heal the relationship that has been injured. It is difficult to ask for forgiveness, just as it is difficult to forgive someone who has caused pain. The paradigm created here is that the one who has been ignored and overlooked, the one who has experienced the pain (in this case, God), calls out.

"*Vayikra*" is a call of invitation, a call designed to remove the fear of rejection and to begin the process of renewal. It is a call that echoes throughout the whole book of *Vayikra*.

Around the *Shabbat* Table

1. The bringing of a sacrifice is a public act. Everyone who sees it knows that the person bringing it committed an accidental transgression. What effect do you think that the public nature of the sacrifice had upon the person asking for forgiveness?

2. Now that we no longer have the daily sacrifices of the Temple, Maimonides writes that an individual's prayers have assumed the role of achieving atonement (Laws of Prayer 1:4–6). What do you think are the positive and negative aspects of this change?

3. The paradigm of forgiveness set forth in *parsha Vayikra* is that the party who is hurt initiates the healing. Do you identify with this model of forgiveness? Have you ever had a relationship mended in a similar way?

SHABBAT LUNCH: Approaches to Prayer

The *parsha* of *Vayikra* concentrates on the sacrificial system of the Temple. For the last two thousand years, however, the Temple sacrifices have been replaced by the prayer service, which takes place primarily in the synagogue. Instead of actually coming to Jerusalem, Jews now direct their hearts toward Jerusalem. The peak moment of this directing of one's heart occurs during the silent standing prayer called the *Amidah*. The Mishnah states that during the *Amidah*, even if a snake were to wrap itself around a person's leg or a king were to ask a question, one should not interrupt this moment of prayer.

What is supposed to occur during these moments of prayer? While standing in total silence, what is the one praying trying to achieve? What should one be thinking?

Among the many philosophies of prayer developed by Jewish thinkers over the last 2,000 years, two radically divergent approaches can be found in the writings of Samson Raphael Hirsch, one of the leaders of German and all Western European Jewry during the nineteenth century, and Rav Kook, the first chief rabbi of the state of Israel.

Rabbi Shimshon Raphael Hirsch writes that:

There are two Divine services: the inner Divine service [prayer] and the outer, active, Divine service [in the whirl of life]. The inner Divine service should serve as a *preparation* of the outer one and should realize, in it, its main purpose.

This fulfillment of the Divine will in our inner self can come to its perfection only *by bringing about a change in our thoughts and emotions*—namely, by evoking and rejecting, and by bringing to life and reviving thoughts and emotions in our inner self.

"*Hitpallel*" (to pray), from which "*tefillah*" (prayer) is derived, originally meant to *deliver an opinion about oneself, to judge oneself* . . . Thus it denotes to step out of active life in order to attempt to gain a true judgment about oneself, that is, about one's ego, about one's relationship to God and the world . . . It strives to infuse mind and heart with the power of such judgment as will direct both anew to active life—purified, sublimated, strengthened.

For Hirsch, prayer represents a cognitive, analytical opportunity for self-judgment. Prayer is a "means," a vehicle through which people strive to examine their behavior and to find concrete resolutions for improving their course of action. The clarity and effectiveness of these insights were the signs of a successful prayer experience.

Rav Kook espouses a more mystical approach to prayer:

Prayer does not come as a remedy [asking for something], rather as the expression of the understanding that *the soul is continually praying*. It [the prayer of the soul] flies and embraces its lover [God] without any break or separation . . . . The *perpetual prayer of the soul* continually tries to emerge from its latent state to become revealed and actualized, to permeate every fiber of life of the entire universe.

For Rav Kook, the moment of prayer is one of listening and connection with one's essential spiritual self. In contrast to Hirsch, Rav Kook views prayer as neither analytical nor introspective. It does not focus on evaluating one's latest behavior, nor does it serve as preparation for the outer, active whirl of life. For Rav Kook, prayer is an opportunity to filter out the multitude of voices and demands that continually monopolize one's attention and to listen to the divine voice within oneself. Every person is created in the image of God, and this "divine spark" is always speaking, communicating to the individual his or her uniqueness. During prayer one strives to hear the "perpetual prayer of the soul."

The rabbis referred to prayer as "the work of one's heart." One should experience a "change of heart," a transformation, during prayer. For both Rabbi Shimshon Raphael Hirsch and Rav Kook, successful prayer is a life-changing occurrence.

Around the *Shabbat* Table

1. Organized Jewish prayer is intended to be a synthesis of spontaneous individual prayer and organized communal prayer. Can you think of any drawbacks or potential dangers of prayer experiences that possess only one of these two qualities?

2. In this unit we encountered two approaches to prayer: Rabbi Shimshon Raphael Hirsch views prayer as an analytic moment of self-judgment aimed at improving one's behavior. Rav Kook views prayer as a meditative moment of listening to one's deepest voice. With which of these two outlooks do you identify most? Can you think of an alternative approach to prayer?

3. What do you think are the major obstacles that preclude meaningful prayer experiences? How might they be overcome?

Seuda Shlishit: A Child's Flute

In the eighteenth century, a new movement, "*Hasidut,*" arose in Judaism, that stressed the centrality of prayer. Its founder, known as the Ba'al Shem Tov (1700–1760), taught that while learning and knowledge are important in the service of God, above all else, God desires the faithful devotion of one's heart (in Hebrew: *kavannah*). All else, even learning Torah and doing mitzvot, are vehicles to help generate clinging (*devekut*) to God. The following story, precariously balancing on the antinomian edge of *Hasidut*, was one of the Ba'al Shem Tov's classics.

A villager who went to town every year on the High Holy Days to pray in the synagogue of the Ba'al Shem Tov had a son who was so simple that he could not even learn the Hebrew alphabet, much less a single prayer. And because the boy knew nothing, his father never brought him to town for the holidays.

Yet when the boy reached the age of thirteen and became responsible for his actions, his father decided to take him to the synagogue on Yom Kippur, lest he stay at home and, in his ignorance, eat on the holy fast day. And so they set out together—and the boy, who had a little flute on which he used to play to his sheep, unbeknownst to his father, put the flute into his pocket.

In the middle of the service, the boy, touched by the power of the prayers, suddenly said, "Father, I want to play my pipe!"

The horrified father scolded his son and told him to behave himself. A while later, though, the boy said again, "Father, please let me play my pipe!" Again his father scolded him, warning him not to dare; yet soon the boy said a third time, "Father, I don't care what you say, I must play my pipe!"

"Where is it?" asked the father, seeing that the boy was uncontrollable.

The boy pointed to the pocket of his jacket, and his father seized it and gripped it firmly so that the boy could not take out his little flute. And so the hours passed with the man holding onto his son's pocket. The sun by now was low in the sky, the gates of Heaven began to close, and it was time for the final prayer of the day (*Ne'ilah*).

Halfway through the closing prayer, the boy wrenched the pipe free from his pocket and his father's hands, put it to his mouth, and let out a loud blast that startled the entire congregation. As soon as the Ba'al Shem Tov heard it, he hurried through the rest of the service as he had never done before.

Afterward, when asked by his followers why he had hastened through the remaining prayers, he told them that "when this little boy played his flute, all your prayers soared heavenward at once and there was nothing left for me to do but finish up."

Around the *Shabbat* Table

1. According to Jewish mysticism, the ideal way to pray is like a little child. What do you think is so admirable about a child's prayers?

2. If God is omniscient, knowing both our needs and merit, what is the purpose of prayer?

3. What was your most powerful prayer experience?

Tzav

FRIDAY NIGHT MEAL: The Source of Fire

As already noted, many of the *parshiyot* (portions) of the Torah come in pairs, with the second *parsha* expanding and deepening the ideas introduced in the previous week's *parsha*. This week's *parsha*, *Tzav*, develops themes present in last week's *parsha*, *Vayikra*, and concludes the account of the preparations necessary for the installation of the Tabernacle (Hebrew: *Mishkan*), the holy sanctuary at the heart of the camp of the Jewish people.

While there are many similarities between the two *parshiyot*, several striking distinctions should be noted. First, although both *parshiyot* concern bringing sacrifices, *Vayikra* dealt with the offerings brought by *individual* members of the Jewish people, whereas *Tzav* discusses the sacrifices brought by the *priests* (*kohanim*). The sacrifices brought in *Vayikra* were primarily voluntary offerings brought *after an individual had sinned*, as an expression of his desire to repair a damaged relationship with God. In contrast, the *olah* sacrifices, which the *kohanim* were commanded to bring at the beginning of *Tzav*, were to be brought daily, at sunrise and sunset, *regardless of the behavior or inclinations of the kohanim*. The *olah* (meaning: "to go up"), is the only sacrifice that is completely burnt in the altar, whereas all of the other sacrifices have parts that are permissibly eaten either by their owners or by the *kohanim*.

In addition, the beginning of this week's *parsha* repeatedly emphasizes the fire that burned continuously on the altar, "... It is the *burnt* offering, which shall be *burning* upon the altar all night until the morning, and the *fire* of the altar shall be kept *burning* in it. And the *kohen* shall ... take up the ashes which the *fire* has consumed with the *burnt* offering .. and the *fire* upon the altar shall be kept *burning* in it; *it shall not be put out*. And the *kohen* shall *burn* wood on it every morning ... The fire shall ever be *burning* upon the altar, *it shall never go out*" (Leviticus 6:2-6).

The "continual fire" was the source of all fire in the Tabernacle. From it, the lights of the Menorah, the fire of the altar, and all other fires were kindled. Yet even after all of the other fires were lit or when there was no need to light fires from it—that is, when this fire served no practical function—the *kohanim* were still commanded to maintain it. It was prohibited to extinguish even one ember of this fire, since the Torah states "it shall never go out."

The Torah forbids the wanton destruction of any element of nature, yet aren't the daily burning of the *olah* sacrifice and the continual fire on the altar examples of waste? Are these two examples of destruction, or is there a creative process and intention underlying these acts?

Both of these cases of apparent destruction and waste can be resolved by a single, unifying principle. The Tabernacle, physically placed at the heart of the Jewish encampment, symbolized the heart of the Jewish people. Just as the heart pumps blood to all parts of the body, so too, every quality of the Jewish people emanated from this central source. The health and purity of the heart ultimately determine the well-being of the whole organism.

How does one maintain a healthy, pure heart? The midrash states that the *olah* offering was a force of purification, brought exclusively to "purge impure meditations of the heart." It served as a daily reminder for the *kohanim* (and consequently for all of the Jewish people), to prevent their innermost thoughts from wandering and becoming corrupt or commonplace. Similarly, the continual fire, when seen in the context of the Temple environment, was supposed to remind its viewers of the need to eradicate, or to burn away, all nonessential and dispensable thoughts.

The Tabernacle (and subsequently the Temple) were not places of magic. Ultimately, they were structures that enabled the human beings working in them to elevate and transcend their physical realities. Later in Jewish history, many of the prophets bewailed that the services occurring in the Temple were empty acts, bereft of spiritual intent. The degree to which the *kohanim* were focused on their tasks determined the worthiness of the entire Temple existence. Thus, the continually burning fires and the daily reminder of the burnt *olah* offering helped to keep the meditations of all who saw them properly directed. In the end, as the Talmud states, "God desires [the purity and sincerity of] one's heart."

Around the *Shabbat* Table

1. Unlike Greek mythology, in which Prometheus was punished for stealing fire from the gods, the Torah affirms the human use of fire and directs the Jewish people to continually burn fires in their holy places. What might this difference indicate about the different approaches of Greek mythology and Judaism regarding the relationship between God (or the gods) and humanity?

2. The hasidic master S'fat Emmet explains that there are two kinds of fire: fire that consumes and fire that gives light. Can you think of examples of this paradigm in Judaism? In personal growth and/ or relationships?

3. The fire continually burning was supposed to excite and vitalize all those who saw it. Which aspect of Judaism makes you the most enthused?

SHABBAT LUNCH: Vegetarianism

This week's *parsha*, *Tzav*, deals with the Temple animal sacrifices, some of which were completely burned upon the altar and some of which were eaten by either the *kohanim* (priests) or the owner of the animal. Rav Kook writes that in the messianic age, all sacrifices will be vegetarian, brought from either flour mixtures or plants (*Olat HaRa'ayah*, p. 292).

Does this imply that, in the future, the human diet will also become vegetarian? Is there either a Jewish imperative to eat meat or an inclination toward refraining from eating meat products? On what grounds would Judaism advocate a vegetarian diet?

Originally, in the Garden of Eden, man was given permission to eat only seed-bearing herbs and fruits. In this garden paradise, which included no trace of death, man could eat only foods that carried within them the powers of creating further life.

Ten generations later, after the flood, Noah was given permission to eat animals. "Every moving thing that lives will be food for you; just like the green herb have I given you all things" (Genesis 9:3). Humanity's relationship with the animal world was drastically altered. The previous harmony was shattered. Now "the fear of you and the dread of you will be upon every beast of the earth, and upon every bird of the air, and upon all that moves upon the earth . . ." (Genesis 9:2). The primary limitation placed upon humanity now was the prohibition of eating the blood of an animal.

The third stage of human–animal relations occurred after the Jewish people's exodus from Egypt, during the forty years of their wandering in the desert. Now the Torah prescribed that every time one wanted to eat meat, the animal had to be brought to the Tabernacle at the center of the camp to be slaughtered. The proximity of the killing of the animal to the place of greatest holiness imbued the physical act of slaughtering with a sense of holiness and raised the act of eating to a spiritual plateau.

The fourth and final stage occurred when the Jewish people entered the Promised Land. Moses tells the people, "When the Lord your God will enlarge your border . . . and you will say, 'I will eat meat', because you long to eat meat; then you may eat meat to your heart's desire" (Deuteronomy 12:20). Once in the land of Israel, the Jewish people were allowed to eat meat whenever and wherever they wanted, without the stipulation of bringing the animal to the place of greater holiness.

In his work *The Vision of Vegetarianism and Peace*, Rav Kook writes of the paradoxical nature of Jewish vegetarianism. According to Rav Kook, the moral ideal is to refrain from harming all animals. He notes that the verse that gives permission to the Jewish people to eat meat in Israel also subtly infers a concealed disdain for this inclination. The emphasis upon, "and you will say, 'I will eat meat,' because *you long to eat meat* . . . . " implies that God allowed the Jewish people to eat meat only as a concession to their insatiable "heart's desire." He writes that the reason that Jewish law requires us to cover up the blood spilled of a slaughtered animal is to hide our shame over having desired to eat the animal in the first place. The day will come, he writes, when every human being will feel a natural repulsion over spilling the blood of an animal, and the world will evolve to a more sensitive and developed moral plane.

On the other hand, Rav Kook strongly cautions against the displaying of great kindness for animals at the expense of directing kindness toward other human beings. The human arena should always remain our primary focus. Only those who have developed a high degree of compassion in all of their life's engagements should seek to actualize this level of mercy toward animals.

It is told that Rav Kook ate a tiny morsel of meat on *Shabbat* to symbolize both the yearning for the vegetarianism of the Garden of Eden as well as the awareness that we have not yet achieved this status and must not delude ourselves that the world has already attained an advanced moral level. The result of living this paradox deepens the longing to advance and perfect this world.

Around the *Shabbat* Table

1. In contrast to Rav Kook, who sees meat-eating as a concession to human desire, Jewish mystical works view the ingestion of an animal as the greatest kindness one can perform, because in eating the animal, a person elevates its nature from the animal to human, and thus elevates the animal to a higher spiritual plane. What do you think?

2. According to Jewish law, an *am ha'aretz* (an ignorant, boorish person) is prohibited from eating meat (*Pesachim* 49b). Why do you think that this is so?

3   Are you or have you ever considered becoming a vegetarian? For what reasons?

Seuda Shlishit: Compassion for Animals

Though *Tzav* deals primarily with the sacrificing of animals, both the letter and spirit of the law in Judaism stress the compassion that one should always extend to all creatures. The Talmud (*Bava Metziah* 85a) records that almost two thousand years ago, the leader of the Jewish people, Rabbi Judah Ha Nasi (the head of the Sanhedrin), was punished for an uncompassionate act and then, because of his kindness, was forgiven.

> Once, a calf was being brought to slaughter. It ran away and placed its head in the corner of Rabbi Judah's robe, and cried pitifully. Rabbi Judah said to it, "Go [to your slaughter], for this is why you were created."
>
> At that time it was declared [in Heaven], "Since Rabbi Judah showed no compassion for the calf, let grief and misfortune come upon him."
>
> His suffering was removed because of a compassionate act: One day, the maidservant of Rabbi Judah was sweeping his home. She found baby weasels lying there and was about to sweep them out. Rabbi Judah

said to her, "Leave them, for it is written, 'And His [God's] compassion is for all of His creations'" (Psalms 145:9).

At that moment it was declared [in Heaven], that "since he was merciful, let us be merciful with him," and his grief and misfortune were removed.

Around the *Shabbat* Table

1. The Talmud (*Eruvin* 100b) states in the name of Rabbi Yochanon that "if the Torah had never been given, we would have learned modesty from the cats, not stealing from the ants, faithfulness from the dove, and courting rituals from the chicken and rooster." What else do you think one might learn from animals?

2. While owning and caring for pets may be a sign of compassion for animals, it may also lead to caring for animals at the expense of caring for human beings. What do you think are the pros and cons of having pets?

3. What is the greatest act of compassion toward animals that you have performed? That you have witnessed?

Shemini

FRIDAY NIGHT MEAL: An Obsession with the Holy

Tragedy strikes. The very first episode of human initiative in the book of Leviticus ends in calamity. Just like the Torah's description of the Garden of Eden, in which Adam and Eve spend preciously little time in paradise before the onset of crisis and expulsion, so too, in this week's *parsha* the joy of the Jewish people is regrettably brief. On the eighth and final day of the erection of the Tabernacle, people bring sacrifices, Moses and Aaron bless the people, a miraculous fire from heaven accepts their offerings, and the people rejoice.

In the very next verse, tragedy strikes. A heartbreaking drama ensues seconds after this moment of exultation, as Aaron's eldest sons, Nadav and Avihu, are struck down while entering the Tabernacle to burn their incense offering. "And Nadav and Avihu, the sons of Aaron, took each of them his censer, and put fire in it, and put incense on it, and offered *strange fire* before the Lord, which He had not commanded. And a fire went out from the Lord, and devoured them, and they died before the Lord" (Leviticus 10:1, 2).

One moment the Jewish people are jubilant, and the next moment there are no words to describe this dreadful loss. "... And Aaron was speechless" (Leviticus 10:3).

What happened? What possessed Nadav and Avihu to offer this "strange fire" that "God had not commanded"? Weren't they aware of both the sanctity and hazard surrounding the Holy of Holies?

Nadav and Avihu were the prospective leaders of the generation after Moses and Aaron. They alone had been singled out by name at Mount Sinai to ascend with Moses and Aaron. "And God said to Moses, 'Come up to the Lord, you and Aaron, *Nadav and Avihu*, and the seventy elders of Israel ... '" (Exodus 24:1). The Midrash explains that they had been selected to eventually replace Moses and Aaron, yet because of an apparent flaw in their leadership qualities, they would never fulfill their destiny.

What was the fatal shortcoming of Nadav and Avihu? They offered a "strange fire," which was "strange" because it had not been commanded by either God or Moses. Why would they have dared to break the rules of the Tabernacle and ostensibly enter without having been invited by either God or Moses?

According to the Midrash, Nadav and Avihu brought the "strange fire" because they were intoxicated! The future leaders of the Jewish people, the next in line to be the High Priest in the Tabernacle— drunk?! The Midrash arrives at this conclusion based upon the fact that the next section of the Torah (Leviticus 10:8–11) prohibits priests from drinking wine or strong drink while performing their service. "And the Lord said to Aaron, saying, 'Do not drink wine or strong drink, neither you nor your sons with you, when you enter the Tent of Meeting [Tabernacle], lest you die.'" The startling juxtaposition of the deaths of Nadav and Avihu with this restriction against drinking is the probable basis for the Midrash's assertion.

Nevertheless, the answer of the Midrash begs the question: Why was there concern that the priests might drink wine to excess? We do not find such prohibitions with regard to the judges, prophets, or other public figures. Why was the Torah only worried about intemperate drinking of priests in the Tabernacle or the Temple?

The rabbis understand that wine possesses a liberating quality that sometimes leads to disgraceful behavior but can also enable a person to reach spiritual heights. The Talmud established that *Kiddush*, *Havdalah*, weddings, circumcisions, and other holidays should all be accompanied by the drinking of wine. "The rabbis taught, [it is written] 'Remember the Sabbath day and make it holy.' Remember it through [the drinking of] wine" (*Pesachim* 106a). The drinking of wine temporarily frees people of their personal inhibitions and thus may enable them to come more in touch with their spiritual identity.

What might have happened to Nadav and Avihu? Inspired by the celebrations of the people and in ecstasy over the completion of the Tabernacle, the future leaders of the Jewish people may have been overtaken by their spiritual fervor. Their passion for holiness brought them to disregard the known strictures of the Tabernacle and violate the boundaries of the "Holy of Holies." Their fervent passion to become closer to God was ultimately self-destructive.

The Tabernacle, the very place that was supposed to be the source of life, brought about the death of two of the people's leaders. In the shadow of tragedy, Aaron becomes voiceless. His emptiness reverberates throughout the whole community. The lesson of the dangers of uncontrolled individual passion has been taught to the Jewish people.

Around the *Shabbat* Table

1. One of the possibilities suggested by the Talmud to explain the nature of the "Tree of Knowledge of Good and Evil" in the Garden of Eden is that it was a grapevine. Given what is known about wine, why do you think that this possibility was suggested?

2. Sometimes an impulsive act does not occur as an isolated circumstance but rather represents the actualization of certain qualities or tendencies long present in an individual. The only other information about Nadav and Avihu that the Bible discloses is that they

did not have any children. The Midrash infers from this that neither of them ever married. There is a tradition that one should not
begin the study of Kabbalah (mystical tradition) until one is married. What do you think is the rationale for this? Could there be a
connection to the fates of Nadav and Avihu?

3. Have you ever known someone whose enthusiasm for a project
    or work has caused them to lose sight of "the bigger picture"? What
    were the consequences? How did the person regain a healthier
    perspective of his or her undertaking?

SHABBAT LUNCH: *"Yuhara"*

And Nadav and Avihu, the sons of Aaron, took each of them his
censer, and put fire in it, and put incense on it, and offered strange
fire before the Lord, *which He had not commanded.* And a fire
went out from the Lord, and devoured them, and they died before
the Lord. [Leviticus 10:1, 2]

Nadav and Avihu were punished for conducting themselves beyond
the letter of the law. They were spiritually gifted though fervently
independent personalities, and they died while attempting to scale
previously unprecedented spiritual heights. The Talmud ascribes a
number of different causes for their deaths. Among them, the Talmud states that Nadav and Avihu sought to express their religious
beliefs regardless of preexisting social norms and did not confer
respect to their generation's leaders. "They instructed rulings of law
while in the presence of Moses, their teacher" (*Eruvin* 63a).

Should one's religious behavior be limited by preexisting social
norms? Does expressing oneself independently necessarily constitute a problem? Can religious conformism and social pressure become negative influences and thwart personal growth?

The Mishnah (*Berakhot,* Chapter 2) discusses a potential conflict between personal religious inclinations and the prevailing communal custom. Although it is a mitzvah to recite the *Shema* every

night, special exemption is given to a bridegroom on his wedding night, because the rabbis assume that he will be so overtaken with excitement and tension that he will not be able to recite the *Shema* with its proper level of concentration. What if, nevertheless, the groom feels that he will be able to control himself and that he will not be distracted by his nervousness, and he chooses to recite the *Shema*? Should he be allowed to recite it, or should he be forced to yield to the accepted custom of exemption?

The Mishnah concludes with Rabbi Shimon ben Gamliel's statement that "not all that choose to take the '*name*' should (be allowed to do so)." This "*name*" that not all are allowed to take is the appellation reserved for one who is commonly regarded as having extraordinary piety in all of one's behavior. Only one who is already recognized by the community as having achieved a very high spiritual level should be allowed to forgo this exemption and recite the *Shema* on one's wedding night. For anyone else, this would be considered an act of *hubris*, of exaggerated or false religious devotion.

The rabbis wanted to inhibit spiritual pretension and affectation. They wanted to deter sporadic, ostentatious exhibitions of piety and to limit immoderate flourishes of religious grandiosity. They created a legal category, referred to in Hebrew as *yuhara* (literally: making a mountain of oneself), to prohibit such displays of religiousity. The rabbis were aware that spiritual devotion could be motivated by a desire for attention, behavior intended to create the impression of honor and righteousness. Any religious behavior that is not commensurate with one's recognized conduct and position within the community is suspect of being self-serving and possibly pompous. Public forms of prayer were considered to be especially susceptible to acts of *yuhara*, and excessive bowing, standing for the entire service, or choosing to stand next to the rabbi were all considered to be haughty expressions of religiosity.

This category of *yuhara* is intended to serve as a moral check for the Jewish society, impelling each individual to build an integrated life of spirituality, harmonious with his or her community. Nadav's and Avihu's instructing while in the presence of their own teacher,

Moses, reflect their desire to use Torah to advance their personal standing within the community. Their greatest legacy is a warning against acts of *yuhara*.

Around the *Shabbat* Table

1. Why might religious observance be especially prone to exaggerated public displays of spirituality?

2. The Talmud states that a blessing only resides with one who does kind acts in private. Why do you think this is so?

3. Have you ever witnessed any incidents of *yuhara* in Jewish life?

Seuda Shlishit: Painting a Shul

This *parsha*, *Shemini*, describes the dedication of the Tabernacle, the structure erected by the Jewish people that would serve as the channel for receiving God's blessing. After Moses and Aaron came out of the Tabernacle and blessed the people, " ... the Glory of God appeared to all of the people" (Leviticus 9:23). Ever since the destruction of the Second Temple, for almost 2,000 years, Jews have tried to make synagogues places of blessing and sanctity.

The Rebbe of Ruzhin was the head of a prominent hasidic dynasty. When the time had come to repaint his shul (synagogue), a contest was held to see who would be the most worthy of receiving the honor of painting the Rebbe's shul. Hundreds of artists demonstrated their talents. Finally, four were chosen. It was decided that each artist would be given one wall to work on and two weeks to complete his task.

The first artist painted a mural of the story of Creation.

The second artist painted the giving of the Torah at Mount Sinai.

The third artist depicted the coming of the Messiah and the World to Come.

The people of the town were very excited. Never before had a shul been decorated with such vivid and inspiring pictures. They all wondered how the fourth artist could possibly match the works of his three predecessors.

The fourth artist walked into the shul and sat down, staring at the other three scenes. He sat there for one day, and then another day, for three days, a week, and then for ten days. People began to whisper, "He will never finish, he doesn't know what to do. Maybe he should not have been chosen." The artist continued to sit and gaze at the walls.

All of a sudden, the artist stood up, and in a frenzy started to work on his wall. He finished it in one day.

It was Friday night. Everyone was ready to receive of *Shabbat*. The Rebbe of Ruzhin walked into the shul. He looked around, admiring the work of all four artists. Then he turned toward his hasidim, and said, "All of the artists are wonderful, but the fourth artist is the most precious Jew in this town."

On his wall, he had created a mirror that reflected the work of the other three artists. His creativity had included the creativity of all of the others.

Around the *Shabbat* Table

1. If you were assigned to paint a mural on a synagogue wall, what would you paint?

2. Eight hundred years before the dynasty of the Rebbe of Ruzhin, Maimonides objected to murals and mosaics that might distract the worshiper during the prayer experience. What do you think is the role of aesthetics in the experience of prayer?

3. What synagogue or setting have you found to be the most conducive to your praying?

Tazria/Metzorah

FRIDAY NIGHT MEAL: Dealing with Loneliness

The two *parshiyot* (portions) of *Tazria* and *Metzorah* are often read together during the yearly cycle of Torah readings. Prior to these *parshiyot*, the structure of the Jewish camp has been established and certain guidelines have been established to ensure its stability (see "*Shemini*"). The Holy of Holies is at the center of the encampment, surrounded by three concentric rings of public domain. The precisely detailed arrangement of the camp enables the twelve tribes and the individuals therein to understand their roles in maintaining the purity and holiness of the nascent Jewish society. A model community based on personal uniqueness, mutual respect, and balanced cooperation is in the process of being achieved (see "*Vayechi*").

Yet no human society functions without crises and breakdowns. Now that the system of the community has been instituted, the *parshiyot* of *Tazria* and *Metzorah* detail a number of individual cases that threaten to dissolve the order and harmony of the Jewish people. The central personalities of these *parshiyot*, the new mother and the leper, both have to leave their families, suffer temporary exile (either outside their homes or outside of the Holy of Holies), and finally bring a sin-offering sacrifice before they are allowed to return to their homes and rightful places in the camp.

At first glance, the title figures of these two *parshiyot* could not seem more different. The first, the birthing mother epitomizes a life-giving force. After carrying life within her for nine months, she now has brought a new being into the world. In contrast, the second title figure, the leper (*metzorah*), experiences a form of living death. His skin turns deathly white, his hair falls out, his body is plagued with ghastly afflictions.

In addition, the origin of their conditions seems to be utterly dissimilar. The birthing woman, having brought a new life into this world, has not only performed a wholly natural and positive act but has helped to fulfill the first mitzvah given to humanity, namely, to "be fruitful, multiply, and replenish the earth" (Genesis 1:28). The leper (*metzorah*), however, suffers the consequence of sinful or aberrant actions. His leprosy is, in fact, a physical expression of a moral shortcoming, as the Midrash ascribes numerous causes of leprosy (*tzara'at*), ranging from idolatry to selfishness. The most common cause of leprosy mentioned in the sources and commentators is *lashon hara* (gossip or slander). The two other incidents of *tzara'at* in the Torah both occur in the contexts of improper speaking about other individuals.

Why, then, are these two seemingly disparate cases juxtaposed? What offense has the new mother committed to warrant exile? Moreover, why should the birthing mother and the leper share the similar fates of having to leave their places of abode and bring sin offerings before they are allowed to resume their previous lives?

They seem to be reflecting physical states resulting from entirely different circumstances. Yet at their source, the new mother and the leper have both experienced profoundly similar emotional states.

The Talmud (*Niddah* 31b) states that the new mother must bring a sin-offering after having given birth because in the midst of her birth pains, she swears that she will never return to her husband, so as to preclude repeating the agony of childbirth. At the most intense moment of childbirth, the mother screams a scream of utter loneliness, of emotional isolation. No one can understand her pain; no one is able to share the depths of her mood or spirit. It is her experience alone.

The *metzorah* (leper) has spoken *lashon hara*. His punishment is to dwell entirely alone, outside of the camp, until he has been cured. His punishment befits the transgression of gossiping, as the one who defamed and thus divided the community must now sense the very same loneliness. One of the primary motivations for speaking *lashon hara* is the need to bond and discover a way to relate with others. The loneliness one feels impels him or her to speak negatively about others, to search for any possible means of connection.

The new mother and the leper have both experienced moments of heartfelt loneliness. This sense of loneliness may ultimately have debilitating effects on the functioning of the Jewish community, as it potentially undermines the family relationships and social cooperation vital to a healthy society. Eventually, the mother will need to return to her husband. Eventually, the leper needs to develop productive ways to interact with other members of society. Their feelings of loneliness should not remain scarring moments, haunting them forever. The fabric of society cannot afford to be weakened by their feelings, no matter how natural or justified they may be. To be enabled to confront and move beyond these experiences, both of these personalities must temporarily leave their homes and undergo periods of actual separation, of loneliness.

Tragically, one rarely truly appreciates something until it has been lost. The temporary "losing" of their former place amid the Jewish camp hopefully instills in the new mother and leper a greater desire to return and become productive members of their society. Their recent traumas of loneliness should ultimately serve to bond them with those whom they have left.

Around the *Shabbat* Table

1. Another explanation for the new mother's bringing of a sin-offering is that the sin-offering is a response to a form of "spiritual postpartum depression." The exhilaration of carrying life and bringing a new being into this world may be followed by a severe emotional letdown, an anticlimactic return to reality. Do you think that moments of depression or gloom naturally follow emotional peaks?

2. The Talmud (*Moed Katan* 5a) states that when people would come near to the leper, he was supposed to call out, "Impure, impure," thus imploring them to pray for him. How else do you think that this would influence his healing?

3. How do society or families today enable individuals to overcome their experiences of loneliness? What mechanism(s) would you suggest to help facilitate this? Have you ever found loneliness to be beneficial?

SHABBAT LUNCH: Seeing One's Moral Self

The Torah's obsession with the *metzorah* (leper) is difficult to understand. Over 100 verses describe the physical symptoms of the *metzorah,* ranging from the swelling and discoloring of the skin, to spots, sores, and baldness. There seems to be an inordinate detailing of the sickness and healing of the *metzorah.*

The commentators are quick to clarify that the *tzara'at* (leprosy) of the Torah should not be confused with the medical disease of leprosy, more likely known in the Torah as *shcheen.* The *metzorah* was not examined by a doctor but by the *kohen* (priest). The Talmud posits that no one was declared a *metzorah* on *Shabbat,* holidays, or during wedding celebrations, the times of greatest social gatherings, since *tzara'at* was not contagious.

What did this person do that he became afflicted with *tzara'at*? The Talmud states that the cause of *tzara'at* was the speaking of *lashon hara* (gossip). The rabbis of the Talmud ask, "Why is the *metzorah* different [from all other transgressors] that he must dwell utterly alone, outside of the inhabited camps? ... Because he caused a division (estrangement) between husband and wife, and between friends [through his gossiping]; therefore, the Torah demanded that he now must remain alone. The Talmud continues, "Rabbi Yehuda ben Levi said, 'Why is the *metzorah* different that he must sacrifice two birds upon becoming pure? ... 'The Torah demands of one who has performed an act of "chirping" (*lashon hara*), that he must bring a "chirping" sacrifice'" (*Erchin* 16b).

Why did the *metzorah* become so ugly? Why is it necessary that we are informed of the gruesome details of the *metzorah's* plague?

The ugliness of the *metzorah* is not a punishment, rather, a reflection of his true self. The physical symptoms of *tzara'at* serve as a mirror of the person's moral repulsiveness. The *metzorah* is forced to stare at the dissolution of his physical self with the understanding that it signifies his moral dissolution. The detailed picture drawn by the Torah of the *metzorah* emphasizes the agony that he must endure, knowing that his entire community witnesses the outcome of his moral failings. Amid physical and emotional pain, the *metzorah* himself is visited by the ugliness of his actions. Ultimately, the goal is not to punish the *metzorah*, but to have him repent.

Apparently, in the time of the Temple, the most effective way to convey this message was to actually see the consequences of one who spoke *lashon hara*. Today, hopefully, this lesson is learned through reading of the frightful fate of the *metzorah*, who was guilty of not guarding his tongue.

Around the *Shabbat* Table

1. Why do you think that *lashon hara* was deemed such a serious crime by the rabbis?

2. Do you think that one's physical appearance is affected by one's moral behavior? Did you ever physically feel beautiful (or ugly) because of something that you did?

3. If you could see your moral self, what would be your most beautiful quality? Your most ugly quality? If you could see the moral appearance of others, who would be the most beautiful person whom you know? Why?

Seuda Shlishit: Acher's Brit Mila

In the book of Genesis, Abraham was 99 years old when he had his *brit mila* (circumcision), and his first son, Yishmael, was circumcised at 13. In this week's *parsha*, the Jewish people are told to circumcise their sons on the eighth day after birth. The *brit mila* represents the first public act between the parent and the child.

The Jerusalem Talmud (*Hagigah* 7b) records the ill-fated *brit* and rite of passage of Elisha ben Abouyah.

Elisha ben Abouyah is almost never referred to by his name in the Talmud. He is simply known as *Acher*, the "Other." A student of Rabbi Akiva, he forsook the Jewish way of life and became the foremost apostate of the Talmud. The Jerusalem Talmud attributes the source of his apostasy to a declaration made by his father at his *brit mila*.

Elisha's father, Abouyah, was one of the most notable personages in Jerusalem. On the day of his son's *brit*, Abouyah invited all of the important figures in Jerusalem and seated them in one room. In a second room, he seated Rabbi Eliezer and Rabbi Yehoshua. The guests began to eat and drink, to sing and dance. Rabbi Eliezer said to Rabbi Yehoshua, "While they are engaging in their world, let us engage in ours."

The two rabbis began to learn and discuss matters of Torah. After discussing the Five Books of Moses, they discussed the Prophets, and then the rest of the Holy Writings. Fire descended from the heavens and encircled them. Abouyah said to them, "Rabbis, what are you doing?! Have you come here to burn my house down?" They replied to him, "Certainly not. We were sitting and reviewing words of Torah, and then the Prophets, and then the holy Writings. And the words were as blazing as when they were given at Mount Sinai, and, just as at Mount Sinai, the letters were surrounded by fire. As it is written, 'and the Mountain blazed with fire up to the heavens.'"

Abouyah said to them, "Rabbis, if this is the power of Torah, then for the whole life of my son, I will dedicate him to Torah."

Since Abouyah's intention was not pure, the Torah learning of his son did not last.

Around the *Shabbat* Table

1. What was wrong with Abouyah's response? What do you think would have been the proper response to the rabbis' learning of Torah and the descending of fire?

2. Can you offer several reasons why his father's declaration might have led Elisha ben Abouyah to eventually go astray?

3. Why do you think that the Talmud considered it especially important that the motivation for learning Torah be "pure?"

Acharei Mot

FRIDAY NIGHT MEAL: Returning to Life

The opening verse of *Acharei Mot*,"And the Lord spoke to Moses after the death of the two sons of Aaron, when they approached before the Lord, and died" (Leviticus 16:1), seems superfluous and unrelated to the rest of this week's *parsha*.The deaths of Nadav and Avihu have already been described in *Shemini* (see *"Shemini*: An Obsession with the Holy"). We already know what happened to them. Furthermore, the continuation of this week's *parsha* is, on the surface, unconnected to their fate. Nevertheless, the death of Nadav and Avihu serves as an introduction to this *parsha*, becomes the title of the *parsha* (*Acharei Mot*:"After the Deaths"), and somehow sets the theme that will affect everything that comes thereafter.

Why does this week's *parsha* begin with this seemingly uncon- nected statement about the deaths of Nadav and Avihu? How is their fate relevant to this week's *parsha*?

Acharei Mot is composed of three chapters, each with a distinct theme:

1. the service of the High Priest on Yom Kippur (Chapter 16)

2. the regulations of eating meat and personal sacrifices (Chapter 17)

3. the defining of the sexual mores of the Jewish people (Chapter 18)

Each of these topics has been dealt with briefly in previous sections of the Torah. *Tetzaveh* outlines the clothing and sacrificial duties of the priests; *Shemini* enumerates forbidden foods, and *Tazria* specifies the laws regulating the new mother. In this week's *parsha*, however, these three subjects are linked together for the first time.

The majority of the laws of the first of these topics, Yom Kippur, concerns the service of the High Priest. Yet one enigmatic command is also directed to the Jewish people: "You shall afflict your souls" (Leviticus 16:29). The Torah repeats this command a number of times, never explicitly defining what this "afflicting of souls" entails.

The Mishnah (*Yoma* 8:1) clarifies the nature of these afflictions: "On Yom Kippur it is forbidden to eat, drink, wash, anoint oneself, wear [leather] shoes, and have sexual relations." These six restrictions are arranged in three pairs, depicting three categories of life. Eating and drinking are necessary for an individual's *physical* survival. Washing and anointing are requisite for the *social* domain of human interaction. Though perhaps less obvious, the prohibitions against wearing of shoes and sexual relations can be seen as referring to the *spiritual* realm—at his encounter with the burning bush, Moses is ordered, "Do not come near: take your shoes off your feet, for the place upon which you are standing is holy" (Exodus 3:5). Because of its potential to bring a new soul into this world, the Mishnah understands that sexual relations possess the sanctity of the Holy of Holies.

Though Yom Kippur is often understood primarily to be a day of fasting, these additional prohibitions reflect a more powerful and inclusive message: Yom Kippur is a day dedicated to the total cessation of human activity and creation, on which the physical, social, and spiritual drives are denied. Affliction is thus the suspension of all growth. The day of affliction, the holiest day of the year, is essentially a day of death.

The next two chapters of *Acharei Mot* return us to the most powerful physical drives propelling humanity: eating and sexual relations. Immediately after scaling the spiritual heights of Yom Kippur, the day of transcending human needs, the Torah returns to the reality of human existence. The step away from life must serve, ultimately, as a catalyst and invitation to return to the passions of life, now attuned with greater moral and spiritual refinement.

Returning to the original question: Why did *Acharei Mot* begin with a flashback to the fate of Nadav and Avihu? The entire *parsha* is read in the shadow of their deaths. Nadav's and Avihu's spiritual passion eclipsed their physical worlds. The lesson of Yom Kippur can only be properly understood "after the death of the two sons of Aaron, when they came near before the Lord, and died" (Leviticus16:1). The experience of Yom Kippur is not an end, in and of itself, rather the vehicle through which the Jewish people are able to better sanctify their very human, physical realities.

Only after reminding us of the deaths of Nadav and Avihu can the afflictions of Yom Kippur occasion a day of death that enhances and empowers life.

Around the *Shabbat* Table

1. The rabbis of the Talmud expanded on the Day of Atonement of the Torah and transformed it into a day of utter cessation of creation, simulating one's death. Why do you think they decided that this was its most appropriate form of expression?

2. Maimonides divided his encyclopedic work of Jewish law, the *Mishneh Torah*, into fourteen books. In the book entitled *Kedusha* (Holiness), he included only the laws of eating and sexual relations. Why do you think that he did this?

3. Do you think that more fully developing one's spiritual qualities necessarily diminishes one's physical life? Have you ever seen examples of this?

SHABBAT LUNCH: Modes of Change

And this will be an eternal statute for you, that in the seventh month, on the tenth day of the month, you will afflict your souls, and do no work.... [Leviticus 16:29]

This week's *parsha*, *Acharei Mot*, details the procedure of Yom Kippur, the Day of Atonement. The ultimate goal of this day is to serve as a catalyzing force for change.

Why should an individual change? Does this presuppose that there is something wrong with him or her? Furthermore, how does this change, or the awareness for the need to change, transpire?

The Torah presumes that every individual possesses both free will and an infinite potential for development. Not only does every individual have the capacity for change, but change is intrinsic and essential to his or her very being. Rav Kook understood that the human being was part of the evolutionary process (not to be confused with Natural Selection, which includes humanity's development from the monkeys) of the world, and that periods of stagnation deny the natural growing process of life. He wrote that "the doctrine of evolution that is presently gaining acceptance in the world has a greater affinity with the secret teachings of the Kabbalah [Jewish mysticism] than all other philosophies. Why shall we not compare the events of general existence to the events in the life of an individual person or any other creature?" Change does not need to happen because of some shortcoming in the individual. The world is in a continuous stage of evolution, and therefore, in order to be in harmony with the world, the individual must also continually develop and grow.

There are a multitude of forces, ranging from physical to emotional to spiritual, which may encourage a person to make a change in his or her life. Regardless of the actual change at hand, Rav Kook writes that change most likely occurs in one of two forms, sudden or gradual.

1. Sudden change comes about as a result of a certain *spiritual lightning bolt* that enters the soul. At once the person senses . . . that he has become a new being; already he experiences inside himself a complete transformation for the better. This form of change dawns on a person through some inner spiritual force whose sources are entirely mysterious.

2. There is also a gradual form of change. No sudden flash of illumination dawns upon the person to make him change for the good, but he feels that he must mend his way of life, his will, his pattern of thought. By heeding this impulse he gradually conditions himself to becoming a good person, reaching higher levels of purity and perfection. [*Lights of Repentance*, Chapter 2]

The first process of change, sudden change, is intuitive and inexplicable. It is the result of a sudden awareness, an epiphany or realization, that the person cannot quite fathom yet understands is personally true. This insight is given neither to articulation nor to reasonable explanation, yet it resonates convincingly within the individual. The second process of change, gradual change, lends itself to rational formulation and evaluation. Incrementally, the person examines his or her life and judiciously determines whether his or her path is progressing in a beneficial direction, at a healthy pace.

Rav Kook's two processes of change have their origins in the two sources of life within the individual: the heart and mind. Both the heart and the mind continually push for growth and greater life. These two sources express themselves in the drives for sudden (*heartfelt*) and gradual (*rational*) change. A life of growth results from listening to and synthesizing both of these voices.

Around the *Shabbat* Table

1. Rav Kook wrote that a deep understanding of the process of evolution should bring about a perpetually optimistic outlook on life.
   Why?

2. In the excerpt previously quoted, Rav Kook writes of a "spiritual
   lightning bolt." Elsewhere, he writes that "each time that the heart
   feels a truly spiritual stirring, each time that a new and noble
   thought is born, we are as though listening to the voice of an angel of God who is knocking, pressing on the doors of our soul,
   asking that we open our door to him." Have you ever experienced
   this kind of heartfelt inspiration?

3. Rav Kook describes two different kinds of change: sudden and
   gradual. With which of these two processes do you most identify?
   Do you know someone who typifies the other process?

Seuda Shlishit: On the Verge of Conversion

This week's portion, *Acharei Mot*, details the Temple service performed by the High Priest on Yom Kippur. In the time of the Temple
in Jerusalem, the practices of Yom Kippur included the special service of the High Priest, the sacrificing of animals, and the sending
out of the scapegoat. Though none of these practices have been
observed since the destruction of the Temple in the year 70, the
power and spiritual intensity of Yom Kippur has continued to change
the lives of countless Jews nonetheless.

When Franz Rosenzweig (1886–1929) was 27 years old, he made
the necessary preparations to convert to Christianity. Rosenzweig
had been raised in a minimally Jewish home, and a number of his
friends and relatives had already left Judaism. On July 7, 1913, he
himself finally made the decision to convert. Rosenzweig, destined
to become one of the leading Jewish theologians of Western Europe,

resolved not to enter Christianity without any religious identity but rather to come to it as a Jew. He would fulfill this intention by attending Yom Kippur services in Berlin later that year.

Rosenzweig never completed his plan of action; he never converted to Christianity. Instead, his life was forever changed by his experience during the Yom Kippur services that he attended in Berlin. Several days later, he wrote to his mother, "I seem to have found the way back, about which I had tortured myself in vain and pondered for almost three months." Many years later he would write, "Anyone who has ever celebrated the Day of Atonement knows that it is something more than a mere personal exaltation, or the symbolic recognition of a reality such as the Jewish people; it is a testimony to the reality of God which cannot be controverted."

In 1921, Franz Rosenzweig completed his magnum opus, *The Star of Redemption*. Writing on postcards from his bunker during World War I, Rosenzweig blended the concepts of Humanity, the Universe, and God, with the themes of Creation, Revelation, and Redemption, and formed them into a single coherent Jewish philosophy. After World War I, together with Martin Buber, Erich Fromm, Gershom Scholem, and other notable German intellectuals, Rosenzweig helped to found the "Free Jewish House of Learning," which was a paradigm and center of Jewish learning for its duration.

In *The Star of Redemption*, Rosenzweig wrote that on Yom Kippur, "man is utterly alone ... everything lies behind him ... he confronts the eyes of his judge in utter loneliness, as if he were dead in the midst of life."

For Franz Rosenzweig, on his momentous Yom Kippur of 1913, everything did indeed "lie behind him." From that moment on, his new life commenced.

Around the *Shabbat* Table

1. Prior to his Yom Kippur experience, Franz Rosenzweig wrote that one of the shortcomings of Judaism (or of Jews) was its lack of passionate faith. Would you agree?

2. Rosenzweig wrote that "Everything earthly lies so far behind the transporting into eternity during this [Yom Kippur] confession, that it is difficult to imagine that a way can lead back from here into the cycle of the year." Did you ever experience anxiety or find it difficult to return to life after Yom Kippur?

3. Did you ever have a life-changing moment on Yom Kippur? Do you know anyone who did?

Kedoshim

FRIDAY NIGHT MEAL: Spiritual Masters

As has already been noted, the *parshiyot* (portions) of the Torah often come in twosomes. In such instances, the first *parsha* establishes the basic ideas, while the second develops and deepens the themes presented in the first. The previous *parsha*, *Acharei Mot*, set the essential minimal boundaries for acceptable social behavior. Now, *Kedoshim* will attempt to advance this standard to higher and more profound levels.

"And the Lord spoke to Moses saying, 'Speak to all the congregation of the children of Israel and say to them, 'You shall be holy, for I, the Lord your God, am holy'" (Leviticus 19:1, 2). At Mount Sinai, God promised the Jewish people that they would become a "holy nation" (Exodus 19:6). Now each person is individually commanded to fulfill this calling. They are not summoned to become "good," or "honorable," or "especially worthy." They are required to become "holy."

Only recently the Jewish people had been slaves in Egypt. What were they supposed to think when they were now told to become "holy"?! At this moment in history, what did "becoming holy" mean to the Jewish people?

Rashi understands this directive as referring to the minimal standards governing eating and sexual behavior introduced at the end of last week's *parsha*. He writes that by virtue of adhering to these strictures one necessarily becomes "holy." The call to become holy does not carry with it new patterns of actions; rather, it describes the state attained through the fulfillment of the laws previously conferred.

Commenting on Rashi's explanation, the Ramban understands that becoming "holy" extends beyond the eating and sexual regulations mentioned in *Acharei Mot*. Ramban writes that a person can satisfy all of the particulars of these laws (by not eating prohibited foods and not engaging in sexual relations proscribed by the Torah) and still demonstrate loathsome behavior through *excessively indulging* in his or her physical drives. The challenge of "becoming holy" is reflected in the exertion of self-control precisely within the guidelines set by Torah law. One should not eat immoderately or yield unrestrainedly to one's sexual drive. This type of conduct reflects being an "abomination within the domain of Torah law."

For the Ramban, the call to become "holy" is the Torah's setting of a standard that goes beyond the "letter of the law." Where laws no longer reign, where the authority of society is unable to demand compliance, there individuals are exhorted to master themselves and to become "holy."

According to this understanding of the Ramban, could one ever actually become "holy?" Can one ever totally master the proper involvement and direction of one's physical drives?

Other religions and cultures have understood the concept of "holiness" to involve some form of detachment from this-worldly behavior. "Holy" people lead ascetic lives entailing the denial of physical commitment and pleasure. In such clearly defined circumstances, holiness becomes attainable—one becomes holy through relinquishing certain patterns of behavior. Obliterating certain drives may, in fact, be easier than trying to sustain and direct them.

According to the Ramban, the challenge of living a holy life involves continually aspiring to neither deny nor become controlled by one's physical drives. The question is not: "Is this act allowed or prohibited?" but rather, "Although permitted, am I at this moment expressing the fact that I have been created in the image of God?"

In last week's *parsha*, the "letter of the law" prohibitions concerning eating and sexual behavior were established. The separation of these two *parshiyot* reflects the assumption that the human being develops in stages. In *Acharei Mot*, one is commanded to discriminate between permitted and proscribed behavior. Then, in *Kedoshim*, one is charged to perpetually elevate the realm of behaviors that are technically allowable.

The question of last week's *parsha* was: "Is it allowed or not?" Now the question is: "Is it holy?"

Around the *Shabbat* Table

1. According to the Ramban, how a person spends his or her spare time would be a strong indicator of his or her true character. Why? Do you agree?

2. According to one of Rav Kook's foremost students, Rav Harlap, there is a subconscious voice in each individual trying to convince him or her not to improve, not to try and become more "holy." Do you agree? Have you ever felt this?

3   Is there anyone whom you would call *kadosh* (holy)? Why?

SHABBAT LUNCH: Commanding Love

" . . . And you will love your neighbor as yourself . . . " (Leviticus 19:18). Two thousand years ago, Rabbi Akiva said that this maxim was the guiding rule of the entire Torah. This commandment has been quoted by an untold number of religions and cultures. Yet there remains a very disturbing and enigmatic dimension to this commandment: How can the Torah presume to command an emotion?

Aren't emotions, by their very nature, beyond the dictums of one's control? How can the Torah tell me to love someone whom I do not love? For those whom one already loves, there is no need for a commandment; rather, it is precisely to those whom one does not naturally like or love that this commandment refers—how can the Torah assume that a human being will be able to love everyone?

Over 100 years ago, Samson Raphael Hirsch, one of the leading rabbis of Western Europe, offered this commentary:

> The loving of our neighbor as we love ourselves is practically impossible to carry out ... (rather) we are to rejoice in his good fortune and grieve over his misfortune as if it were our own. We are to assist at everything that furthers his well-being and happiness as if we were working for ourselves, and must keep trouble away from him as assiduously as if it threatened ourselves. This is something which does lie within our possibilities and is something which is required of us—even toward somebody whose personality may actually be highly antipathetic to us ... Nobody may look upon the progress of another as a hindrance to his own progress, or look on the downfall of another as the means for his own rising, and nobody may rejoice in his own progress if it is at the expense of his neighbor.

Hirsch understood that this verse was not directing a person to bond emotionally with other people but rather to act as if he loves the person and to outwardly care for all other beings—something that does lie within an individual's control.

In his discussion of the commandment "And you will love the Lord your God," Maimonides equates a person's love with his or her level of knowledge of the other. "According to the level of knowledge will be the level of one's love, if a little—then a little, if a lot—then a lot" (Laws of Repentance 10:6). The demand to love is instructing one to learn more about each person. If one finds the actions of another to be loathsome, then one must strive to understand the possible origins and reasons for such behavior. This deeper knowledge and perception of the other will engender greater empathy and positive feelings.

The hasidic masters, epitomized by the S'fat Emmet, also grappled with the problem of commanding one's emotions. They offer a third and uniquely hasidic resolution:

> The philosophers challenge this idea and say: "How is it possible to command love? Isn't love an abstract idea which is dependent on the nature of the person; can a person love simply by virtue of being thus commanded?"
>
> However, the answer is inherent in this question. Because the verse commands us to love, we must conclude that it is potentially possible for each individual to love, if only he does what is necessary to arouse this love.

According to this approach, one's love for another is primarily a function of one's own ability to love. Each person must develop and expand his or her own capacity to love. If they fully develop their loving potential, then people will be able to love all beings.

Countless interpretations have been offered to resolve the question of the commanding of love. Hirsch focuses on one's external behavior; Maimonides equates love with knowledge of the other; and the S'fat Emmet believes that loving another begins with one's own ability to love. These three thinkers represent three prototypes of this guiding rule of Torah, "Love your neighbor as yourself."

Around the *Shabbat* Table

1. In context, the commandment of "love your neighbor" reads as follows: "Do not take revenge and do not hold a grudge against the children of your people, love your neighbor as yourself, I am the Lord." How are the other parts of this verse connected to loving one's neighbor?

2. Why do you think that the commandment is not to "love your neighbor," rather that one should "love your neighbor *as yourself*"? What understanding of human nature do these two additional words add?

3. With which of these three previously mentioned approaches do you most identify? Do you know anyone who typifies a different approach of love? How do you resolve the problematic nature of commanding an emotion?

Seuda Shlishit: Silent Acquiescence to Sin

It is very difficult to criticize one's friends or peers. Nevertheless, this is the command presented in this week's *parsha*: "Do not hate your brother in your heart, *you must certainly reprove your peer*, and do not bear sin on his account" (Leviticus 19:17). (See "*Vayigash*: Giving/Taking Advice.") The Talmud (*Shabbat* 54b) states that "anyone who could possibly have prevented someone from transgressing and does not prevent it, will eventually receive the punishment for that sin." One's lack of protest or rebuke upon seeing an immoral act is tantamount to the approving of that act. The Talmud (*Gittin* 55b, 56a) relates a tragic example of this type of silent acquiescence:

> The destruction of Jerusalem came through Kamtza and Bar Kamtza. A certain man had a friend named Kamtza and an enemy named Bar Kamtza. He once made a party and said to his servant, "Go and bring Kamtza." The man went and brought Bar Kamtza [by mistake].
> When the man [who gave the party] found him there he said, "Aren't you my enemy! What are you doing here? Get up and leave!"
> Said the other, "Since I am here, let me stay, and I will pay you for whatever I eat and drink."
> He said, "No."
> "Then let me give you half the cost of the party."
> "No," said the other.
> "Then let me pay for the whole party."

He still said, "No." He took him by the hand and put him out.

Said Bar Kamtza, *"Since the rabbis were sitting there and did not stop him, this shows that they agreed with him.* I will go and inform against them to the Government."

He went and said to the Emperor, "The Jews are rebelling against you." He said, "How can I tell?' He said to him, "Send them an offering and see whether they will sacrifice it [on the altar]." So he sent with him a fine calf. While on the way, he [Bar Kamtza] maimed its upper lip, or some say on the white of its eye, in a place where we [Jews] consider it to be unfit for sacrificing but the non-Jews do not.

The Talmud concludes that because the Jews would not offer the sacrifice, the Emperor thought that they were rebelling. Consequently, the Temple was destroyed, its sanctuary was burnt, and the Jewish people were exiled from their land.

Around the *Shabbat* Table

1. Why do you think that the rabbis did not intervene on Bar Kamtza's behalf at the party? Why do you think that the Talmud ascribed the destruction of Jerusalem to the failure of the rabbis present at the party to reprove the host?

2. Do you think the host could have done anything to restore the damaged honor of Bar Kamtza? What?

3. Do you know of any examples of religious or political leaders who have publicly reproved others even though it endangered their popularity?

Emor

FRIDAY NIGHT MEAL: Cycles in Time

These are the special days of the Lord, holy gatherings, which you
should proclaim them at their special times. [Leviticus 23: 4]

*E**mor** introduces a list of the major holidays of the Jewish calendar. While in the previous *parsha*, *Kedoshim*, the Jewish people
had been instructed to become a holy people, now they are charged
to recognize and observe holiness in time. Prior to this week's
parsha, the Jewish people had been told to observe *Shabbat*, Rosh
Chodesh (the new moon), and Passover. But now for the first time,
they are told to observe all of the major festivals: Passover, Shavuot,
Rosh Hashana, Yom Kippur, Sukkot, and the eighth day of Sukkot
(which was considered to be an independent holiday).

Although this week's *parsha* lists the full roster of biblical Jewish holidays, later in the Torah, in the book of Deuteronomy, the list
of holidays include only Passover, Shavuot, and Sukkot, with no
mention of *Shabbat*, Rosh Hashana, or Yom Kippur. The three holidays of Passover, Shavuot, and Sukkot thus seem to comprise a distinct unit and cycle of time.

What distinguishes Passover, Shavuot, and Sukkot from the other special days of the Jewish calendar?

Passover, Shavuot, and Sukkot are unique in that they each reflect historical, agricultural, and national realities.

Historically, these three holidays each reflect a significant event in the development of the Jewish people: Passover celebrates the Jewish people's exodus from Egypt, Shavuot traditionally commemorates the giving of Torah at Mount Sinai, and Sukkot recalls God's care for the Jewish people during their wandering in the desert.

Agriculturally, Passover is celebrated during the time of planting in the spring. The Torah refers to its time of celebration as the month of *Aviv* (Deuteronomy 16:1), the springtime. Shavuot is called "the holiday of the first-fruits (*bikkurim*)" (Numbers 28:26), as it is celebrated at the time of the first harvest. Sukkot is celebrated at the time of the major harvest, as the Torah says, "You shall observe the feast of booths seven days, in your gathering of your grain and wine" (Deuteronomy 16:13).

On a national level, in Deuteronomy, all three of these holidays are described as pilgrimage holidays, being fully observed only in Jerusalem: "Three times a year shall all the males appear before the Lord your God in the place which He shall choose; in the holiday of the unleavened bread [Passover], in the holiday of weeks [Shavuot], and in the holiday of booths [Sukkot]" (Deuteronomy 16:16).

Furthermore, the progression between these three holidays reflects a paradigm of growth in the relationship between the Jewish people and God. Passover, the first of these holidays, commemorates the birth of the Jewish people and the beginning of their relationship with God. The Passover seder accordingly focuses on children, as we see from the four questions, the four types of sons, and so forth. The seven-week period between Passover and Shavuot represents the springtime of the relationship between God and the Jewish people, that is, the period of youth. Shavuot represents God's betrothal of the Jewish people, with the giving of the Ten Commandments symbolizing an engagement ring. Finally, this relationship between God and the Jewish people reaches adulthood during the holiday of Sukkot. The *sukka* (booth) symbolizes a *chuppa* (wedding canopy), as the relationship between God and the Jewish people is consummated.

Within this national cycle of time is woven another cycle, from Rosh Hashana until Yom Kippur, which reflects a process of individual of growth and change. One opinion in the Talmud understands Rosh Hashana as commemorating the sixth day of Creation, the day on which Adam and Eve were created. Thus, on Rosh Hashana we remember the moment of creation of the human being and not a specifically Jewish historical event. The ten days from Rosh Hashana until Yom Kippur are referred to as the "ten days of repentance," signifying a process of personal, individual introspection and growth.

The ten days of repentance between Rosh Hashana and Yom Kippur interrupt the national cycle of events from Passover through Sukkot. When taken altogether, the interweaving of these two cycles forms an annual drama of personal and national growth. At Passover and Shavuot the Jewish people's relationship with God is created and developed. Yet before there can be ultimate national bonding (the wedding of Sukkot), each Jew has to focus and amend his or her individual life. Only then, as individuals and as a nation, are we ready to culminate this relationship at Sukkot. Thus, it comes as no surprise that, although there is an obligation to rejoice on all of the holidays, only on Sukkot, the culminating holiday of these two cycles, does the Torah state that we should be completely happy, "*v'hayeetem ach sameach*" (Deuteronomy 16:15).

Around the *Shabbat* Table

1. Do you relate more to the national or individual aspects of the Jewish holidays?

2. During the rabbinic period, Hanukah and Purim were added to the Jewish calendar. In the last fifty years, a number of new holidays have entered the Jewish calendar: Israel Independence Day,

Jerusalem Day, Holocaust Remembrance Day. Have you found ways to make these days meaningful?

3.   Which holiday of the calendar is the most significant for you? Which custom of that holiday do you appreciate most? Why?

SHABBAT LUNCH: The One Not Chosen

This week's *parsha* deals primarily with two subjects: the special status of the *kohanim* (priests) and the holidays of the Jewish calendar. Both the priests and the special days are referred to as being holy, *kadosh*. In addition, the Torah relates that priests who have suffered certain bodily injuries may not enter the most holy *kadosh* places of the Tabernacle. Thus, found in this *parsha*, are distinct levels of holiness in person, place, and time.

The selection of the *kohanim* enabled a percentage of the Jewish people to focus exclusively on sacred matters, without the pressures of earning a livelihood and owning land. A reciprocal relationship existed between the *kohanim* and the Jewish people: in return for the community providing their physical sustenance, the *kohanim* provided spiritual guidance and direction for the nation.

The choosing process, however, is always fraught with dangers and complications. By definition during the selection process, someone has not been chosen; someone has been left out. How will this person feel about not having been chosen?

Throughout the Torah, the choosing of a person has almost always resulted in feelings of animosity toward the person who was chosen. In the book of Genesis, God chose Abel's offering and rejected that of his brother Cain, resulting in Cain's becoming distraught and killing his brother. When Jacob chose Rachel over her sister Leah, the result was " . . . and the Lord saw that Leah was hated . . . . " (Genesis 29:31). Though the Torah never states that Jacob hated Leah, Jacob's choosing of Rachel engendered feelings of being hated within Leah. Similarly, the strife between Joseph and his brothers resulted from Jacob's choosing of Joseph. "And when his brothers saw that their father loved him more than all of his brothers, they hated him . . . " (Genesis 37:4).

The problematics involved in choosing can be found not only within families, but also among nations. The rabbis understood that God's choosing of the Jewish people aroused the animosity of the other nations. The Talmud (*Shabbat* 89a) derives this from a subtle play on the words *Sinai* and *sin'ah* (hatred): "Why was it called 'Mount Sinai?' Because it was at that mountain, when the Jewish people were chosen, that the hatred (*sin'ah*) of the other nations for the Jews came into the world."

The blessing given to Abraham was that "in you all the families of the world shall be blessed" (Genesis 12:3). Ultimately, the hope of the Jewish people is to convey to the nations of the world that their being chosen was not a rejection of the other nations but was intended to bring benefit and blessing to them.

Around the *Shabbat* Table

1. Perhaps partly to avoid arousing feelings of animosity, the *kohanim* were known for their love of the Jewish people. Before giving their benediction to the people, they would say a blessing stating that they should "bless the people in love." Can you think of any examples from the Torah (or from life), in which someone was separated out and did not incur hatred? How was this accomplished?

2. Why do you think that not being chosen provokes antagonism? Why do you think that this hostility is directed toward the one chosen, rather than the one who chooses?

3. Have you ever resented someone else for being chosen?

Seuda Shlishit: Moshe the Cobbler

This week's *parsha*, *Emor*, describes the major holidays of the Jewish calendar, Passover, Shavuot, Rosh Hashanah, Yom Kippur, and Sukkot. The discussion of these holidays is preceded by a reminder to observe *Shabbat*, the weekly holiday on the Jewish calendar: "Six days will work be done; but the seventh day is the sabbath of solemn rest, a holy gathering; you will do no work; it is a sabbath to the Lord in all your dwellings" (Leviticus 23:3).

A story is told of Moshe the cobbler and his efforts to refrain from work on *Shabbat*.

There was once a poor cobbler named Moshe. Moshe felt he had nothing of value in his life. He had never really accomplished anything: his shoes never came out right, there was never enough food in his house, he would never be a scholar. It seemed that anything that Moshe touched was doomed to fail. Everyone knew that poor Moshe was one of those people who would never succeed, and, in his heart of hearts, Moshe knew this more than anyone else.

One Friday night, after singing *Kiddush* off-key, and then having the most modest of meals, Moshe and his wife went to sleep.

Suddenly, in the middle of the night, Moshe's wife was woken up by the joyous singing and dancing of her husband. "Moshe," she screamed, "What's gotten into you?"

"I just had a dream," he replied. "A most wonderful dream. I dreamt that a messenger from the king had knocked on my door and told me that I had just been appointed to be the head of the king's army, that I would wear silken robes with medals, ride in a golden chariot, and that everyone would have to honor me, just as they honor the king himself. I asked the messenger, 'Is there anything that I have to do?' and he replied, 'Only to check the troops.'

"I asked him, 'How often do I have to review the troops?' and he told me for just fifteen minutes every day. 'Every day?' I asked. 'Yes,' he replied.

"Even on *Shabbat*?' 'Yes,' he replied. 'Every day for fifteen minutes.' Then I told him that I was deeply honored, but that I would have to refuse. How could I work even for one minute on *Shabbat*?"

At this point, Moshe's wife could no longer control herself. "Moshe, why are you singing and dancing?!! Even in your dream you didn't succeed; you didn't take the job!"

Moshe turned to her and smiled, perhaps the first real smile of his life. "Don't you see, my dear, I'm singing and dancing because now I realize that I really do have something of value in my life. Something that is even more precious than all of the honor in the king's kingdom."

Around the *Shabbat* Table

1. What do you think gave Moshe the strength to resist the king's offer?

2. How do you think that refraining from working on *Shabbat* affects one's life during the other six days of the week?

3. Do you know anyone like Moshe the Cobbler, someone who has not achieved external success but who has found "something that is even more precious than all of the honor in the king's kingdom?" What did they find? What would it be for you?

Behar/Bechukkotai

FRIDAY NIGHT MEAL: A Closing of Hope

The two *parshiyot* (portions), *Behar/Bechukkotai*, are often read together as one unit. Together they close the book of Leviticus, which began with the voice of God calling to Moses out of the Tabernacle in the heart of the camp.

How would we have expected this book to end?

The *parsha Behar* enumerates the laws of the Sabbatical (seventh) year and the Jubilee (fiftieth) year, and stipulates the caring for the poverty-stricken.

> *"When you come into the land which I give you, then the land will keep a Shabbat to the Lord.* Six years you will sow your field, and six years you will prune your vineyard and gather in its fruit; but in the seventh year the land will have a *Shabbat Shabbaton,* a *Shabbat* for the Lord, you will not sow your field or prune your vineyard ... And you will count for yourself seven *Shabbatot* of years, seven years seven times, and you will have the space of seven *Shabbatot* of years, forty-nine years ... *And if your brother grows poor, and his well-being fails while with you, then you will strengthen him."* [Leviticus 25]

Contrary to what might have been expected at the end of Leviticus, there is no mention of sacrifices, no reference to the Tabernacle or the priests; rather, the uniquely Jewish laws of land ownership and social commerce are described. During the seventh year, all debts would be remitted and the land would lie fallow. During the Jubilee year, most of the land that had been sold during the previous forty-nine years would be returned to its original owner, and Jewish slaves would go free. The *shofar* would be blown, the year would be sanctified, and the economic organization of the Jewish people would be restored to its original and natural condition. Those who had become poor could once again garner hope that their plight would be relieved and that they could begin anew during the next seven-year cycle.

Why does Leviticus move from the world of sacrifices to that of economic and social welfare? What could the Jewish people have been thinking as they received these mitzvot of the Sabbatical year and the treatment of the poor? They had never even seen their land, much less owned any of it. Rashi asks, "What is the relevance of being told of the Sabbatical year at Mount Sinai?" It would be years and years before the Jewish people would come in to the land, conquer it, and divide it up into the appropriate tribal sections. Even then, there would be an additional seven years before they could fulfill the commandment of resting during the Sabbatical year! Why did they need to learn about this commandment precisely at this moment in their incipient history?

Furthermore, the theme of the Sabbatical year had been previously introduced in the *parsha* of *Mishpatim* in the book of Exodus (Exodus 23:11). Why were these laws not included there? Why do the laws of the Sabbatical and Jubilee years recur at this critical juncture, in the concluding messages of the book of Leviticus?

For twenty-four chapters, the Jewish people have been exhorted to become a holy people. Now, at the conclusion of the book of Leviticus, the two themes of *Behar* represent the true tests of the spiritual development of the Jewish people:

1. Will they have the spiritual strength not to work the land during the sabbatical year?

2. Will they have mercy and care for the poor, their powerless brethren?

Taken together, these two themes offer new hope for their society. The Jewish people have just fled from Egypt, where the strong enslaved the weak, the rich exploited the poor. This was their only model of social existence. Now they are being told that their society must be different and that there will always be hope for the less fortunate. No one will forever be financially burdened; within each person's lifetime his or her debts will be annulled and their land will be returned. No one will be abandoned; the treatment of the poor would become the focus of Jewish spirituality.

Economic and social laws do not form the core of the book of Leviticus, which concentrates on the centrality of the Tabernacle and the role of the priests and sacrifices in maintaining the holiness of the Jewish encampment. By choosing to close with these two themes, national holiness has transitioned into economic and social concerns.

Around the *Shabbat* Table

1. How do you think that returning land and annulling debts during the seventh year would affect the economic structure of the society?

2. It was customary that during the Sabbatical year, the farmers would go to Jerusalem to study Torah. Are there any modern equivalents to this in your society?

3 What would you most want to do if you were to be given a Sabbatical year?

SHABBAT LUNCH: Deceitful Words

Is one allowed to window-shop? Am I allowed to walk into a store and ask the price of an item, if I have no intention of buying it?

This week's *parsha* states, "You should not defraud another, but you will fear your God, for I am the Lord your God" (Leviticus 25:17). Earlier in this *parsha*, the Torah already warned against financial fraud: "If you sell an object to your neighbor, or buy from him, you will not defraud one another" (Leviticus 25:14). What kind of fraudulent acts might have been excluded by the first commandment? What types of fraud does the second prohibition include?

The Mishnah states that "just as there may be deceit in monetary matters, so too, there may be deceit in verbal discourse. A person should not say [to a shopkeeper], 'How much does this item cost' if he has no intention of buying it. If a person has changed his life for the better, one should not say to him, 'remember your earlier actions . . .'" (*Bava Metziah* 58b). The Talmud adds, "If one became ill or suffered family tragedies, don't talk to him the way that the friends of Job spoke to him, saying, 'Recall, now, was there ever someone that was innocent who perished?' (Job 4:7). If donkey-drivers ask for grain, one should not send them to someone's home if one knows that he does not have any grain to sell [in order to embarrass that person]." Even calling someone by a derogatory nickname to which the person has become accustomed constitutes a form of verbal fraud, according to Jewish law, even if the person does not object to being called by the name.

What is the common denominator of these examples? What separates this type of speech from *lashon hara*?

These cases carry with them a trace of falseness and deception. If confronted, the speaker could always claim that his intentions were positive and pure—that is, he could claim that he really did intend to buy the object or that he really did think that there was grain at the home to which he sent the donkey drivers. In its most severe form, this type of verbal deceit can be acutely damaging, as, unlike cases of gossip, direct slander, or defamation, here the injured party has no potential recourse. The speaker can always claim, "I intended no harm, I meant well."

The Talmud posits that verbal deceit is more severe than monetary deceit, as the latter is possible to repay, while there is no way of alleviating the pain caused by deceitful words. Furthermore, while personal profit may provoke one to financially deceive another, there is no such incentive in cases of verbal damage and deceit; there is no benefit to be accrued, the speaker acts purely out of ill will.

This section of the Talmud concludes: "Since the time of the destruction of the Temple, the gates of prayer have been locked ... But even though the gates of prayer are locked, the gates of tears have not been locked ... Rav Hisda said, 'All of the gates are locked, except for the gates of those hurt by deception.'" The rabbis said that words and feelings that sincerely emanate from the heart have the power to enter the heart of another. So, too, the pain that is caused through subtle and guileful words can break a heart and has the power to break through the "locked gates of heaven."

Around the *Shabbat* Table

1. If a person asks the price of an item with no intention of buying it, he has falsely raised the hopes of the shopkeeper. Can you think of additional reasons why this practice should be forbidden? Can you think of ways to overcome this problem?

2. What ramifications do you think that verbal deception may have for the field of advertising?

3. The Talmud states (*Bava Metzia* 58b) that the "placing of one's eyes" on merchandise if one does not have the money to purchase it is also a form of fraud. Yet in this case, there is no other party involved. How do you understand this form of deception? What are the implications of this for the popular pasttime of window-shopping?

Seuda Shlishit: The *Tzaddiks'* Response

"You should not defraud another, but you will fear your God, for I am the Lord your God" (Leviticus 25:17). In this *parsha*, the Torah cautions against the use of deceitful words (see: "*Behar/Bechukkotai*: Deceitful Words"). What might be a person's response to having been misled?

Two leading rabbinical figures were, perhaps, unusual in their reactions to verbal deception:

The Rebbe from Szanz, noted for his giving of *tzedakah*, was once misled by the father of a bride. It once happened that the father of a bride came to ask the Szanzer Rebbe for money. In his community, it was customary for the bride's father to buy two *tallitot* (prayer shawls) for the prospective groom, one for the weekdays and one for *Shabbat*. The father told the Rebbe that he did not have enough money to buy the *tallitot*. The Rebbe prepared to give the father the necessary funds.

Suddenly, the elder son of the Rebbe cried out, "Abba, the man is a liar! I saw him in the store just yesterday buying two *tallitot*!" The man turned pale and raced out of the Rebbe's room.

The Rebbe put his head in his hands and moaned, "*Oy vey, oy vey*! How could my son have done such a thing. *Oy*!" The Rebbe leaned over and spoke very softly to his son. "Son, do you know what you have done? This man has a lot of expenses for the wedding. He simply thought that I would be more sympathetic to a request for money for something ritual, something sacred, than for other things. That is why he asked for money for the *tallitot*. Now, quickly run after him and bring him back here."

It is told that the Rebbe from Szanz did not forgive his son until he (the son) had helped to raise money for the whole wedding.

The Rebbe from Salant was once misled by a poor man shortly before Passover. The poor man asked him, "If I do not have enough money to buy wine, can I fulfill the obligation of seder night by drinking four cups of milk?" The Rebbe replied that one cannot ful-

fill the mitzvah of the four cups by drinking milk, and then gave the
poor man an extremely large amount of *tzedakah*.

When asked why he had given the man so much money, the
Rebbe replied, "You see, he wasn't only asking about the wine.
Through his question (by asking specifically about milk), he was
hinting to me that he also did not have enough money to buy meat
for the seder. I gave him money for both wine and meat."

Around the *Shabbat* Table

1. How are these two cases different from other forms of verbal deception?

2. Martin Buber once said that it is not hard to answer the question
that was asked, but it is very difficult to answer the question that
was not asked. What do you think gave these rebbes the perception to answer the questions that were not asked? Do you know
anyone else who has this quality?

3. When did you last respond to a question that someone was too
embarrassed to ask? Did someone ever do this for you?

Numbers

Bamidbar: Final Preparations

G eneral Introduction to the book of *Bamidbar*:
The fourth book of the Torah, *Bamidbar*, spans the 40 years of
the wanderings of the Jewish people in the desert. It chronicles their
journeys from Mount Sinai to the plains of Mo'ab, which border the
land of Israel. Unlike the two books of the Torah that immediately
precede it, few commandments are given to the Jewish people in
Bamidbar; rather, this book focuses on the crises, failures, and suc-
cesses of the Jewish people during their wanderings in the desert
and the lessons they learned from them.

In Genesis, Abraham is chosen, his mission is determined, and
the twelve sons of Jacob become the prototypes of the twelve tribes
of the nation. In Exodus, the Jewish people emerge and are given
the Torah at Mount Sinai. In Leviticus, the laws concerning holiness,
whether regarding the priests and the Tabernacle or involving general interpersonal relations, are transmitted. Now, the Jewish people
are finally ready to begin their travels as a nation. Unlike when they
departed from Egypt, they are now equipped with both their religious guidelines—the Ten Commandments—and their social and
holy center, the Tabernacle.

The numerous incidents recounted in *Bamidbar*, such as the people's complaints for meat and water, the spies' fear of entering the Promised Land, the rebellion of *Korach* and his cohorts against Moses, and the cursing of the Jewish people by *Bila'am* are ostensibly one-time events in the history of the Jewish people. They are unique predicaments brought about by this singular period in history. The Jewish people will never again leave Egypt to travel to the Promised Land; the Jewish people will never again wander in a desert.

Why is there a need, then, to eternalize these seemingly one-time events into a book of the Torah? Why must they be remembered for all of time?

Each event in the book of Numbers epitomizes a situation that is destined to take place in each and every generation of the Jewish people. The crises that are recorded here are not "one-time" events; rather, they constitute prototypes that recur continually throughout Jewish history. Countless events must have occurred to the Jewish people during their 40 years of wandering; however, only those that will revisit the Jewish people in the future are recorded in this book.

This week's *parsha*:

The first subject of this week's *parsha* is the counting of the Jewish people. Unlike the previous census, taken in the *parsha Ki Tissa* (Exodus 30:12), in which the Jewish people were counted as individuals upon contributing half a shekel to the building of the Tabernacle, now they are counted according to their respective tribes, in other words, "The numbering of the tribe of Reuben, forty-six thousand, five hundred ... the numbering of the tribe of Simeon, fifty-nine thousand, three hundred" (Numbers 1:21, 23). Furthermore, here the Torah states, "Take the sum of all the congregation of the children of Israel... from 20 years old and upward, *all that are able to go forth to war* in Israel ..." (Numbers 1:2).

The second subject is the arrangement of the camp of the Jewish people into three concentric circles. At the innermost circle was the Tabernacle and its service, known as the "camp of the *Shechinah*" (the Holy Presence). The next circle, surrounding the Tabernacle, was divided into four regions, three populated by the Levites (*levi'im*) and one by the priests (*kohanim*). This circle was called "the camp of the Levites." This camp was devoted primarily to the care of the Tabernacle and matters of holiness. The remaining twelve tribes (Joseph received a double portion, as his tribe was divided between Efraim and Menashe) were organized into four groups of three, surrounding the camp, comprising what would be referred to as "the camp of Israel." In short, three very carefully structured circles of tribes formed the shape of the Jewish society.

Why does the book of *Bamidbar* begin with these procedures? Why were the counting of the Jewish people according to their tribes and the arrangement of the tribes into a well-organized system the first two events in the book of *Bamidbar*?

Before beginning their travels to the Promised Land, the Jewish people had to learn that they were not traveling as a mass of individuals but as a carefully orchestrated collective whole, with every person linked and responsible both to his or her community (tribe) and to the whole Jewish community. The Jews were not being counted as individuals but rather as potential soldiers preparing to serve in defense of the whole Jewish people.

The book of *Bamidbar* depicts the drama of a people in transition from slavery to freedom, from dependence to self-reliance. The Jewish people are now beginning to find their own way, both physically and spiritually, as a nation. This week's *parsha* outlines the final preparations before commencing this journey. The sanctuary is positioned at the people's center, the community alliances are publicly proclaimed, and the awareness of risking one's life for the sake of the entire nation is affirmed.

Around the *Shabbat* Table

1. King David ordered the counting of the Jewish people (2 Samuel, Chapter 24), and then regretted his action, referring to it as a great sin. Is there any danger inherent in counting people? Have you ever been "counted" as part of something? How did it make you feel?

2. The Jewish people no longer have a Tabernacle or sanctuary at their center. What do you think is the focal point of the Jewish people, of your own society? What would you like to be at its center?

3. In this *parsha*, the counting of the Jewish people and the arrangement of their camp is intended to foster a sense of national identity. How does one learn to think of one's own identity in national terms? How central is national identity in your life?

SHABBAT LUNCH: Adolescent Growth

In Hebrew, the most holy name of God has four letters—"yud, heh, vav," and a second "heh." These four letters, together with the very first point of the first letter, represent five units that correspond to the five books of the Torah. Though the very first point of the first letter, the point at which the quill touches the parchment, is virtually imperceptible, it directs the path for the continuation of the writing. Symbolically, this infinitesimal point represents the moment of conception. It determines all future development. This first point corresponds to the first book of the Torah, Genesis, which, like the embryonic process, holds within it the concealed raw material and potential for all impending growth.

The first letter of God's name, "yud," the smallest of all the letters, dangles unsupported in the air. It symbolizes birth and the beginning of actual life, the nascent stages of being. This "yud" corresponds to the second book of the Torah, Exodus, in which the Jewish people are born and precariously begin their first stages of life.

The second letter of God's name, "heh," reflects the continuous growth and expansion of this birth process. This letter corresponds to the third book of the Torah, Leviticus, in which the Jewish people establish their camp and build the Tabernacle.

The first point of writing, together with the first two letters of God's name, compose a single unit denoting conception, birth, and growth. This reflects the process occurring in the first three books of the Torah,

The third letter of God's name, "vav," corresponds to the fourth book of the Torah—Numbers, or *Bamidbar*. This letter, written as a straight vertical line, symbolizes an arrow pointing directly downward, toward the earth. The "vav" represents the transition from a "heavenly" existence to actual life in this "earthly" world. During the first three books of the Torah, the Jewish people were continually guided by "heavenly" direction. God chose Abraham, brought the Jewish people out of Egypt, and gave them the Ten Commandments. This chain of events set the stage for the Jewish people to act in this world, and now, in *Bamidbar*, they embark on their struggle to actualize their latent potential.

The book of *Bamidbar* thus represents the adolescence and young adulthood of the Jewish people, their movement from the supervision and parental care of childhood to the responsibility and independence of adulthood. This process is fraught with hazards, instability, and not a small number of crises.

The frame of mind necessary for this transition from dependence to independence is summarized in an expression in a mishnah that describes the educational and spiritual guidance necessary for each stage of life, from the age of 5 to 100 (*Pirkei Avot* 5:25). The period from 20 to 30 is designated as the time "*to pursue.*" The transition from dependence—from fulfilling the directives of a higher source, be it God or a parent—to independence, and finding one's own way, is full of "pursuit."

What does "to pursue" imply about this stage in life? Why are ten years necessary for this endeavor?

The road to independence is never straight or simple. The Jewish people wandered in the desert, struggling with issues of authority, rebellion, jealousy, and fear. The many years that the mishnah allocates to this process of self-discovery reflect the depth and complexity of this passage to maturity. To achieve independence, a person must be willing to explore and probe countless alternatives. "Pursuit" entails questioning, challenging, dreaming, and examining new ways of living and thinking. Through this process one begins to crystallize a personal outlook on life, cast in the uniqueness of his or her own personality and experience. The goal of this process is not simply to be unique but to be authentic; to fully believe in one's life rather than to live a life of imitation, mere acceptance, or fear of the unknown.

For the Jewish people, this process commenced with 40 years of wandering in the desert. The divine and parental hand of God gradually withdrew and the Jewish people were left to learn from their mistakes and to forge their own identity. On the path to independence, only by making earthly mistakes and struggles can we strive for heavenly perfection and guidance.

Around the *Shabbat* Table

1. The Talmud explains that one of the unique qualities of a desert is that it is utterly devoid of personal ownership or control. How else would you describe the uniqueness of the desert and what its effect might be upon a people? Have you ever spent time in a desert, in the Sinai? How did it affect you?

2. The mishnah, which describes the years from 20 to 30 as the time of "pursuit," describes the years from 30 to 40 as the time of "strength (or power)." What qualities do you think this exemplifies?

3. What do you think happens to a person who never "pursues"? What characterizes your decade of "pursuit"?

Seuda Shlishit: Old and New Flags

Every one of the children of Israel will camp with his own *flag*, with the insignias of their father's house.... [Bamidbar 2:2]

As they camped in the desert, each tribe of the Jewish people was marked by its flag. The unique color and design of each flag denoted the individual attributes and role that the tribe was supposed to play within the nation. With the emergence of the Zionist movement, the quest for a modern flag for the State of Israel began. Though today the Israeli flag is one of the most well-known symbols of the State, over 100 years ago, neither its colors nor design had been determined.

Theodore Herzl recorded his idea for the flag in his diary: "Perhaps a white flag with seven golden stars. The white background would represent our new and pure life; the stars would represent the number of daily hours one would work in our society." Herzl approached Baron Hirsch, one of the leading Jewish benefactors of his time, with the initial thoughts of his plan, but it was never accepted. Other designs, including a Lion of Judah or a golden Star of David were also suggested, though none achieved significant popularity.

The source of today's blue and white flag came from David Wolffsohn (1856–1914), Herzl's associate and companion, who became the second president of the World Zionist Organization. Wolffsohn writes that "this matter (the design of the flag), caused me considerable distress. Suddenly, an idea popped into my head and everything became clear. In fact, we already had a flag—the *'tallit,'* whose colors were white and dark blue ... I instructed that a white flag with two dark blue stripes and a *Magen David* (Star of David) in its center be made. It was immediately accepted as the national flag."

Numerous theories abound as to the meaning of the colors and the *Magen David* of the flag. Dark blue (in Hebrew, *tchelet*), the color originally intended for the *Magen David*, symbolizes the shade of water on the horizon, where it seems to blend into the sky. This signifies the uniting of the earthly and heavenly domains (Talmud, *Menachot* 43b). The two intertwining triangles composing the *Magen David* may represent the weaving together of the three sections of the Bible—Torah, Prophets, and Writings—with the three stages of time: past, present and future.

In addition to the significance of its design, Rabbi Joseph Soloveitchik writes that since its acceptance, the flag has assumed a new level of holiness. He writes that according to Jewish Law, a Jew who was killed in an act of anti-Semitism is buried in his or her bloodied clothes because the clothes acquire an element of sanctity through the blood that was spilled on them and also deserve a proper burial. All the more so, he writes, the flag of the State of Israel has acquired a spark of holiness by virtue of the thousands of Jews who have fallen in its defense. Honoring the flag of Israel is a sign of respect for their self-sacrifice.

Around the *Shabbat* Table

1. What do you think might the six points and the two triangles of the *Magen David* might represent?

2. Today, the stripes of the flag of Israel are not *tchelet* (dark blue) but rather a lighter shade of blue. At the inception of the state, the flag-makers had difficulty creating a dark blue dye that would not fade in the strong sun of the Middle East. A lighter, more durable, shade was therefore adopted. Suggestions have been made to return to the original dark blue shade and/or to add a Lion of Judah to it. What do you think?

3. What would you have suggested as the symbols of the flag of Israel? What spontaneously comes into your mind whenever you see the flag?

Naso

FRIDAY NIGHT MEAL: Parts of the Whole

In Genesis, Abraham was told, " ...and you will be a blessing" (Genesis 12:2). Abraham acquires the power to bless people's lives, to help them unite the physical and spiritual domains, to transform their awareness of the world. Now, six generations later, God's promise to Abraham is finally being fulfilled. This gift, in the form of the Priestly Blessing, is conveyed to Moses and Aaron:

> "May the Lord bless you and keep you;
> May the Lord make His face shine upon you, and be gracious to you;
> May the Lord lift up His face to you, and grant you peace."
> [Numbers 6:24-26]

Everything seems to be in place for the Jewish people to begin their mission. In last week's *parsha*, the organization of the camps of Israel was precisely defined. In this week's reading, the Jewish people have been endowed with the power to affect and elevate the world through their conduct, culminating with the Priestly Blessing. In next week's *parsha*, the Jewish people will finally depart from

Mount Sinai and begin their journeys as an autonomous people. Yet one last piece is missing. For some reason, immediately preceding the Priestly Blessing, this week's *parsha* dwells on a number of paradigms of socially problematic behavior: (1) one who has stolen from a convert, (2) the *Sotah*, a woman suspected of being unfaithful to her husband, (3) the Nazirite, one who has taken an oath not to cut his hair or drink wine or strong drink.

Why are these cases mentioned before the Jewish people are ready for their mission? Is it by chance? Why has the Torah chosen this moment to discuss these problems?

An important principle is conveyed through the presentation and placement of these cases. Their presence illustrates that even with God's providential care in the desert, even with the wisdom of the Torah and leaders like Moses, Aaron, and Miriam, every human society is fraught with vices and failings. There will always be problems. There can be no blessing, no potential to perfect the world, if Jewish society has not first healed itself. Jewish society is not measured through external excellence and achievements but by its morality and its compassion for those who have, for whatever reason, stumbled morally. The value and well-being of Jewish society is determined by how well it facilitates the return of these individuals into its mainstream. No one is superfluous.

On a different level, a number of hasidic commentators see these cases representing classic human failings. The thief has been physically tempted and hurt the community. The *Sota* has failed to remain emotionally faithful to her husband and has hurt the family unit. The Nazirite has moved to a spiritual excess, presenting an extreme relationship between the human being and God. The physical, emotional, and spiritual drives are all capable of consuming and controlling an individual.

Despite their failings, and the damage or pain they consequently inflict on the community, family, and spiritual dimensions of Jewish society, they remain part of the Jewish people. Before the Jewish people are able to bless others, they must themselves become whole; they must care for the health and welfare of each member.

Around the *Shabbat* Table

1. The Nazirite strove to live on a higher spiritual level, refraining from a number of human activities (drinking wine, cutting his hair, etc.) and thus separating himself from the rest of society. Some commentators regard this effort as praiseworthy, while others judge it negatively. What do you think? What would be a modern example of this behavior?

2. Which of these drives (physical, emotional, and spiritual) do you think is the most difficult to control and direct positively for the majority of people? For you?

3. What blessing would you give to the Jewish people?

SHABBAT LUNCH: Home Schooling

This week's *parsha* states that when the Levites reach the age of 30 they should begin to perform the service of the Tabernacle. Yet in next week's *parsha* the Torah states that they should begin their service from 25 years and upward. The Talmud (*Chullin* 24a) resolves this apparent contradiction by stating that the Levites started learning their trade at 25, and began to actually work at the age of 30.

The formal education of the Levites began at the age of 25. What is the ideal age to begin schooling in general?

The Talmud (*Bava Batra* 21a) relates four steps that led to the creation of the public school system in Judaism:

> Rav Judah said in the name of Rav: "Truthfully, the name of that man, Joshua ben Gamla, should be blessed, for if not for him, then the learning of Torah would have been forgotten from all of Israel! *For at first*, if a child had a father, his father taught him, and if he had no father, then he did not learn at all ... *Then* they made a decree that teachers of children should be appointed in Jerusalem ... Even so, if a child had a father, then the father would take him up to Jerusalem and have

him taught there, and if not, then he would not learn at all. *Therefore*, they ordained that teachers should be appointed in each region, and that boys should enter school at the age of sixteen or seventeen. They did so, and if the teacher punished them they would rebel and run away from school. *Finally*, Joshua ben Gamla came and ordered that teachers of young children should be appointed in each district and town, and that children should enter school at the age of six or seven."

Though Joshua ben Gamla is remembered favorably, it seems that his approach was accepted reluctantly by Judaism. Despite their seemingly limited chances for success, two other options were adopted beforehand and were discarded only after they had failed. Apparently, the rabbis were reluctant to have children between the critical ages of 6 to 16 removed from their home atmosphere.

Why was the option of public schooling not desired by the rabbis? What drawbacks might they have been worried about? Why was the home considered to be the ideal educational setting?

First of all, the relationship between the parent and child is not contingent upon the child's understanding of the material; their bond began long before the child commenced learning and will continue afterward. Thus, the whole learning process ideally transpires in an environment of love, support, and caring. Unlike teachers who most likely instruct the child for only one year, acquiring a limited perception of the child, parents have watched their child grow during his or her whole life, hopefully observing his or her unique qualities, idiosyncrasies, and needs.

Second, the goal of parent–child education differs from that of a teacher–student relationship. The goal of a classroom setting is to convey material. Students are tested on how well they have understood the content of the classes. There is a yearly syllabus and projects, often determined before the students enter the classroom. In contrast, home schooling can be geared to a child's individual needs and qualities. In home schooling, the goal is not to transmit a set amount of material within a limited period of time but to convey values and lessons of life, which may take years to impart. The parent educates the "being" of the child, transmitting a way of life, rather than the material of the yearly syllabus.

Finally, the classroom setting creates an environment of comparison and competition (see "*Bereshit*: Aggression"), often at the expense of individual expression. Teachers learn how to "control" a classroom, and the establishment of order and discipline are essential skills to master. Individual students who may learn in a slightly different fashion or pace may be labeled as "problematic" or "disruptive." Students may begin to perceive themselves as being either "gifted" or "slow." The parent–child education, precisely because it affords itself a longer scope of time, is more likely to be free from the problematic consequences of comparison, labeling, and the rigid structure endemic to the classroom.

Home schooling has the potential to create an environment in which a loving parent who understands the unique qualities, needs, and learning patterns of his or her child can bequeath an education of a lifetime. However, as noted by the Talmud almost 2,000 years ago, this ideal vision is rarely realized. As a result, the creation of the formal public school safeguarded the future of the learning of Torah.

Around the *Shabbat* Table

1. In light of the selection from the Talmud quoted previously, Judaism understands that a teacher should see him- or herself as a surrogate parent. What ramifications might this approach have for the classroom setting?

2. Why do you think that home schooling broke down? What other differences are there between these two educational settings?

3. Did the classroom setting help or hinder your educational development? Has your education reflected any of the ideas expressed here? How do you hope to educate your children?

Seuda Shlishit: A Twentieth Century *Nazir*

> And the Lord spoke to Moses, saying, "Speak to the children of Is-
> rael and say to them, 'When either a man or woman will pronounce
> a special vow of a *Nazir* to separate themselves to the Lord, he
> shall *abstain from wine and strong drink...no razor shall come
> on his head ... and he shall be holy, and shall let the locks of
> the hair of his head grow.*" [Numbers 6: 1-5]

The drinking of wine and other strong drink is considered to be a
primary form of social interaction; refraining from cutting one's hair
is regarded as an antisocial act. The vows of the *Nazir* (Nazirite)
served to distance the *Nazir* from society and, it is hoped, bring him
or her to a new and higher level of spirituality. During the Temple
period, one could assume Nazirite vows for a limited or extended
period of time. After the destruction of the Second Temple (70 C.E.),
the observance of the Nazirite lifestyle appears to have disappeared,
and for centuries there has been no record of individuals becoming Nazirites.

Nevertheless, one of the most unusual and extraordinary figures
of Jerusalem during this century was known universally simply as
"the Nazir." Rav David HaKohen (1886-1972)—philosopher, mystic,
teacher, and writer—was recognized in Jerusalem by his long beard
and flowing locks of hair, a contemporary *Nazir*.

Born to a rabbinic family near Vilna, the Nazir studied with the
leading rabbis of Europe during his adolescent years. He continued
his academic studies at universities in Germany and Switzerland,
preparing a doctorate on the philosophy of religion, heavily influenced by the ideas of the German philosopher Hermann Cohen. In
1916 he met Rabbi Abraham Isaac Kook and began a lifelong relationship as his friend and disciple. For thirty years, the Nazir collected and edited Rabbi Kook's writings, eventually producing his
three-volume epic called *Lights of Holiness.* The Nazir's own work,
The Voice of Prophecy, comparing Jewish and Greek attitudes to-

ward spirituality, won the Maimon Prize for literature.

While in Switzerland during World War I, the Nazir began to lecture at the University of Basel, achieving great success and popularity. Fearful that these accomplishments might engender feelings of pride or conceit, he decided to accept vows of a *Nazir*. For the rest of his life, the Nazir did not cut his hair, or drink wine or other intoxicating liquor. He became a lifelong vegetarian, and each year, for the forty days prior to Yom Kippur, he would abstain from all non-holy conversation. Legends abound of his refraining from sleep while studying through the night.

The Nazir chose his path in the search for holiness and prophecy. Strikingly, his choices did not remove him from involvement with his contemporary society. He raised his son, Shear Yashuv HaKohen, as a *Nazir* until the age of Bar Mitzvah. While still a lifelong vegetarian, Shear Yashuv chose to end his Nazirite behavior at the age of 16, eventually becoming the rabbi of the Israeli Air Force and serving as the chief rabbi of Haifa. The Nazir's son-in-law, Rabbi Shlomo Goren, was the rabbi of the Israeli Army and then chief rabbi of Israel.

After the death of Rav Kook in 1935, for over thirty years, the Nazir did not leave his room, studying and writing most of the day. During the Six-Day War, as soon as the Israeli army regained the area of the Kotel (Western Wall), his son-in-law, Army Chaplain Shlomo Goren, sent his jeep for the Nazir, who is reputed to have been the first nonmilitary figure to reach the Wall. In his book, General Motte Gur, the leader of the paratrooper force that captured the Old City, reports that the soldiers stood in awe and amazement as the long-haired, aged rabbi, the Nazir, clutched the stones of the Western Wall.

Around the *Shabbat* Table

1. When the *Nazir* (of the Torah) finished the period of being a Nazirite, he or she brought a sin-offering sacrifice. The commentators are divided over whether the "sin" of the *Nazir* was his or

her *initial decision* to refrain from these activities, or whether it was the decision to *end* the period of being a *Nazir* and return to normal life. What do you think?

2. How might one evaluate whether the manifestations of a spiritual drive are healthy and productive or peculiar and unbalanced? What would you suggest to someone who wanted to grow spiritually?

3. Do you know individuals who have developed their spiritual side while still maintaining an involvement in mainstream affairs of society?

Behaalotekha

FRIDAY NIGHT MEAL: Grumbling, Again

After almost a year of experiencing life-changing revelations, receiving the Ten Commandments, organizing themselves into distinct social units, and growing into a people with collective guidelines and a national vision, the Jewish people depart from Mount Sinai.

How would they look back upon their experience at Mount Sinai? What were their feelings as they left Mount Sinai?

Nachmanides quotes a midrash that "they left Mount Sinai in joy, like a child fleeing from school, exclaiming, 'lest (God) give us more commandments.'" They could not wait to leave. Their perspective of the whole experience had shrunk into seeing only the burden of the rules placed upon them. Now, at last, they had the chance to run away from school.

This attitude of grief and resentment quickly found expression: "And the people complained . . . " (Numbers 11:1). The Torah never discloses the substance of their grumbling. Apparently, the content is not central to their leaving. Rashi states that "they simply sought

any pretense to grumble, in order to distance themselves from God."
Regarding the unusual word used here by the Torah to denote their
complaining (*k'mittonanim*), Samson Raphael Hirsch comments,
"The people were as if mourning over themselves. They looked on
themselves as already dead, and mourned over their very selves!"

Momentarily, their flight from Mount Sinai and subsequent grumbling finds concrete expression in the Torah. " . . . And the children
of Israel also wept again, and said, 'Who will give us meat to eat? We
remember the fish, which we ate freely in Egypt; the cucumbers,
the melons, the leeks, the onions, and the garlic, but now our soul
has dried away; we have nothing to look at except the *manna*'"
(Numbers 11:4-6). Now Egypt, the land of slavery and persecution,
evokes fond memories; the house of bondage is transformed into a
home for which they nostalgically yearn.

Upon hearing the last round of complaints, Moses seems to break
down. When the people had complained of lack of water and food
immediately after their departure from Egypt (Exodus 15:24-16:10),
Moses had interceded with God on their behalf. He had prayed for
them and shown great compassion. But now, one year later, Moses'
resolve seems to be broken:

> And Moses heard the people weeping throughout their families . . . and
> Moses said to the Lord, *"Why have You afflicted Your servant? Why
> have I not found favor in Your sight, that You place the burden of
> this people upon me? Did I conceive this people? Did I give birth to
> them?* . . . Should I have to carry them like a wet nurse carries a baby?
> . . . From where should I have meat to give to this whole people when
> they cry to me? . . . I am not able to bear this people alone, it is too
> heavy for me. And if You deal like this with me, please kill me . . . and
> let me not see my own wretchedness. [Numbers 11:10-15]

What happened to Moses? Why doesn't he intercede on behalf
of the Jewish people? How can it be that one year ago he said, "Forgive their sin, and if not, please blot me out of Your book . . ." (Exo-

dus 32:32), but now he pleads with God to let him abandon the people?

Rav Soloveitchik explains that now, after the Jewish people's latest outburst, Moses' assessment of the needs of the people, and of his relationship to them, has radically changed. Initially, Moses understood that the transformation of the mass of slaves into a holy people would be achieved through education and that his role was primarily that of a teacher. Moses deemed himself capable of this task, and indeed history has accorded him the appellation of "Moses Rabbenu" (our teacher). Now, however, Moses' language reflects his realization that more than they need a teacher, they need a parent. "Did I conceive this people? Did I give birth to them? . . . Should I have to carry them like a wet nurse carries a baby?" This role is quite different.

Unlike the teacher, who primarily conveys information and deals with intellectual faculties, the parent must understand and nourish all of the qualities of the child's personality. The role of a parent involves endless caring and nurturing. While the teacher can retain his or her own identity, parents must suspend their own needs while raising a small child.

Moses accepted the responsibility to teach the Jewish people and felt himself worthy of this challenge. But after their continual outbursts, after their seeking pretenses in order to grumble, Moses realized that more than a teacher was needed; a parent was essential to enable the Jewish people to mature into a stable people. For this role, he doubted his capabilities.

God granted Moses' request. "And the Lord said to Moses, 'Gather to Me seventy men of the elders of Israel . . . and the Lord took of the spirit that was upon him, and gave it to the seventy elders" (Numbers 11:16, 25). No longer would Moses have to bear the Jewish people by himself.

Around the *Shabbat* Table

1. What do you think Moses' admission of inadequacy says about him as a leader? How do you think that the appointment of the seventy elders affected Moses' position as the leader of the Jewish people?

2. "Running away from Mount Sinai" is considered to be an eternal metaphor. Why do you think responsibility is often shirked? Is it possible to overcome this feeling? If you had been amidst the Jewish people at Mount Sinai, is there any law in particular from which you would have wanted to run away?

3. Have your Jewish role models been more like teachers or parents? Which do you think you need more? Which has been more effective?

SHABBAT LUNCH: The Most Humble

And the man, Moses, was very humble, more so than all the men that were on the face of the earth. [Numbers 12: 3]

In one of its most sweeping statements, the Torah defines the uniqueness of Moses. Not just "humble," not just "very humble"—Moses was the "most humble human being," beyond the scope of all of the rest of humanity.

The Torah never attributes such superlatives to Abraham, Isaac, or Jacob, or to Sarah, Rebecca, Leah, or Rachel. In fact, very rarely does the Torah ascribe qualities to any of its major figures (Noah and Jacob being notable exceptions). Furthermore, Moses has many character traits, yet this one alone is singled out.

Why does the Torah place such emphasis on this quality of Moses? What distinguishes the "humble" person?

Humility is often confused with meekness or timidity; the docile or obsequious personality may be mistakenly called humble. Yet throughout his period of leadership, Moses demonstrated assertiveness and courage. He stands up to Pharaoh, boldly breaks the tablets of the Ten Commandments, and continually resolves crises among the Jewish people. In what way, then, is Moses "humble"?

Humility is *not* continually deferring to other opinions or believing that one does not have special gifts; rather, humility is believing that one's special talents, are, in fact, gifts. Each person has been granted unique and special powers with which to effect positive change in this world. The humble person understands that he has been bestowed with these powers not for personal fulfillment but rather for influencing the world. Personal abilities are always accompanied with the requisite obligation and responsibility of using them productively. Unlike the self-centered personality who looks upon his or her achievements with a sense of personal accomplishment, the humble individual removes the "I," or the ego-fulfillment, from the centrality of the task at hand. There is a very subtle though poignant altering of subject and emphasis: it is not that "*I*" am performing these tasks, but rather: *these tasks* need to be accomplished by me.

Ironically, humility is the primary quality necessary for successful leadership. Only a person who is not concerned with self-fulfillment can clearly perceive the intended objective. Only a person who does not confuse this greater vision with concerns of self-esteem can become an ideal leader. Moses did not seek out a leadership role. When Moses was originally approached by God to lead the Jewish people out of Egypt (Exodus, Chapter 3), he declined, asserting that he was not suitable for the part. When God offered to destroy the Jewish people and to create a new people from Moses, he protested.

The Talmud (*Tannit* 7a) states that the quality of humility is essential for learning Torah. The learning of Torah should not be exploited to build up one's own reputation; rather, one should learn in order to fulfill the task of improving the world. Ultimately, the Talmud (*Shabbat* 89a) states that because Moses was humble and was not concerned with his own self-image, he was rewarded by having the Torah called *Torat Moshe*, the "The Torah of Moses."

Around the *Shabbat* Table

1. Rav Kook writes that true humility strengthens one's resolve and is reflected in a growing sense of happiness; in contrast, despondency or despair reflect perversions of true humility. Why?

2. Do you know of any leaders today whom you would consider to be humble?

3. Have you struggled with feelings of pride over your personal achievements?

Seuda Shlishit: Education of a Child-Rebbe

From the age of 25 until 50 years old, the Levites tended to all matters of holiness in the Tabernacle and, eventually, in the Temple. Moses was ordered to "separate out the Levites from among the children of Israel; and the Levites shall be Mine [God's]" (Numbers 8:14).

It is not simple to raise a child to become a religious leader. The hasidim relate the following educational approach:

The Rebbe was about to die. He had served his people well for a long time, and now he was prepared to move on to a better world. Before he died, he called together his closest disciples and carefully advised them how to raise the future Rebbe, his son.

The Rebbe passed away, and his son was proclaimed as the new Rebbe. Though only a child, the new Rebbe had already been recognized as a wondrous prodigy. People came from all over to ask him their most personal and difficult questions; his answers did not disappoint them. He tirelessly served his followers, soon becoming beloved by all those in the community.

Yet every afternoon, his father's closest disciples would mysteriously lead him to a place that no one ever discovered. Every afternoon, for several hours, the young Rebbe's whereabouts were a mystery to all.

Legends abounded about the miracles that he wrought during these times. "Surely," claimed one of his followers, "he is traveling in the most holy of worlds." Another asserted with the greatest confidence, "He is praying for all those who are suffering. He doesn't want us to see his tears." They argued incessantly over his possible feats. Was he studying the secrets of the Kabbalah? Was he bringing the Messiah?

Years passed, and the child-Rebbe became aged. He now realized that his time was approaching to be called to the heavenly court.

His faithful followers approached him one last time. "Rebbe," they hesitantly asked, "can you finally reveal to us where you went during those times when the advisers stole you away? What were you doing? All of these years, we could never truly fathom your mysterious disappearance."

With benevolent love, the Rebbe's eyes caressed his followers. "You must understand," he began, "that my father was the most wise of men, the most loving of fathers. He knew what my future held for me. Therefore, he carefully bade his advisers to carry me away and occupy me during every afternoon of my childhood. They would bring me to a room, and there, they would give me a box. What was in the box? Marbles. Every afternoon, my father wanted to be certain that I would play marbles."

Around the *Shabbat* Table

1. Why do you think that the Rebbe instructed that his son play marbles?

2. In *Pirkei Avot* (Ethics of the Fathers 5:25) it is stated that children should begin to learn Torah at the age of 5. Based upon this, the rabbis instruct that parents should not try to teach their children how to read before the age of 5; rather, the early years should be safeguarded for experiential forms of education. What do you think?

3. What would be adult equivalents of playing marbles? What is yours?

Shelach Lekha

FRIDAY NIGHT MEAL: Generations of Crying

The Jewish people leave Mount Sinai, they are only a few days' journey from the Promised Land. Yet this generation will never enter the land. They will "wander in the wilderness for 40 years . . . According to the number of the days in which you spied out the land, 40 days, each day for a year, you will bear your transgressions" (Numbers 14:33, 34). Because of the sin of the spies, the entire generation is sentenced to wander for forty years, dying homeless in the desert.

What went wrong? What was the sin of the spies?

Twelve spies, the leaders of each of the tribes, were sent to examine the Promised Land. In the book of Deuteronomy, Moses relates that it was neither his nor God's idea to send spies to explore the land; rather, the people proposed the plan, and Moses acquiesced. "And you all came near to me [Moses] and said, 'We will send men before us, and they will search out the land, and bring us back word by what way we must go up, and into what cities we will come'" (Deuteronomy 1:22). After 40 days, the spies brought back the following report: "We came to the land where you sent us, and indeed it flows with milk and honey; and this is the fruit of it. *But* (*effes*) the people are strong that dwell in the land, and the cities are fortified, and very great . . ." (Numbers 13:27, 28).

Was this purely a scouting report? In the account of the spies, which would become known in history as the "evil report," a single word ignominiously stands out: "but" (*effes*). Instead of objectively recounting their mission, the spies passed judgment that entering the land would be too great a challenge for the people. The spies continued: "[It is a] land that consumes its inhabitants, and all the people that we saw in it were men of great stature. There we saw the giants . . . and we were like grasshoppers in our own eyes, and so too we were in their eyes." The spies, the leaders of the Jewish society, succeeded in breaking the hearts of the people, "and the people wept on that night" (Numbers 14:1).

What were these leaders of the Jewish people afraid of?

The *Zohar* states that the spies "were misled by a false reasoning. They said (to themselves): If the Jewish people enter the land, then we (the spies) will be superseded, since it is only in the wilderness that we are considered worthy to be leaders." The spies were afraid not of being defeated by "the men of great stature," but of losing their own stature within the community. The leaders sought to protect their individual fortunes and insidiously misled the people. They were concerned that the present social framework would change once the people entered the land, and they were troubled by the fact that their type of leadership was appropriate only for this particular time, for a people in transition.

According to the Talmud, not only did the generation of the Exodus suffer, but "God declared that 'since [in the desert] you cried for no valid reason, I swear that every future generation will also cry on this day'" (*Tannit* 29a). The day on which the spies returned with their evil report, the ninth of Av, was destined to become the most calamitous day in Jewish history. The mishnah records five catastrophes that occurred on the ninth of Av, including the destruction of the First and Second Temples.

Whenever the leaders of the Jewish people place their self-interest before the national concerns, or whenever the leaders of the Jewish people regard themselves as insignificant, "we were like grasshoppers in our own eyes," then the echoes of the crying on that night still resound. Part of the lesson of the spies is knowing what is truly worthy to cry about.

Around the *Shabbat* Table

1. Before the spies departed, Moses changed the name of one of the spies, Hoshea, meaning "one who *has* saved us," to Yehoshua (Joshua), meaning "one who *will* save us." Moses already had an inclination of the intentions of the spies and wanted to empower Joshua to withstand their machinations. Do you know anyone who has become empowered, or has better withstood the forces of social pressure, through changing his or her name?

2. How does one's self-perception affect one's behavior? What is the difference between seeing oneself as "small as a grasshopper" and being very humble?

3. The events of the generation of the desert are considered to be eternal paradigms, occurring in every community and generation in our history. Do you think that we have learned the lesson and overcome the failure of the spies, or are there still symptoms of this failure in our times?

SHABBAT LUNCH: Attitudes toward the Land of Israel

The sin and tragedy of the spies prevented the generation of the desert from entering the Land of Israel. For the last 2,000 years, other obstacles, ranging from poverty and danger to ideological opposition to *aliyah* ("ascent," the Hebrew term for moving to Israel), have stood in the Jew's path to Israel. During the last century, many waves of *aliyah* have come to Israel, for many utterly distinct reasons and goals.

Theodor Herzl (see: "*Vayakhel/Pekudei*: Building Dreams") called the Jews to return to Israel to evade the harsh anti-Semitism of Europe. Similarly, another early Zionist thinker, Leon Pinsker, wrote that the existence of the Jews as a nonassimilated, separate, ethnic entity in Europe would forever arouse the hatred of the nations. These Zionist thinkers sought a haven for the Jews, entertaining even the possibilities of Uganda and Argentina.

In 1904, at the age of 48, A. D. Gordon came to Israel, where he worked as a manual laborer in the vineyards of Petach Tikvah, and then moved to the Galilee. Gordon began to formulate what would eventually be referred to as "the religion of labor." Asserting that the human's relationship to God had become severed through the detachment from nature, Gordon called for an almost mystical rejuvenation of the soul through physical labor and connection to the soil. This bond to nature would enable the people to rediscover their spirituality and to regain a sense of cosmic unity and holiness.

A different kind of Zionism was advocated by rabbis who supported *aliyah* because it would enable the fulfilling of particular mitzvot that were impossible to observe while living outside of Israel. These include tithing the produce of the land and refraining from working the land during the Sabbatical year.

The first chief rabbi of Israel, Abraham Isaac Kook, combined the idea of the mystical holiness of the land and their respective mitzvot. He wrote that the holiness of the land did not simply enable the Jews to perform a few more mitzvot, but transformed all of the mitzvot and all of their lives. Its effect upon the Jewish people was something that was impossible for one's cognitive powers to fully appreciate. "The Land of Israel is not something external, not an external national asset, or a 'means' to create collective solidarity . . . [rather it] is an essential constituent bound to the life-force of the people" (*Orot*). Just as a flower can only thrive in its proper soil, so, too, the thought, life, and action of the Jewish people can only truly flourish in the Land of Israel. The development of this national awareness is necessary to bring about the salvation of the world.

Around the *Shabbat* Table

1. In 1889, Ahad Ha'am (pseudonym of Asher Hirsch Ginsberg) wrote "The Wrong Way," in which he vigorously criticized the early Zionist movement for placing a premature emphasis on settlement in Israel. Ahad Ha'am advocated that more cultural and educational work be done outside of Israel, as a precursor to mass *aliyah*. What do you think are the most significant cultural or educational achievements presently occurring outside of Israel? In Israel?

2. What do you think has been the effect of the return to Israel on the Jewish people as a whole? What challenges do you think it presents for the State of Israel?

3. With which of the approaches to *aliyah* discussed in this unit do you most identify?

Seuda Shlishit: Fruits of Paradise

Moses instructed the spies to explore the land of Israel. He told them to check "whether the land is fat or lean, whether there are trees in it or not . . . and bring back the fruit of the land" (Numbers 13:20). The spies returned with pomegranates, figs, and clusters of grapes. They showed the fruit to the people and told Moses, "We came to the land where you sent us, and indeed it flows with milk and honey, and this is the fruit of it" (Numbers 13:27). The bounty of the fruit of the Land of Israel was an indicator of its being blessed.

During talmudic times, when faced with a choice of eating fruit grown in Israel or in the Diaspora, many rabbis favored eating those indigenous to the land. A legend relates that the *Orach Chayim*, a leading Jerusalem rabbi, would only eat produce grown in Israel.

Is there something unique about the fruit that grows in Israel and draws its nourishment from the land? Certainly, countries all over the world produce delicious-tasting fruit. What is special about something that has grown in Eretz Yisrael?

The Talmud relates the remarkable qualities of one particular fruit of Israel, "the fruit of *Ginosar*," grown near the lake of Galilee.

> Rabba Bar Bar Chana recounted: "One time we accompanied Rabbi Yochanan to eat the fruit of *Ginosar*. If there were one hundred of us, each one of us would give him ten pieces of fruit. If there were ten of us, each one would bring him one hundred pieces. Each bundle of one hundred pieces would fill up a basket of almost one hundred pounds of fruit. Rabbi Yochanon would eat all of them (!), and then swear to us that it was as if he had not eaten anything, that he was not yet full ... Rabbi Shimon Ben Lakish would eat them until he became dazed [confused and bewildered]. [*Berakhot* 44a]

The fruit of *Ginosar* had such wonderful qualities that the rabbis stated that it was good that it did not grow in Jerusalem, for if it did, people would come up to Jerusalem in order to eat its fruit, rather than to experience the city itself.

No one knows exactly what was so special about this particular fruit. The Midrash, however, proposes a theory, based on its name. *Ginosar* may be the conjunction of two words: *Gan* (garden) and *Sar* ("prince" or "guardian angel"). The fruit of *Ginosar* was the yield of a royal, perhaps heavenly, garden. One could eat it without becoming full, like Rabbi Yochanan. On the other hand, it had the power to cause someone to lose touch with this world, like Rabbi Shimon Ben Lakish.

Thus, the fruit of this heavenly garden, like the fruit of the original Garden of Eden, could be both special and perilous at the same time.

Around the *Shabbat* Table

1. The rabbis of the Talmud (*Berakhot* 40a) speculate and disagree over the type of fruit that was on the "Tree of Knowledge of Good and Evil" in the Garden of Eden. A number of theories are offered regarding the fruit that was the original cause of sin; a grapevine, fig tree, and wheat (!) are offered as possibilities. In what way could each of these fruit be seen as responsible for sin?

2. According to Jewish mystical sources, each piece of fruit carries within it a force of life, a soul, and the fruit grown in the Land of Israel is considered to have an additional level of holiness. When one eats and becomes nourished by this fruit, one absorbs the vitality of the Land. The mishnah focuses on a play on words and states that the "fruit" that one eats ultimately influences the "fruit" of one's labors. Has your behavior ever been influenced spiritually by the types of fruits (or food) that you eat?

3. What fruit do you think would be most similar to the "fruit of *Ginosar*" today?

Korach

FRIDAY NIGHT MEAL: Rebellion

Korach, Moses' cousin, fomented the first rebellion in Jewish history. Together with his group of followers, he harshly and directly attacked the leadership of Moses and Aaron. The Mishnah states that Korach and his group epitomize an unholy alliance united for personal gain, and he is condemned in rabbinic writings for having acted from impure motives. "What controversy was not in the Name of Heaven [for righteous ends]? The controversy of Korach and all of his company" (*Ethics of the Fathers* 5:20).

What was Korach's complaint?

> Now Korach, the son of Yitzhar, the son of Kehat, the son of Levi, and Datan and Aviram . . . took men. And they rose up before Moses, together with two hundred and fifty leaders of the community, men of renown. They gathered themselves together against Moses and against Aaron, and said to them, "You take too much upon yourselves. All of the congregation is holy, every one of them, and the Lord is among them, why do you raise yourselves up above the congregation of the Lord?" [Numbers 16: 1-3]

At first glance, it seems that Korach's complaint is quite legitimate. Isn't, in fact, the whole congregation holy? Didn't the Torah
state at Mount Sinai, "And you shall be to Me a kingdom of Priests
and a *holy nation?*" (Exodus 19:6). Isn't Korach simply being a leader
of the people, standing up for them and defending their rights? Why
does Moses immediately distrust Korach's motivation?

Three signs alert Moses to the true nature of Korach's intentions.

First, Korach's personal background leading up to his allegations.
Why does Korach protest against Moses and Aaron precisely now,
rather than during the first year of their leadership? According to
the Midrash, Korach had a personal reason for inciting the rebellion
now:

> What induced Korach to quarrel with Moses? He was envious of the
> position bestowed upon Elitzaphan, the son of Uziel, whom Moses had
> appointed to be prince over the sons of Kehat. Korach argued: "My
> father and his brothers were four in number: Amram, Yitzhar, Hevron
> and Uziel. The two eldest sons of the first-born son, Amram, [Moses
> and Aaron], have assumed important positions; thus who should be en-
> titled to receive the second level of ranking if not myself, since I am
> the son of Yitzhar, who was the second-born? Yet, who has been ap-
> pointed as prince of the tribe, if not the son of the fourth-born and
> youngest brother, Uziel?! (Numbers 3:30). I hereby protest against him
> [Moses] and will undo his decision."

Second, the masses of people aligned with Korach aroused
Moses' suspicions. Some protested against the positions of leadership assumed by Moses and Aaron, "You take too much upon yourselves"; others griped over the lack of success of their leadership—
"Is it a small thing that you have brought us up out of a land flowing
with milk and honey (!), to kill us in the wilderness . . . " (Numbers
16:13). In a classic example of demagoguery, Korach banded together
an array of malcontents, each burning with his own issue. Their
particular issues became secondary to launching a frontal attack on
Moses and Aaron.

Third, the style of Korach and his assembly was excessively brusque and contemptuous of Moses and Aaron. Two of Korach's co-conspirators, Datan and Aviram, refused to meet with Moses. "And Moses sent for Datan and Aviram ... and they said, 'We will not come up'" (Numbers 16:12). They were not interested in engaging in a discussion with Moses, but in lowering his standing in the eyes of the community.

As discussed earlier ("*Shelach*: Generations of Crying"), the crises of the generation of the desert are considered to be inherent in every generation. Unlike the spies who wanted to *maintain* their personal standing within the community, Korach and his assembly sought to *advance* their communal status and power. The test of Moses as a national leader was to discern the merit and integrity of his challengers. Ultimately, Korach, who craved to raise his status, was plunged into an endless descent when the earth opened its mouth and swallowed him alive. "They, and everything they owned, went down alive to *She'ol*, and the earth closed upon them and they perished from among the congregation" (Numbers 16:33). Just as Datan and Aviram had unwittingly predicted, Moses' challengers did not "go up"; rather, they descended forever.

Around the *Shabbat* Table

1. Which of the three factors mentioned previously (the background, alignment, and style) is the most characteristic of disingenuous political protests and movements?

2. Some commentators maintain that Korach wanted to eliminate the hierarchy within the Jewish people and to establish a populist ruling body. If so, should Moses have resisted this initiative? What are the advantages and disadvantages of a hierarchical political system?

3. Is there "a voice of Korach" within each person? The author of one of the earliest hasidic writings, the *Tanya*, states that it is almost

impossible to perform an act of pure giving, without any intention of receiving something in return. How is it possible to check whether one's behavior is wholly benevolent or mingled with personal concerns?

SHABBAT LUNCH: The Afterlife

And it came to pass . . . that the ground split beneath them [Korach and his followers]. The earth opened her mouth, and swallowed them up, and their houses, and all the men that were allied with Korach, and all their goods. They, and all that belonged to them, went down alive to *She'ol* [the nether world], and the earth closed upon them, and they perished from among the congregation. [Numbers 16:31-33]

Korach had impugned the authority of Moses and, together with all of his family and followers, was swallowed alive. Yet the Torah mysteriously notes later that "The children of Korach did not die" (Numbers 26:11). The Talmud (*Sanhedrin* 110a) and its commentaries explain that the children of Korach descended with him to *She'ol* (purgatory), but because of their remorse over their actions, a special place was created for them there. Somewhere in the depths of *She'ol*, says the Talmud, they forever sing, "Moses and his Torah is true, and we are impostors."

How does Judaism understand what happens to someone after death?

Notwithstanding several references to this obscure region *She'ol*, the Torah does not directly address the issue of life after death. Furthermore, there seems to be no consensus in the sources of what happens in the Afterlife.

Some commentators, based on an allusion in the first book of Samuel (25:29) which describes the soul being "tossed about, as if from a slingshot (*kaf hakalah*)," understand that the first stage of life after death is characterized by perpetual affliction and agony of the soul. In this stage, the soul watches and reviews its life *again and again*, feeling increasing distress over moments wasted and decisions poorly made. The remorse felt over each unfulfilled moment of life serves as a "cleansing process" (*tikkun*) for the soul, which provides correction for the person's failures in this world. Until one feels complete regret over each nonactualized moment, the soul is forced to "toss and turn" without rest.

Though not mentioned in either biblical or talmudic sources, the Kabbalah described an intricate system of reincarnation (*gilgul neshamot*), in which the soul, after departing from one's body, would return to the physical world in succeeding generations. Rabbi Moshe Chaim Luzzatto, an eighteenth-century mystic and author, wrote that a soul would continually be united with a new body until it had fulfilled its destined purpose in this world; each new cycle would perfect flaws of a previous life. Luzzato wrote, though, that it is impossible for human beings to understand why or how this occurs. Nevertheless he considered himself (Moshe/Moses) and his wife, Tzipporah, to be somehow the incarnations of the souls of their biblical namesake, Moses and Tzipporah.

Following a more rationalist approach, Maimonides wrote that one should not dwell on matters of the Afterlife, because "concerning all of these things, a person will not understand them until they happen . . . they are not the essence of Judaism" (Laws of Judges, 12:2). Similarly, the Maharal of Prague (1525–1609) wrote that the "The World to Come" is not mentioned in the Torah so that one will focus all efforts and attention to the perfection of this world.

The whereabouts of the children of Korach remain a mystery.

Around the *Shabbat* Table

1. Which of the approaches mentioned above (Luzzato, Maimonides, or Maharal) appeals most to you? Why?

2. Did you ever know someone who had a near-death experience or "saw their life flash before their eyes"? How did it affect them?

3. Do you ever think about the Afterlife? Does this affect or concern your present living?

Seuda Shlishit: Leading Astray

Korach's pride caused him to lead himself and his followers astray. He exploited his position of leadership for personal gains.

Two hundred years ago, the hasidic rabbi, Ya'akov Yosef of Polonnoye (d. c.1782), bitterly castigated the leaders of his generation for their egotistical behavior. One of the foremost students of the Ba'al Shem Tov and a major ideologue of the hasidic movement, he caustically wrote of "two plagues" of his generation:

> Our souls are sick of listening to *hazzanim* (cantors), for in every fine and pious community the plague has spread. They sin and bring others to sin. When they prolong their melodies without end, the people gossip in the synagogue, interrupting the silence of prayer at times when it is forbidden to interrupt. Therefore the *hazzan* brings evil upon himself and upon others. Originally, I heard, he sang devoutly and without payment, for the *hazzan* was the most important person in the city ... But in the course of time, when the generation was no longer pure, only the melody remained, while the *hazzan* ceased to pray at all ... Woe for the disgrace! How has he the shamelessness to stand up as the advocate, the messenger of the congregation ... ?
>
> A plague has spread among the rabbis regarding the sermons they preach on the Sabbath before Passover and on the Sabbath of Repentance (the *Shabbat* before Yom Kippur). For the principal purpose of the sermon should be to show the people the path upon which they should tread ... But at the present time it is otherwise, for the rabbis use most of their sermons to display their brilliance and their knowledge, while toward the end they just mention a few laws regarding Passover and none at all on the Sabbath of Repentance. [*Toldot Ya'akov Yosef*]

Around the *Shabbat* Table

1. Have you ever encountered examples of the "two plagues" that Rabbi Ya'akov Yosef spoke about? Have you encountered cantors or rabbis who did not exhibit these qualities? Who?

2. Rabbi Ya'akov Yosef did not seek to abolish positions of leadership, but rather to instill these positions with a new vitality. He wrote at length of the *tzaddik* (the holy or completely righteous leader)—a figure who would serve as the connection between "the heavens and the earth," between God and the people, regarding all matters of life. The establishment of this position aroused the anger of the more conventional leaders, who feared that it would encourage an almost cult-like circle of followers. Have you ever met someone who you would consider to be a *tzaddik*? Do you share the concerns of those who opposed this institution?

3. Have you ever been in a position of leadership in which you struggled with feelings of vanity over your accomplishments?

Chukkat

FRIDAY NIGHT MEAL: Mysteries

The name of this week's *parsha*, *Chukkat*, comes from the term *chok*, which refers to decrees that reflect the mysterious and inexplicable ways of God. Unlike *mishpatim*, laws that the human being can potentially comprehend, *chukim*, by definition, remain beyond the scope of human comprehension and are utterly unfathomable. The *parsha* begins with the preeminent example of a *chok*, the purification of a person who has become defiled (through contact with a dead body) by sprinkling the ashes of a red heifer over him or her. This *parsha* symbolizes that which is beyond human understanding; thus, it comes as no surprise that its unifying theme is the reality and mystery of death.

In this week's *parsha*, the Torah jumps almost imperceptibly from the *second* year of the wandering of the Jewish people in the desert to the *fortieth*. The generation of the Exodus from Egypt, the generation that had cried over the evil report of the spies, has died. The deaths of Moses' sister, Miriam, and brother, Aaron, are also related in this week's *parsha*.

One of the most baffling and perplexing events of the *parsha* is God's punishment of Moses—forbidding him to lead the Jewish people into the Promised Land.

After the death of Miriam, the Jewish people complained about their lack of water. God then tells Moses:

> Take the rod, and gather the assembly together, you, and Aaron your brother, and *speak* to the rock before their eyes; and it will give forth its water, and you will give the congregation and their beasts drink. And Moses took the rod from before the Lord, as He commanded him. And Moses and Aaron gathered the congregation together before the rock, and he said to them, "Hear now, *you rebels*; will *we* bring water out of this rock for you?" And Moses lifted up his hand, and *hit* the rock with his stick *two times*; and the water came out abundantly, and the congregation drank, and their beasts also.
>
> And the Lord spoke to Moses and Aaron, "Because you did not believe in Me, to sanctify Me in the eyes of the children of Israel, therefore you will not *bring* this congregation in to the land which I have given them." [Numbers 20:8-12]

What exactly was Moses' sin? What could have been so wrong that the faithful leader of the Jewish people for forty years would never finish his life's task of bringing the people into the land?

The exact nature of Moses is never revealed in the Torah. Numerous theories abound. According to Maimonides, Moses' sin was his outburst of anger in front of the whole congregation, calling them "*you rebels*" (Introduction to *Pirkei Avot*, Chap. 4). Maimonides assumed that a leader of Moses' stature should have been able to control his frustration. Rashi writes that Moses was told to "*speak* to the rock," and by *hitting it* he reduced the profoundness of the moment. Nachmanides attributes the source of Moses' mistake to his hitting the rock *twice*, as if two different sources of the miracle were communicating with him.

Moses does not utter a word of protest upon receiving his punishment of not bringing the people into the land. The punishment appears to focus on the failure of leadership, since it implies that he no longer merits *bringing* the people into the land.

Forty years earlier, when the Jewish people complained over the lack of water in the desert (see "*Beshallach*: Growing Pains"), Moses was told to hit the rock to bring forth water (Exodus 17:1-7). Forty years later, Moses hears a similar complaint, yet now it arises from a different generation. Nevertheless, *he responds in exactly the same manner as before*: he hits the rock. Perhaps one of the qualities of leadership is knowing how to react differently to each situation, never relying upon earlier accomplishments, and Moses' response had not changed despite the elapsing of time and changing of the generation.

Notwithstanding the countless attempts to understand this moment in history, it appears that it will forever remain a *chok*, an eternal mystery, hidden both to the Jewish people and Moses.

Around the *Shabbat* Table

1. Which of the various explanations of Moses' sin mentioned previously do you think is the most plausible? Why do you think that the Torah never disclosed the actual reason?

2. This week's *parsha* remains one of the most mysterious in all of the Torah. Why do you think that the Torah sets forth rules or experiences that are, by definition, beyond human understanding?

3. Despite receiving notification of this heartbreaking punishment, Moses continued to lead the people until his death. How have you grappled with your greatest disappointment?

SHABBAT LUNCH: Anger

In this week's *parsha*, once again, the people complain about their life in the desert. Before Moses hits the rock, he reprimands them, saying, "Hear now, you rebels; from this rock shall we bring forth water for you?!" (Numbers 20:10). Moses, who had previously been described as the "most humble man on the face of the earth" (Numbers 12:3), seems to explode in anger. As discussed previously, according to several commentators, including Maimonides, it was because of this outburst that Moses was punished and not allowed to lead the Jewish people into the Promised Land.

Anger is sometimes provoked by seemingly insignificant annoyances or by feelings of wounded pride or self-respect. Yet neither of these explanations seem applicable to Moses. After selflessly guiding the people for almost forty years in the desert, why did Moses suddenly become so enraged?

The Talmud (*Tannit* 4a) explains that a person's yearning for truth and the improvement of the world can also lead to exasperation and short-temperedness. This anger is not a result of feelings of personal affront or injury; rather, it is motivated by a sense of frustration and despair over the increasing gap between an ideal world and the present reality. Leaders are especially subject to these feelings of disappointment. Maimonides writes that when community leaders perceive the need to reprove their constituents, they should "*show a face*" of anger, while never *actually* becoming angry. In order to effectively discipline the community, leaders should appear to be angry, they may assume a facade of harshness or severity, but they should remain calm and level-headed within.

For a moment, Moses *actually* became angry. He lost perspective of the nature and the emotional make-up of the people and lost sight of what they needed and why they complained. For a moment, he did not focus on their needs but on his own pain, and he was overcome with his frustration at not having successfully raised the people beyond their immediate needs. Thus, his anger was not educational, but personal.

The Torah, of course, never prohibits becoming angry. As seen from the fact that even Moses got angry, it is apparently an aspect of human nature that is impossible to completely sublimate or deny. Nevertheless, anger was considered to be self-indulgent and was strongly condemned by the rabbis of the Talmud and major Jewish thinkers.

The primary danger inherent in becoming angry is losing self-control. The Mishnah (*Pirkei Avot* 4:18) states that it is futile to try and comfort others when they are furious or outraged, as they are incapable of listening and reasoning clearly. The Talmud states that one who becomes angry is virtually committing idolatry; either one *controls oneself*, or one becomes *controlled* by something else. The *Zohar* remarks that during consuming moments of rage, it is as if one is under the spell of the "drug of death."

Perhaps audaciously, the Talmud (*Berakhot* 7a) discusses what God asks for during God's own prayers. God's first prayer is, "Let it be My will that My mercy will conquer My anger."

Around the *Shabbat* Table

1. The mishnah of *Pirkei Avot* (5:11) cites four types of personalities:

    1. Easy to become angry and easy to be pacified
    2. Hard to become angry and hard to be pacified
    3. Hard to become angry and easy to be pacified
    4. Easy to become angry and hard to be pacified
        Which type are you? Do you know anyone who fits the third category?

2. The seventh blessing of the *Amidah* (silent standing prayer) can be understood as a request to be granted the strength not to be-

come upset over the countless, though minute, irritating moments during the day. How can this be achieved?

3. Have you ever shown a "face of anger" while remaining calm within? What enabled you to control yourself?

Seuda Shlishit: Learning How to Die

This week's *parsha*, *Chukkat*, deals with the mystery of death.

The great hasidic masters approached the moment of passing without panic or fear.

When the hour arrived for Rabbi Simcha Bunam from Psyshcha to depart from the world, his wife stood by his bedside and wept bitterly. He said to her, "Be silent—why do you cry? My whole life was only that I might learn how to die."

On the day of his death, the Ba'al Shem Tov told his followers, "I am not worried about myself, for I know clearly that I shall go from this door and immediately enter another door." He sat down on his bed and told his students to stand around him. He prayed with great concentration and devotion, until the syllables of his words could no longer be distinguished. He told them to cover him with blankets and began to shake and tremble as he used to do when he prayed the Silent Prayer. Little by little he grew quiet. They waited until they saw that he had begun his journey through the next door.

Before his death, Rabbi Abraham Joshua Heschel from Apt moaned bitterly over the exile of his people and over the fact that the Messiah had tarried in coming. Finally he cried out, "The Rabbi of Berditchev said before he died that when he arrived up there he would not rest nor be silent, nor would he allow any of the holy ones to rest or be silent until the Messiah would come. But when he came there, the beauties and wonders of heaven overwhelmed him, so that he forgot about this. But I," concluded the Rabbi of Apt, "I shall not forget."

Rabbi Sussya from Plozk raised his head at midnight and recited the verse "At midnight I rise to praise You," and with these words his soul departed from him.

Around the *Shabbat* Table

1. What do you think that Rabbi Simcha Bunam of Psyshcha meant
    by "My whole life was only that I might learn how to die?"

2. The Ba'al Shem Tov told his followers, "I am not worried about
    myself, for I know clearly that I shall go from this door and imme-
    diately enter another door." How do you think that this understand-
    ing of death might affect the way in which one lives?

3. Do you know anyone who is not afraid of the mystery of death?

Balak

FRIDAY NIGHT MEAL: A Contentious Witness

This week's *parsha*, *Balak*, is arguably the most unusual story in the whole Torah. Its primary figures include two non-Jews—Balak, the king of Mo'ab, and Bila'am, the leader and spiritual force of Midyan—as well as Bila'am's mule, who both talks and sees angels. The *parsha* does not impart Jewish law, and virtually no active role is taken either by individual Jews or the Jewish nation.

What is the message of this *parsha*? What eternal struggle is being depicted here? Furthermore, why does this struggle occur precisely at this moment in the travels of the Jewish people?

The book of *Bamidbar* chronicles the growth of the Jewish people from their second to their fortieth year in the desert. It describes a journey from childhood to adulthood, from dependence to independence. Last week's *parsha*, *Chukkat*, recounted the deaths of Miriam and Aaron. The Jewish people were aware that Moses would not bring them into the Promised Land, and thus soon they would be utterly bereft of the leaders who brought them out of Egypt and nurtured them during their forty years in the desert. Their present condition seemed full of confusion and vulnerability. They had already suffered a multitude of crises, including having been misled by those in positions of authority (the spies) and being witness to a failed rebellion (*Korach*). Soon, upon leaving the desert, their existence would be drastically transformed; no longer would they be graced with the *manna* from heaven or God's unambiguous presence. What would give them the strength to carry on?

In this *parsha*, Balak, the king of Mo'ab, is nervous over the impending approach of the Jewish people. He has previously witnessed the Jewish people request to pass through the land of the Emorites on their way to the Promised Land. Sichon, the Emorite king, denied them passage and launched war against them. In the ensuing battle, he and his people were conclusively defeated. Though the Jewish people harbored no intentions of conquering Mo'ab, their previous victory worried Balak. Concerned that he did not possess the military resources to defeat the Jewish people, he summoned Bila'am to weaken them through his power of speech. "Please come now and curse this people for me, for they are too mighty for me. Perhaps together we may defeat them, and I [Balak] will drive them out of the land, for I know that whomever you [Bila'am] bless will be blessed, and whomever you curse will be cursed" (Numbers 22:6).

Bila'am complied with Balak's request and attempted to denounce the Jews. Yet each time he opened his mouth, only blessings came forth. Three separate times Bila'am disappointed Balak with his words of praise for the Jewish people:

Who can count the dust of Jacob, and number a quarter of Israel? Let me die the death of the righteous, and let my last end be like his [Jacob's]. [Numbers 23:10]

God has not beheld iniquity in Jacob nor has He seen perverseness in Israel, the Lord his God is with him, and the trumpet blast of a king is among them.... Behold, the people will rise up as a great lion, and lift up itself as a young lion; it will not lie down until it eats of the prey.... [Numbers 23:21, 24]

How goodly are your tents, Jacob, and your dwellings, Israel. Like the winding brooks, like gardens by the river's side, like aloes which the Lord has planted, and cedar trees beside the waters . . . it will eat up the nations, its enemies, and will break their bones, and pierce them through with its arrows. It lies down like a lion, and like a great lion, who will stir him up? Blessed is he that blesses you, and cursed is he that curses you. [Numbers 24:5-9]

The story of Bila'am comes to clarify to the Jewish people who they truly are and what singular powers they possess. Testimony, conceptually and legally, is suspect when it comes from someone who has a vested interest in giving it. Thus, according to Jewish law, relatives may not serve as witnesses for each other. Only when the witness will not stand to personally benefit from his or her testimony is it most likely to be totally valid and truthful. Bila'am was offered riches and honor from Balak to denounce the Jewish people. Yet, as Bila'am himself stated, "[it is] the word that God puts into my mouth, that I shall speak" (Numbers 22:38).

Ironically, precisely because of his evil character and intentions, the praise that he eventually uttered is regarded as being thoroughly impartial and truthful. Bila'am had no vested interest in praising the Jewish people. Only his utterances could truly convey to the Jewish people their power and righteousness. His words, "How goodly are your tents, Jacob, and your dwellings, Israel," have been incorporated into the daily prayerbook. In the midst of the confusion and vulnerability of the Jewish people, who faced the daunting prospect of becoming independent, comes the voice of Bila'am to remind them of their remarkable gifts, blessings, and potential.

Around the *Shabbat* Table

1. In rabbinic literature, despite the fact that Bila'am praised the Jewish people, he is portrayed very negatively. The mishnah *(Pirkei Avot* 5:19) counts him among the four individuals who forfeited their place in the world to come *(Sanhedrin* 10:2). How would you judge him?

2. The Mishnah attributes three qualities to Bila'am: "an evil eye, a haughty temperament, and an insatiable spirit." In contrast, Abraham is said to demonstrate "a good eye, a modest temperament, and a humble spirit." Bila'am was clearly blessed with spiritual powers, yet he could not direct them positively. Do you think that it is unusual for someone to be spiritually gifted yet not righteous? What advice or education would you have given to Bila'am?

3. Did you ever learn something positive about yourself from what an adversary of yours said about you?

SHABBAT LUNCH: Temptation

In this week's *parsha*, Balak, the king of Mo'ab, entreats Bila'am to curse the Jewish people for him. He implores Bila'am, saying, "Let nothing I pray, hinder your coming to me, for I will give you great honor, and anything that you say to me I will do; please come and curse this people for me" (Numbers 22:16, 17). Bila'am could not resist Balak's invitation; the temptation of honor and wealth precluded any possibility of refusal.

Who is the guilty party here? The person who tempted or the person who actually commited the crime?

Judaism affirms that "an individual cannot claim that he was just a messenger perpetrating the transgression" (*Bava Kamma* 79a). The one who actually commits the violation is held responsible, and cannot contend that he was simply following orders. Each human being possesses free will and is consequently held accountable for his actions.

Nevertheless, is the one who tempts completely innocent? Isn't he also responsible for the eventual outcome of his suggestion or request?

An answer can be found in the Torah's prohibition against placing a "stumbling block before the blind" (Leviticus 19:14). What exactly is a "stumbling block?" Is the verse talking only about someone who is physically blind?

The commentators extend the "blind" person in the verse to include two additional categories: "blindness of the mind" and "blindness of the heart."

"Blindness of the mind" refers to someone who is lacking in a particular area of knowledge—that is, who is blind regarding a certain matter. "Not putting a stumbling block in front of the blind" thus becomes an injunction against giving improper advice. The Midrash relates that if a person is not financially astute, one should not encourage him to sell his belongings so that one can then purchase them. Similarly, if someone asks for advice concerning a potential spouse, one should not assure him or her that the spouse is appropriate if he or she is not. Both of these things are considered to be placing a stumbling block before the blind.

"Blindness of the heart" applies to a person who possesses the requisite information, yet who is still *blinded by an uncontrollable desire*. Thus, the biblical prohibition against placing a stumbling block before the blind would admonish us against offering food or drink to someone who may not have the willpower to resist. Similarly, one should not lend money without witnesses, lest the borrower be tempted to deny the transaction.

If people do, in fact, fail because a "stumbling block" was placed in front of them, Jewish law rejects the claim of "I didn't force them; they're adults and they decided for themselves." Precisely because we are human and have weaknesses, we are obligated to help each other overcome "blind spots." Nevertheless, there is no punishment for one who transgresses this injunction. No judge or observer can ever really know what was the true intention behind the bad advice, since the person who gave the advice can always (falsely) assert that "I really had his best interests in mind." The prohibition against placing a stumbling block comes to remind us that we are ultimately held accountable not only for our actions, but for our words, and not only for our words but also for our intentions.

Around the *Shabbat* Table

1. The verse that prohibits placing a stumbling block before the blind begins, "You should not curse the deaf." Why not? Who really suffers? Is there a connection between the two parts of this verse?

2. Applications of the "stumbling block" principle range from the need for clear traffic signs to the restriction of weapons sales nations that cannot be trusted to control them. The field of advertising is especially vulnerable to violations of "putting a stumbling block in front of the blind." Why? Can you think of ramifications of this principle in business, political life, or contemporary society?

3. Have you ever struggled with the sincerity of the advice that you were giving? How did you clarify to yourself that it was truly for the benefit of the receiver?

Seuda Shlishit: Solitary Meditation

It is a people that shall dwell *alone*. [Numbers 23:9]

The non-Jewish prophet Bila'am declared that the Jewish people would forever remain separate from the other nations of the world. Their destiny is to remain singularly alone. Is it a blessing or a curse to be alone?

The hasidic leader Rebbe Nachman of Bratslav wrote extensively of the spiritual value of spending time alone. He insisted that in order to become closer to God, one had to undergo a process of *hitbodedut*, of being alone with oneself. "The only way to fully move beyond one's self and ego, and to become capable of talking directly to God, is through *hitbodedut*." Still today, the essential prayer experience of the Bratslav hasidim takes place in solitude.

Rebbe Nachman wrote of three primary criteria for successful *hitbodedut*:

Time. The essence of *hitbodedut* is at night, when people can free themselves from concerns of this-worldly matters. Even if one thinks that he or she can find moments of focus during the day, the pressures and nonspiritual pulse of the world necessarily impinge upon concentration.

Location. Moments of *hitbodedut* must occur in a special place, outside of populated areas. Even if a person is alone, the effect of being in a place where others have been recently will disturb the purity and intensity of the *hitbodedut*.

Outpouring of one's heart. In *hitbodedut*, one must sincerely and unreservedly open one's heart. Rebbe Nachman notes several stages in this process. An individual should begin simply by trying to talk with God and should not despair if he or she manages only to say a word or two. One should wait and persist in the *hitbodedut* until the effect of being alone in a special place enables one to begin to talk about one's self, one's life, and one's desires. Eventually, this process of speaking moves the individual to an awareness that is beyond speech. Then, in a special place, alone, in silence, one can become, in the words of Rebbe Nachman, "wholly at one with the source of all reality."

Around the *Shabbat* Table

1. A. B. Yehoshua, contemporary Israeli author and winner of the Israeli prize for literature, takes issue with the value of Jewish separatism. He writes that "The need to find difference must be gotten rid of once and for all ... I repeat this simple truth, that the Jewish people is a people like all peoples, and am astonished to discover to what extent it does not appear simple to many ...We must grab hold of this deep-lying notion [of being different] and slowly try to root it out" (*Between Right and Right*, 1982). Do you think that it is possible and/or advantageous to "root out" the separation between the Jewish people and the other nations?

2. Rebbe Nachman describes the importance of finding special times and places to achieve a state of aloneness. What special time of day or place would you choose to foster a "spiritual conversation"? Have you ever experienced a moment of *hitbodedut* like he describes?

3. What do you think are the advantages of meditation? The disadvantages?

Pinchas

FRIDAY NIGHT MEAL: A Covenant of Broken Peace

B ila'am, the main figure in last week's *parsha*, did not succeed in cursing the Jewish people. To the chagrin of Balak, the king of Mo'ab, who repeatedly implored Bila'am to denounce the Jewish people, words of praise continually sprang forth from Bila'am's mouth. Nevertheless, at the very end of last week's *parsha*, the Jewish people are finally entrapped by the sexual promiscuity and idolatry of Mo'ab, " ... and the people began to commit harlotry with the daughters of Mo'ab. And they called the people to the sacrifices of their gods, and the people ate, and bowed down to their gods" (Numbers 25:1, 2). Tens of thousands of Jews are involved in this behavior and incur the wrath of God.

This week's *parsha* opens with God bestowing a "covenant of peace" upon Pinchas: "And the Lord spoke to Moses, saying, 'Pinchas, the son of Elazar, the son of Aaron the priest, has turned My wrath away from the children of Israel, in that he was *zealous* for My sake among them ... Behold, I give to him My *covenant of peace* (*brit shalom*), and he shall have it, and his seed after him, the covenant of an everlasting priesthood; because he was *zealous* for his God, and made atonement for the children of Israel'" (Numbers 25:10–13).

What exactly did Pinchas do? What was his zealousness? Countless good and principled acts are never rewarded in the Torah, so why did Pinchas merit this gift of the "covenant of peace"?

The Torah states that one of the community's leaders, Zimri ben Salu, had publicly flouted the leadership of Moses. According to the Talmud (*Sanhedrin* 82a), in front of the entire congregation of Israel, Zimri issued a public challenge to Moses and dared him to judge whether Kozbi, a Midianite woman, was permitted or forbidden to him. Zimri's question put Moses in an extremely awkward position, since Moses himself had married a Midianite woman, Tzipporah, long before the exodus from Egypt. How could Moses therefore claim that it was proscribed? Moses stood speechless, unable to respond to Zimri's challenge. Witnessing this confrontation and breakdown, the Jewish people began to cry (Numbers 25:6).

Only Pinchas rose above the shock of this trauma. "And when Pinchas . . . saw it [Zimri and Kozbi, the Midianite woman, cohabiting], he rose up from among the congregation, and took a spear in his hand . . . and thrust it through both of them" (Numbers 25:7, 8). With a single thrust, he killed them both. In a moment of unrestrained zeal, Pinchas had stopped the Jewish people from descending to the immorality of the Midianites. Nevertheless, he had brutally murdered a man and a woman.

What is the effect of this action upon Pinchas himself? What happens to a person who has performed an act of violence, even when it is justified or heroic? Nachmanides writes of the unavoidable damage to oneself incurred by engaging in violence, even when it is legitimate and warranted. The very zealousness that Pinchas needed to perform his act of bravery bears within it the power to coarsen and desensitize his being, which may ultimately destroy him. One act of violence may make a succeeding act less offensive, resulting in a spiraling and uncontrollable cycle of zealotry. Having unleashed this power of zealousness, will Pinchas now be able to control it, or will this passion eventually consume and overpower him?

Pinchas is rewarded with the "covenant of peace." He is assured that his essential nature will not become corrupted; he will forever be reminded that his zealousness was for the sake of peace. However, he will always be reminded of the scarring effect of such a violent act. The word in the Torah denoting this covenant of "peace," *shalom*, is written with a broken letter—part of its "vav" is missing. This serves as a reminder that the experience and memory of Pinchas's act will forever diminish the "peace" that he will merit. Pinchas is honored for his valor, for unhesitatingly responding to the crisis at hand. At the same time, however, there is no glorification of zealousness or acts of violence.

Around the *Shabbat* Table

1. Pinchas is rewarded for his action, yet the Talmud (*Sanhedrin* 82a) states that if Pinchas had come to ask Moses' opinion, he would not have been allowed to perform this act. "The one who comes to ask, should not be approved." What do you think that this source reflects on the nature of zealousness?

2. Hasidic leaders wrote that Pinchas was naturally a fiery personality and that he succeeded in directing this trait toward a positive end. Do you know anyone with this "zealous" quality? Have you ever seen it used positively? Negatively?

3. How does one know whether to trust zeal? Is there anything for which you would consider yourself zealous?

SHABBAT LUNCH: *"Shalom Bayit"*

In this week's *parsha*, the institution of the Jewish family is on the verge of breaking down. Tens of thousands of Jews are having sexual relations with Midianite women, and a leader of the Jewish people publicly announces that he intends to cohabit with the daughter of a Midianite leader. Pinchas kills both the Jewish leader and the Midianite woman, thwarts the people's rebellion, and is rewarded with the "covenant of peace" (*brit shalom*).

Even without such external provocation, Judaism regards the survival and health of the family unit to be both crucially important and precariously fragile. In many aspects, the health of the whole community and nation depends on the strength and stability of its individual family units (see:"Home Schooling").The Talmud (*Shabbat* 23b) states that if a person has only one candle to light and must decide whether to use it for *Shabbat* or for Hanukah, the lighting of *Shabbat* candles takes precedence because their light provides *shalom bayit* (peace at home) and supersedes the publicizing of the national miracle of Hanukah.

Yet the expression *shalom bayit* points to an inherent difficulty, since the term *shalom* implies harmony between two potentially conflicting forces. "Peace" is only requisite when there exists the possibility of discord.These two potentially discordant forces seem to form the very keystone of creation.The Talmud (*Bava Batra* 74b) states that "everything that God created in this world, He created male and female"; that is, everything in the world is composed of two essentially different elements, male and female.Though theTorah declares that men and women are essentially equal—"*male and female*, God created *them*" (Genesis 1:27)—nevertheless, they are so utterly different that the Talmud refers to them as two separate species.

Jewish sources highlight some of the primary differences between men and women:

The midrash comments on two seemingly inconsistent verses:

"Honor your *father* and your *mother* . . . " (Exodus 20: 12), and "Every person should fear his *mother* and *father* . . . " (Leviticus 19:3).

Why do these two verses present "mother" and "father" in the opposite order? Why, when discussing "honor," is the father placed first, whereas when discussing "fear," the mother precedes the father? The midrash explains:

> It is a clear and known thing in the eyes of The Creator that a person *honors his mother more than his father, since she speaks often with him.*Therefore the Torah placed the father before the mother concerning the obligation to honor one's parent.
>
> And it is a clear and known thing in the eyes of the Creator that a person *fears his father more than his mother, since the father teaches him Torah.*Therefore the Torah placed the mother before the father concerning obligation to fear one's parent.

While neither parent has a monopoly on speaking with his or her children or teaching them Torah, nevertheless, the midrash reflects a different approach to both of these behaviors on behalf of the father and mother. The mother "speaks often" with the child, denoting a more listening and empathetic personality. The mother attempts to understand the whole world of the child, and this results in a relationship of closeness, described as "honoring." The father, by contrast, is concerned with fulfilling a singular goal—teaching the child Torah. The nature of this "goal-oriented" parent–child relationship is measured by the success or failure of the objective. This is often achieved through reward and punishment and results in a more distant relationship, characterized by "fear."

Shalom bayit is predicated on understanding the differences between the two partners and responding to them accordingly. Often, *shalom bayit* breaks down when one partner expects the other to react exactly like he or she would. Frustrations and disappointments may arise from this type of inappropriate expectation. Clearly, the guidelines of the Talmud are general, and every relationship develops its own unique character and dynamic. The challenge of *shalom bayit,* the creation of a home with peace, harmony, and mutual respect, may be regarded as the first step in the redeeming of the Jewish people and the perfecting of the world.

Around the *Shabbat* Table

1. The Talmud (*Yevamot* 65b, *Niddah* 45b) states that a man is more likely to be concerned with acquiring control and exerting power, whereas a woman is more likely to create situations of cooperation and shared responsibility and authority. Do you agree? What ramifications might this have for *shalom bayit?*

2. The Talmud sanctions the "bending" of the truth in order to maintain *shalom bayit.* "Great is peace, because even God changed [the truth] for its sake" (*Bava Metziah* 87a). Why do you think that in the context of *shalom bayit,* truth is not an ultimate value?

3. Do you agree with the gender differences presented here? Are there any other differences that you would assert? Do you think that the differences are primarily the result of "nature" or "nurture"?

Seuda Shlishit: Religious Extremism

Pinchas exemplifies the quality of zealousness, as he acts on his beliefs without concern for the potentially hazardous or detrimental consequences. Over 1,000 years later, subsequent to the destruction of the Second Temple, another figure becomes synonymous with fervent zealotry.

The Talmud (*Shabbat* 33b) relates how Rabbi Shimon Bar Yochai, one of the foremost rabbis of Talmud and the reputed author of the mystical work the *Zohar,* was forced to flee because of his relentlessly outspoken and zealous behavior.

Rabbi Yehuda, Rabbi Yossi, and Rabbi Shimon (Bar Yochai) were sitting together with Yehuda ben Garim. Rabbi Yehuda began the conversation by saying, "How wonderful are the actions of this [the Roman] nation. They set up marketplaces, constructed bridges, and built bathhouses." Rabbi Yossi remained silent. Rabbi Shimon responded by saying, "Everything they built, they only built for their own benefit. They set up marketplaces—to sit prostitutes in them. Bathhouses—to beautify themselves. Bridges—to take taxes."

Yehuda ben Garim went and spread their words until they reached the Roman authorities. The Romans said, "Yehuda who praised—will be promoted; Yossi who was silent—will be exiled to Tzippori; Shimon who denounced us—will be executed."

Rabbi Shimon and his son went and hid in the *Beit Midrash* [the house of learning]. Every day his wife would bring them bread and water. The decree became more severe . . . and they went and hid in a cave. A miracle happened and a carob tree and spring of water appeared in the cave . . . all day they learned . . . they stayed in the cave for twelve years. [Finally,] Elijah [the prophet] came and announced that the Roman ruler had died and that the decree had been nullified.

Rabbi Shimon and his son went out of the cave. They saw men plowing and sowing fields. Rabbi Shimon exclaimed, "Look at these men, they are forsaking eternal life [the study of Torah] and engaging in the transitory concerns of this world [agriculture]!" Every spot that Rabbi Shimon and his son would place their eyes would immediately be consumed with fire. A voice from heaven called out to them, "Did you leave the cave in order to destroy my world!? Go back to your cave!" They returned to the cave for another twelve months . . .

After the twelve months the voice from heaven called to them, "Leave your cave." They went out . . . it was Friday afternoon, just before *Shabbat,* and they saw an old man running, holding two clusters of myrtle leaves in his hands. They asked him what the myrtle was for. He told them, "To give honor to *Shabbat.*" They asked him, "Isn't one cluster enough for you?" He answered them, "One is for the 'keeping' of *Shabbat,* and one is for the 'guarding' of *Shabbat* [corresponding to the two different times *Shabbat* is mentioned in the Ten Commandments]."

Thereupon Rabbi Shimon told his son, "Look how beloved the mitzvot are to the Jewish people," and his zealousness was calmed.

The burning fire of Rabbi Shimon Bar Yochai was transformed as he realized the possibility of harmonizing the spiritual and physical worlds through the physical enjoyment of *Shabbat*. For hundreds of years, on the anniversary of his death (Lag B'Omer), bonfires are burned throughout Jewish communities, commemorating his passion and zeal.

Around the *Shabbat* Table

1. What does the particular hiding place that Rabbi Shimon Bar Yochai chose—a *cave*—symbolize? What do you think would be today's equivalent of "going into a cave"?

2. The Torah mentions the zealousness of Pinchas; the book of Kings in the Bible relates the zealousness of Elijah; the Talmud speaks about Rabbi Shimon Bar Yochai. Do you think that religious belief is especially prone to extreme behavior and views?

3. How would you have participated in the discussion of Rabbi Yehuda, Rabbi Yossi, and Rabbi Shimon? Do you think that this story has relevance today?

Mattot/Masei

FRIDAY NIGHT MEAL: Traveling *To* or *From*?

How would we have expected the book of *Bamidbar* to end? The book of *Bamidbar* marks the transition from the generation of Jews that worked in slavery in Egypt, to the generation of Jews that was born in the desert and will now enter into the Promised Land. *Bamidbar* chronicles the crises and developments of the Jewish people during their 40 years of wandering, and now, at its close, the Jewish people are on the verge of leaving this desert, the *midbar*.

The final *parsha* of *Bamidbar*, *Masei*, opens with Moses' recounting of all locations of the journeys of the Jewish people during their forty years in the desert. For almost fifty verses, a list of forty-two journeys is mentioned, echoing with the refrain "and they journeyed . . . and they encamped." Place after place is mentioned, most of them never spoken of before or afterward in the Torah, for example, "and they journeyed from Rissa, and encamped in Qehelata. And they journeyed from Qehelata and encamped in mount Shefer . . . " (Numbers 33:22, 23).

Why does Moses remind the Jewish people of all of their travels? What does this list convey to them?

At the beginning of this *parsha*, two different words are used to denote the travels of the Jewish people: "their goings out" and "their journeys." Each expression conveys a distinct state of mind. "Their goings out" denotes a retrospective outlook, of leaving their former home; whereas "their journeys" conveys a future-oriented attitude, with an emphasis on arriving at their destination. Every journey and transition necessarily involves these two moods. During their 40 years of wandering, the Jewish people continually waver between these two frames of mind, sometimes yearning for their former life in Egypt, sometimes yearning for the milk and honey of the unknown Promised Land.

When Moses recounts the forty-two encampments of the Jewish people, he uses one of these expressions exclusively: "and they journeyed." Again and again, the Jewish people hear this refrain, emphasizing their movement *toward* their goal. Furthermore, through recounting their wanderings, Moses enables them to relive their whole experience in the desert. They are reminded that their perpetual wandering was caused by the sin of the spies (see "*Shelach Lekha*: Generations of Crying"), by their fear of entering the land. Regardless of how terrible it might have been, in the eyes of this wandering nation, the concrete reality of Egypt had often been more attractive to them than the unknown reality of the Promised Land. At the end of these 40 years, Moses tries to make the Jewish people see themselves not as traveling *from* their former home but *toward* their desired destination.

The *Zohar* understands the recounting of these forty-two journeys on a mystical level. According to the Kabbalah, God brought the world into being by virtue of the first forty-two letters of the Torah, the forty-two building blocks or stages of creation. The forty-two stations of travel in this *parsha* echo the genesis of the world and reflect a second process of creation, a process that lasted forty years. Moses now tells them that, in fact, a new creation has occurred. The creation of the nation has paralleled the creation of the world.

For forty years the Jews journeyed "by the commandment of God" (Numbers 33:2); for forty years they were dependent upon the leadership of Moses, Aaron, and Miriam. Now they are entering the land and will begin to assume responsibility for their own leadership. Now, they will begin to control their own destiny. They have moved from childhood to adulthood, with all of the ensuing dilemmas and complications.

The route from slavery to freedom, from dependence to independence, has been circuitous, fraught with struggles and crises, both from without and from within. Isaac Abrabanal, who lived at the time of the Spanish inquisition and the expulsion of the Jews from Spain to new lands, wrote that these forty-two temporary stations of dwelling hint to the future, when once again, after their seemingly endless travels, the Jewish people will be gathered together and will come to the Promised Land.

Around the *Shabbat* Table

1. Why do you think that the first act of the first Jew, Abraham (Genesis 12), and one of the first acts of the Jewish people (Exodus 12) was a journey?

2. What do you think the Jews of today would feel if they were reminded of all of the locations of their travels of the last 2,000 years?

3. Has your family changed its location/country of inhabitancy during the last several generations? Did they see themselves as traveling "from" or "toward"?

SHABBAT LUNCH: Wealth

As the Jewish people ready themselves to cross into the Promised Land, two tribes ask Moses for permission not to enter into the Promised Land with the rest of their brethen. The tribes of Reuben and Gad had a great multitude of cattle and were eager to graze their flocks on the lush pastures east of the Jordan. Moses strongly rebukes them for being obsessed with their economic security and for placing their personal affairs before the concerns of the whole Jewish people. The request of these tribes is traditionally seen as synonymous with material greed.

Is there a Jewish attitude toward wealth?

The rabbis offer a number of different answers to the question "Who is rich?" The mishnah in *Pirkei Avot* (4:1) responds, "The one who is happy with his lot." The Talmud (*Shabbat* 25b) states four additional opinions:

> Rabbi Meir says, "Anyone who has pleasure [peace of mind] from his wealth."
> Rabbi Tarfon says, "Anyone who has a hundred vineyards, a hundred fields, and a hundred servants to work them."
> Rabbi Akiva says, "Anyone who has a wife of praiseworthy actions."
> Rabbi Yossi says, "Anyone who has a bathroom near his [dining room] table."

The first answer of the Talmud and that of *Pirkei Avot* seem to be similar. Wealth is not a quantifiable amount; rather, it is an attitude toward one's possessions. Often the acquisition of material wealth is accompanied by feelings of lacking or incompleteness. The acquisition brings a moment of joy but is soon replaced by the feeling of "Now I have this, but I still don't have that." Living in the state of mind of "if only I had that . . ." focuses a person's thoughts on what is missing and reflects a self-perception of deprivation. People who are "happy with their lot" or who have "peace of mind" from their belongings recognize that they will never be able to fulfill all material desires; they are freed from the mindset of eternally desiring something more and are able to enjoy their present situation.

The second opinion, that of Rabbi Tarfon, adds a social element to the understanding of wealth. If a person's possessions can contribute to the community's welfare (e.g., the production of wine), then he or she may be considered rich. The author of the third statement, Rabbi Akiva, who was known for his loving relationship with his wife while living in acute poverty (see "*Vayera*: Getting Closer"), sees true wealth as a function of a caring and meaningful relationship. Rabbi Akiva is stressing a love that not only reflects the closeness between the partners but also benefits the community and others, as evidenced in the phrase "praiseworthy actions."

Perhaps the most surprising answer is supplied by Rabbi Yossi, "anyone who has a bathroom near his [dining room] table." For Rabbi Yossi, symbolically, the truly wealthy person was not someone who continually acquired but rather someone who was able to relinquish his acquisitions. The danger in becoming materially wealthy is that one may become ruled by one's possessions. The ability to part with one's belongings verifies that one is not being controlled by them.

The Vilna Gaon extends Rabbi Yossi's understanding of wealth to the intellectual domain. Only one who is able to continually process and then discard ideas that no longer nourish him- or herself is truly intellectually wealthy.

Around the *Shabbat* Table

1. The tribes of Reuben and Gad were, initially, controlled by their material concerns. Eventually, Moses convinces them to cross into the Promised Land with the rest of the Jewish people and then to return to their fields and cattle (Chapter 32). What would you have said to them?

2. Jewish thinkers have written that, regarding moral behavior and belief in God, there are "tests of poverty" and "tests of wealth." The "test of wealth" is considered to be more difficult than the test of poverty. Why do you think that this is so?

3. Do you know people who exemplify the different answers (to "who is rich?") presented in this unit? With which of these categories do you most identify?

Seuda Shlishit: Wandering Jews

"These are the journeys of the children of Israel, who went out of
the land of Egypt. . . . " [Numbers 33:1]

For forty years, the Jewish people wander in the desert, setting up
and then leaving over forty different campsites. The Promised Land
seems like it will forever elude them.

Over sixty years ago, a group of Jews once again began to wander, in search of refuge. On May 3, 1939, the 937 Jews aboard the
passenger ship *St. Louis* departed from Hamburg and commenced
forty days of wandering at sea. The passengers, many of whom had
already spent time in concentration camps, sought asylum in Cuba.

Denied entry into Cuba, the *St. Louis* futilely pursued landing in
the United States, the Dominican Republic, and other islands in the
Caribbean. Ultimately, to the horror of its passengers, the ship turned
around and headed back toward Germany. Though the predicament
of the suffering Jews aroused international sympathy, Germany's
propaganda minister, Joseph Goebbels, exploited the plight of the
ship to declare to the world that Germany was the only country
willing to offer haven and accept the Jews. Suicide attempts and a
failed mutiny ensued.

In their book *Voyage of the Damned*, authors Gordon Thomas
and Max Morgan Witts describe the despair of the passenger com-
mittee that had to inform the other passengers of their impending
return to Europe:

> A terrible, personal realization touched each member of the passen-
> ger committee. They dared not say it openly, even to each other. Some
> could not bear even to mention it to their wives and children. It was
> inhuman, degrading and endured in private, but it cut deeply into one
> of the most basic of all human needs: the need to be wanted. Instead,
> they had been rejected. Even the New World did not want them; now
> they must rely again on the Old. The committee suffered in silence,
> knowing it was not just an anonymous group of people who had been

turned down, but that they, individually, each one, had had the open door shut in their faces; through them, their entire race had been judged, and found wanting. [p. 264]

Eventually, Belgium, Holland, and England begrudgingly consented to divide the passengers of the *St. Louis* among themselves. Physically and emotionally weary from their forty traumatic days at sea, the majority of these wandering Jews eventually died before the end of the war.

Around the *Shabbat* Table

1. The expression "Wandering Jew" has its sources in anti-Semitic literature, in which it refers to the fate of the sinner who is forced to wander, forever despised and rejected. Nevertheless, the Jewish people understood it as aptly describing their state of living in an imperfect world. Does this expression have a positive or negative connotation for you? Do you consider yourself to be a "Wandering Jew?"

2. The spies described the Land of Israel as "a land that consumes its inhabitants" (Numbers 13:32). The process of wandering naturally precludes one's becoming sedentary or complacent. Constant changes encourage personal development; settling down in one land, by contrast, may foster a greater sense of ease and contentment, hinder growth, and thus, in effect—"consume the inhabitants." Do you think that modern-day Israel is a land that consumes its inhabitants?

3. Was anyone in your family ever forced to leave his or her home? Does this memory affect your identity as a Jew today?

Deuteronomy

Devarim

FRIDAY NIGHT MEAL: Moses' Initiative

An era for the Jewish people is coming to a close. The Jewish people are in transition to a new reality; a reality bereft of God's clear gifts and guidance. Miriam and Aaron have passed away, Moses will be informed of his own imminent death, the mantle of leadership will soon be passed to Joshua.

In the midst of all these developments, a dramatic change subtly occurs.

The familiar expression of the Torah, "And *the Lord spoke* to Moses" is replaced by, "These are the words *which Moses spoke* to all Israel" (Deuteronomy 1:1). Moses, God's reluctant prophet who once stated that he was "not a man of words" (Exodus 4:10), now speaks to the Jewish people for the next thirty chapters of the book of Deuteronomy. Moses, originally "God's mouthpiece" to the Jewish people, now takes the initiative and chooses his own style and words. He recounts many incidents that occurred during the last 40 years, often changing the way they were originally presented in the Torah.

What impelled Moses to take this initiative—to convey his own words to the Jewish people?

Perhaps the key to answering this question is found in the unusual verb used to introduce Moses' speech to the Jewish people: *be'air*. ". . . And Moses began to explain [*be'air*] this Torah . . ." (Deuteronomy 1:5). This word is used only twice in the Torah, here at the beginning of Moses' speech and, later, at the end of Moses' speech (Deuteronomy 27:8). While literally meaning "to explain or clarify," this word alludes to a much deeper process of transmission.

A *be'air* is the Hebrew word for a well. The Torah is often compared to water, and according to Jewish law, there are three possible sources or collections of water which possess purifying qualities: a cistern, a spring, and a well. These three sources reflect distinct approaches to the learning and imparting of Torah.

A cistern is simply an open hole, a receptacle for rainwater. It becomes a source of purity after it has received and stored a significantly large amount water. The cistern is seen as representing the student who is capable of receiving information, storing whatever he or she is told, but never creating or formulating new ideas.

The spring is in many ways the antithesis of the cistern, as it is always refreshing and creative, never allowing its water to remain stationary. It depicts the student who is perpetually in a flowing and creative process, though incapable of receiving ideas from another person.

The third model, the well (*be'air*), is a synthesis of the cistern and the spring. The well is created by digging a deep hole which connects to an underground spring. The well is thus both a source of receiving and storing water (like the cistern), as well as a source for giving and creating anew (like the spring). The *be'air* thus symbolizes the student who first receives knowledge from others and then, through a creative process, transforms what he or she has learned.

For over thirty chapters of the book of Deuteronomy, Moses will select and recount events, interpreting them in light of what the Jewish people need to hear at this juncture in history. His final speech is not a retrospective; he is not looking back nostalgically over the events of the last forty years. Rather, Moses is demonstrating to the Jewish people that during the first four books of the Torah, God began a process that now must be continued by human beings, by the Jewish people. Moses, responsible for the transmission of the Torah, is now ensuring its continued development and its significance to the Jewish people.

The book of Deuteronomy prepares the Jewish people for life after this period of special leadership and care. The Jewish people must now continue this model of a *be'air*; they must develop what they have already received.

Seeds are planted within Torah for the continuation of the relationship between God and the Jewish people. The commentaries relate that after Moses spoke, God agreed to his words.

Around the Shabbat Table

1. The first mishnah in *Pirkei Avot* instructs that a teacher should "teach many students to stand on their own feet." The goal of teaching is not to convey information but to endow students with the ability to independently arrive at their own conclusions and to respond to situations that did not arise while they were with their teacher. Do you know any teachers who managed to accomplish this?

2. Because of Rabbi Elazar Ben Arach's immense creative powers, the mishnah in *Pirkei Avot* 2:8 likens him to an "inexhaustible spring," always flowing with new ideas. Yet later on in his life, he forgot all of his learning, even how to read simple verses. The Midrash explains that after his teacher died, Rabbi Elazar Ben Arach did not follow the other students to the yeshiva at Yavneh but struck out on his own, assuming that because of his great talents, others would soon follow. Though he was exceptionally gifted, others did not follow him, and, left alone, his powers withered. Some commentaries imply that he went deaf. What do you think is the sig-

nificance of his going deaf? Is there anyone whom you would liken to an "inexhaustible spring"?

3. What kind of student are you? Do you consider yourself to be more like a cistern, a spring, or a well?

SHABBAT LUNCH: A "Written" Oral Tradition

Throughout the book of Deuteronomy, Moses retells the Torah through his own eyes. In doing so, he sets a precedent—the teachings of the Torah need to be continually renewed and expanded for each succeeding generation.

By themselves, the teachings of the Torah are not enough to direct society. From the very beginning, the Torah was accompanied by an Oral Law that would interpret and explicate its teachings. The Torah offers essential guidelines for a moral monotheistic life, yet its general precepts lack sufficient detail to serve as a legal basis or to have far-reaching effects upon individuals or a nation. For example, it is written in the Ten Commandments: "Remember the Sabbath day to keep it holy." How is one supposed to do this? Similarly, the Torah commands: "You must honor your father and mother. . . . "What does honoring entail? Are there any limits? No explanations are offered. Standing alone, the commandments, as well as many sections of the written Torah, remain vague and open to innumerable understandings and misunderstandings.

The oral tradition that accompanied the Torah enabled its teachings to be continually applied in fresh and dynamic ways. The rabbis of each generation receive the oral traditions and then decide how to implement them in their contemporary setting. New applications are continually found for eternal principles. Parts of this oral tradition that were no longer considered essential or relevant to the "new" generations would gradually be forgotten.

This dynamic process of the oral tradition continued for over 1,500 years, until approximately 200 c.e., more than a century after the destruction of the Second Temple. Then, amid the deepening Roman persecution and fear of an inevitable fracturing of the Jewish people in exile, the president of the Sanhedrin, Rabbi Judah HaNasi, made a historic decision—the oral tradition would be codified into a set form. It would become known as the mishnah. This code, the mishnah, would set and unify Jewish law for the Jewish people amid their many dispersions.

Rabbi Judah HaNasi faced a dilemma of epic proportions, without precedent in human history—how does one commit an oral tradition to writing? The mass of material in the oral tradition is seemingly endless. *What should be included and what should be left out?* Furthermore, what form or organization should this new "written" oral tradition assume?

Rabbi Judah HaNasi organized the mishnah into six orders, each focusing on a different theme:

1. Agricultural Laws (*Zeraim*)

2. Holidays (*Mo'ed*)

3. Family Law (*Nashim*)

4. Civil Law (*Nezikin*)

5. Objects of Purity (*Kodeshim*)

6. States of Purity (*Taharot*)

The six divisions of the mishnah were organized into three units of two, reflecting the natural, human, and spiritual domains of the world. Furthermore, within each group of two orders a progression can be found from a more physical to a less physical reality; for example, in the natural domain, there is a progression from place to time, while in the human domain, there is a progression from blood relationships to social affiliations.

Domain:	Orders:		
Natural:	Agricultural Laws (*Zeraim*)	→	Holidays (*Mo'ed*)
Human:	Family Law (*Nashim*)	→	Civil Law (*Nezikin*)
Holy:	Objects of Purity (*Kodeshim*)	→	States of Purity (*Taharot*)

Thus, what emerges from the design of the mishnah is a carefully structured work that *gradually directs the Jewish people from the most physical dimension of existence to the most spiritual one.* In order to arrive at the most spiritual subjects (*Kodeshim* and *Taharot*) one first has to understand the Jewish perspective on the physical and human world. Together with the written Torah, this "written" oral law has been guiding the Jewish people for almost 2,000 years.

Around the Shabbat Table

1. The Mishnah attempted to preserve the oral nature of the tradition that it recorded by using a format that raises questions and poses arguments without offering their resolution. Nevertheless, what qualities of oral law are necessarily lost when it is written down?

2. The first five chapters of the Mishnah, which serve as a general introduction to the whole work, discuss the *Shema* and the *Amidah* (standing silent prayer). Why do you think that Rabbi Judah HaNasi chose to begin the mishnah with a discussion of these prayers? What do you think are the educational and religious messages of Rabbi Judah HaNasi's structure of the Mishnah?

3. Do you prefer a written or oral form of learning? What do you think are the advantages of each?

Seuda Shlishit: Forty Years

The book of *Devarim* commences forty years after the Jewish people leave Egypt. "And it came to pass in the fortieth year, in the eleventh month, on the first day of the month, that Moses spoke to the people of Israel . . . " (Deuteronomy 1:3).

Throughout Jewish sources, the number "forty" recurs, denoting the closing of one stage of development and marking the advent of the succeeding stage. The rains of Noah's flood lasted for forty days and forty nights. Isaac was forty years old when Abraham sought a wife for him. Moses remained alone on Mount Sinai for forty days and nights. The spies explored the Promised Land for forty days. Both Elijah and Jonah fled to the desert for forty days. According to the Zohar, the soul waits forty years for the creation of the appropriate body.

The mishnah in *Pirkei Avot* (5:25) sees each decade of life as possessing unique intellectual and emotional qualities. According to the mishnah, the decade of the "forties" reflects a time of "understanding" (*binah*), often expressed through communal responsibility.

During the previous century, the most famous and influential figure in English Jewry, Sir Moses Montefiore (1784–1885), underwent a change of life after his fortieth year. He had acquired great wealth as a stockbroker and associate of the Rothschild banking establishment. At the age of forty, he retired and turned his attention to the Jewish community and Jewish causes throughout the world.

In 1840, when the Jewish community of Damascus was being accused of "blood libel," Montefiore traveled to Constantinople, met with the Turkish sultan, and successfully alleviated the persecution of the Jews. Similarly, he made numerous visits to Russia and Rumania, attempting to improve the social and political conditions of the Jewish communities. At a time when most communities were concerned with their own particular welfare, Montefiore became a ministerial force across the entire Jewish world.

Montefiore visited Palestine seven times, seeking ways to revitalize the Jewish communities there and to promote their economic independence. He devised plans for developing agricultural colonies, as well as textile and printing industries. He encouraged the Jewish population of Jerusalem to move out of the walled city by building one of the first neighborhoods outside the city walls, which has since been named after him, "Yemin Moshe."

After retiring from business at the age of forty, Moses Montefiore devoted the next sixty years of his life to the international affairs of the Jewish people. He achieved public acclaim from the Queen of England and other national leaders for his compassion, idealism, and philanthropy. Toward the end of his life, he was regarded more as an institution than an individual. In 1885, his one-hundredth birthday was celebrated as a public holiday by Jewish communities throughout the world.

Around the Shabbat Table

1. According to Maimonides, Abraham was forty years old when he discovered God. The Ra'avad (a Medieval commentator) disagrees with Maimonides and maintains that Abraham was only three years old when he began to believe in one God. Both of these philosophers choose their numbers symbolically. What do you think is the difference in how they understand the breakthrough of Abraham?

2. Just as the Jewish people wandered with Moses for forty years in the desert, the Talmud (*Avodah Zarah* 5b) asserts that one does not fully understand the intellectual and spiritual depth of the teachings of one's mentor for forty years. Have you ever had a teacher whom you only fully began to appreciate many years afterward?

3. Today, the age of forty is sometimes considered to be the age of mid-life crisis. What do you think is significant about this age? How would you characterize the nature of each decade of a person's life?

Va'et'chanan

FRIDAY NIGHT MEAL: A Different Ten Commandments

This week's *parsha* includes a repetition of the Ten Commandments given to the Jewish people in the book of Exodus. Of all
of Moses' speech in the book of Deuteronomy, this is seemingly the
most superfluous section. The Ten Commandments had been written down, engraved on two tablets. Though hidden away in the Holy
of Holies, the actual wording of the Ten Commandments was extant
and presumably known by the Jewish people. Moses could simply
have reminded the people of the great moment at Mount Sinai, without reiterating the actual words heard there. Why was it necessary
for Moses to repeat the Ten Commandments to the Jewish people?

Not only did Moses repeat the Ten Commandments, he changed
their wording. Why? For forty years, the people had understood one
version of the Ten Commandments. Now, every slight modification
must have cried out to them; even the slightest differences must have
been felt acutely. What did Moses want to achieve through these
changes? (noted in the underlined words in the following chart).

First Set of Ten Commandments Exodus 20:2-14	Second Set of Ten Commandments Deuteronomy 5:6-18
1. I am the Lord your God, Who brought you out of the land of Egypt, from the house of bondage.	(Same as in the first set of tablets.)
2. You will have no other gods beside Me. You will not make for yourself any carved idol, and any likeness of anything that is in heaven above, or that is in the earth beneath, or that is in the water under the earth: you will not bow down to them, nor serve them: for I the Lord your God am a jealous God, punishing the iniquity of the fathers upon the children, upon the third and fourth generation of those that hate Me; but showing mercy to thousands of generations of those that love Me, and keep My commandments.	You will have no other gods beside Me. You will not make for yourself any carved idol of any likeness of anything that is in heaven above, or that is in the earth beneath, or that is in the water under the earth: you will not bow down to them, nor serve them: for I the Lord your God am a jealous God, punishing the iniquity of the fathers upon the children, and upon the third and fourth generation of those that hate Me; but showing mercy to thousands of generations of those that love Me, and keep My commandments.
3. You will not take the name of the Lord your God in vain; for the Lord will not hold him guiltless that takes His name in vain.	(Same as in the first set of tablets.)
4. Remember the Sabbath day to make it holy. Six days you will labor, and do all your work; but the seventh day is a Sabbath to	Keep the Sabbath day to make it holy, as the Lord your God has commanded you. Six days you will labor, and do your work, but the seventh

the Lord your God, on it you will not do any work, you, nor your son, nor your daughter, your manservant, nor your woman servant, nor your cattle, nor your stranger that is within your gates: <u>for in six days the Lord made heaven and earth, the sea, and all that is in them, and rested on the seventh day</u>: therefore the Lord blessed the Sabbath day, and made it holy.

day is the Sabbath of the Lord your God, on it you will not do any work, you, nor your son, nor your daughter, <u>nor</u> your manservant, nor your woman servant, <u>nor your ox, nor your donkey, nor any of your cattle</u>, nor your stranger that is within your gates; <u>that your manservant and your maidservant may rest as well as you. And remember that you were a servant in the land of Egypt, and that the Lord your God brought you out from there with a mighty hand and an outstretched arm</u>: therefore the Lord your God commanded you to keep the Sabbath day.

5. Honor your father and your mother: that your days may be long in the land which the Lord your God gives you.

Honor your father and your mother, <u>as the Lord your God has commanded you</u>; that your days may be prolonged, <u>and that it may go well with you</u>, in the land which the Lord your God gives you.

6. Do not murder.

(Same as in the first set of tablets.)

7. Do not commit adultery.

<u>And</u> do not commit adultery.

8. Do not steal.

<u>And</u> do not steal.

9. Do not bear false witness against your neighbor.

<u>And</u> do not testify in vain against your neighbor.

(table continued) First Set of Ten Commandments Exodus 20:2-14	Second Set of Ten Command- ments Deuteronomy 5:6-18
10. <u>Do not covet your neighbor's house; do not covet your neighbor's wife</u>, or his manservant, or his woman servant, or his ox, or his donkey, or anything that belongs to your neighbor.	<u>And do not covet your neighbor's wife, and do not desire your neighbor's house, his field</u>, or his manservant, or his woman servant, or his ox, or his donkey, or anything that belongs to your neighbor.

Some of the changes seem minor, an additional "and" or "of." Yet, especially in the changes in the fourth and fifth commandments, a pattern may be detected, perhaps revealing Moses' intention behind his rendering of the Ten Commandments.

The Maharal (*Tiferet Yisrael*, Chapter 43) writes that the first four books of the Torah are written from the perspective of the *giver*, while the final book, Deuteronomy, is written from the perspective of the *receiver*. Moses' changes in the Ten Commandments enable the commandments to more deeply penetrate into the lives of the Jewish people. For example: the version of the Ten Commandments in the book of Exodus mandates the observance of *Shabbat* because: "for in six days the Lord made heaven and earth, the sea, and all that is in them, and rested on the seventh day." In Deuteronomy, Moses offers instead a reason for the observance of *Shabbat* that is much closer to the personal experience of the Jews: "Remember that you were a servant in the land of Egypt, and that the Lord your God brought you out from there with a mighty hand and an outstretched arm."

The Midrash states that the tablets of the Ten Commandments symbolize the ring with which God betrothed the Jewish people. Forty years later, Moses' further elaboration reflects the fact that even the human–Divine relationship must be continually renewed and re-sanctified.

Around the Shabbat Table

1. The first stanza of the famous song of the Friday night service (Kabbalat *Shabbat*), "L'cha Dodi," states that the words: "Guard" (*Shamor*, referring to the prohibitions of *Shabbat*) and "Keep" (*Zachor*, referring to the positive mitzvot of *Shabbat*) were both uttered at the same moment, "in one breath of speech." What idea is this assertion trying to convey?

2. How would you explain some of the other changes apparent in the second version of the Ten Commandments?

3. Which of the Ten Commandments would you amplify in order to impact upon other people's lives more powerfully? How would you develop it?

SHABBAT LUNCH: Jealousy

The last of the Ten Commandments, "Do not covet . . . .," is, in many ways, the most difficult one to understand.

First, how can the Torah forbid such a natural, almost instinctive, desire, something of the heart alone?

The Torah commentator Ibn Ezra raises this difficulty and responds with a famous allegory: "Many people were surprised by this mitzvah. How is it possible for a person not to covet in his heart something which is beautiful and appealing to him? I will offer you an allegory: know that when a simple villager who is of sound mind sees a beautiful princess, he will not desire her in his heart . . . because he knows that it is not possible for him to marry her."

So, too, if one understands that it is impossible to acquire the possessions of another, then one's heart will not be aroused to yearn for them.

Second, this commandment changes significantly from the first set to the second set of Commandments. In our *parsha* it begins with "And," and an additional caution of "do not desire" is included. What do these additions signify?

First Set of Ten Commandments: Exodus 20:14	Second Set of Ten Commandments: Deuteronomy 5:18
<u>Do not covet</u> your neighbor's house; do not covet your neighbor's wife, or his manservant, or his woman servant, or his ox, or his donkey, or anything that belongs to your neighbor.	<u>And do not covet</u> your neighbor's wife, <u>and do not desire</u> your neighbor's house, his field, or his manservant, or his woman servant, or his ox, or his donkey, or anything that belongs to your neighbor.

Maimonides (Laws of Theft 1:9-10) understands the verse in Deuteronomy as stipulating two separate prohibitions: (1) Do not covet, and (2) Do not desire. "Do not covet" refers to an emotion that ultimately leads to an action. "Anyone who covets [something] of his friend, and consequently pesters him relentlessly and implores him until he gives it to him, even if he has paid substantially for the object, nevertheless, he has transgressed 'do not covet.'" According to Maimonides, the additional admonition of "do not desire" refers to a "desire is that is something of the heart alone," and this admonition is violated even without any resulting action.

The Midrash states that the additional "*and*" at the beginning of the commandment links it conceptually with the preceding commandments. In Deuteronomy, commandments 6-10 all are now joined together, reflecting a single chain of events. Surprisingly, the sequence of events is in reverse order, beginning with the final commandment! First, one desires the possessions of another person ("do not desire"). This leads to actually trying to acquire the possession through payment ("do not covet"). If this fails, the person may then feel the urge to lie ("do not bear false witness") or steal ("do not steal") the object. Ultimately, this craving may even push the person to murder ("do not murder").

According to the Midrash, the last of the Ten Commandments may actually be the source of all the others.

Around the Shabbat Table

1. In the book of Proverbs (9:17) it is written that "Stolen waters are sweet. . . ." This is understood to mean that as something becomes forbidden, it actually increases in allure. Does this contradict the approach of the Ibn Ezra—that if one knows that something is absolutely prohibited, one will not desire it? Which idea resonates more profoundly for you?

2. Why do you think this prohibition against coveting warranted such great detailing in the Torah?

3. How would you advise someone to overcome "desires of the heart alone"?

Seuda Shlishit: Looking for Jerusalem

And I [Moses] besought the Lord at that time, saying ". . . I implore You, let me go over, and see the good land that is beyond the Jordan, the good mountain region and the Lebanon." But the Lord was angry with me . . . and said to me, "Let it suffice to you, speak no more to Me of this matter. Go up to the top of the mountain and lift up your eyes westward, and northward, and southward, and eastward and behold with your eyes, for you will not go over this Jordan." [Deuteronomy 3:23-27]

Moses was allowed only to see "the good land" with his eyes. The hasidim tell a story of looking for Jerusalem:

Once, across the countryside in Europe, a battle raged. Two armies, hundreds of soldiers, were positioned on opposite sides of the battlefield, fighting with all of their being. Shots rang out and the smoke of gunpowder filled the air.

As the general looked through his binoculars, he suddenly saw a sight that he couldn't believe. An old Jew with a long white beard was hurrying across the battlefield, totally oblivious of the conflict at hand.

Every once in a while, the old Jew would stop, put his hand to his forehead and look out. Then he would shake his head and continue scurrying across the battlefield.

The general called out to him, telling him to stop, but the old man paid no attention to him. He kept running midst the shots and fray of the battle.

The general was so astounded at this sight, that he forgot about the battle and began to run after the old Jew. Panting and racing after him, he called to him to stop. The old Jew looked at him, but then continued to run, stopping only occasionally to look out, as if he were looking for something.

Totally bewildered, the general caught up to the old Jew and screamed at the top of his lungs, "Old man, what are you doing? Don't you know that it is dangerous here, you could get killed!"

Still, the old Jew paid no attention to him, resuming his running. Again the general caught up to him, frantically yelling out, "What are you looking for?! What do you see?!"

The old man turned to him and said, "I am looking for Jerusalem."

The general was dumbfounded. Did he say "looking for Jerusalem?" He shouted back to the old man, "You can't see Jerusalem from here! Jerusalem is miles and miles away! Are you crazy?"

The old man looked as though he could barely wait for the general to finish talking, and then, without even responding, he once again began to run through the battle.

The general followed not far behind, only now he, too, was stopping every now and then, putting his hand on his forehead and looking out.

Finally, exasperated, the general screamed at him, "You can't see Jerusalem from here! I don't see it at all! I don't see anything!"

The old man paused. He took his hand down from his forehead. "You are looking for Jerusalem, but you will never see it. You see, you are looking with your eyes. When you are looking for Jerusalem, you must look with your heart instead."

Around the Shabbat Table

1. One of the prayers of the *Amidah* (daily silent standing prayer) is for the coming of the Messiah:"Quickly cause the offspring of your servant David to flourish . . . for we hope for your deliverance all day long." How do you think it affects one to be constantly "on the look-out" for redemption?

2. Rav Kook writes that Moses was denied entry into the Promised Land in order to forever instill in the Jewish people the yearning to enter it. Why else do you think that God did not allow Moses to come into Israel?

3. What would the "Jerusalem of your heart" look like?

Ekev

FRIDAY NIGHT MEAL: A Bit of Luck

As mentioned previously, the weekly *parshiyot* (portions) frequently come in couplets, with the second *parsha* developing
themes introduced in the first. Often the first *parsha* presents the
physical aspect of an idea, while the spiritual dimension is developed in the next *parsha*. In the *parshiyot Ekev* and *Re'eh*, Moses
cautions the Jewish people about the new and distinct reality of living in the land of Israel. This week's *parsha* describes the *physical*
uniqueness and moral obligations of living in the land of Israel; next
week's *parsha, Re'eh*, will focus on the *spiritual* dimension of the
land.

In this week's *parsha*, Moses tells the Jewish people:

> For the land, into which you go to possess it, is *not* like the land of
> Egypt, that you left, where you sowed seeds and watered them with
> your foot, like a garden of vegetables. The land, into which you go to
> possess it, is a land of hills and valleys, and *drinks water of the rain
> of heaven*. It is a land which the Lord your God cares for; *the eyes of*

the Lord your God are always upon it, from the beginning of the year to the end of the year. [Deuteronomy 11:10-12]

What exactly are the "eyes of the Lord" looking for? What is God watching?

Unlike Egypt, which was watered from the Nile, Israel "drinks water of the rain of heaven." Its produce is dependent upon the gifts of heaven. Rain is not understood to be a purely natural phenomenon; rather, the natural world is intrinsically linked to the moral order, and only if the Jewish people act appropriately will there be rain in the proper quantities and times of the year. The "eyes of the Lord" are thus watching the ethical behavior of the Jewish people.

One recurrent theme of this week's *parsha* is that *God's looking at the Jewish people is a reflection of how the Jewish people look at their own lives, particularly their own success.* As the Jewish people enter the land and struggle for their livelihood, how will they respond to prosperity? How will success affect them? After building good-sized homes and acquiring a measure of wealth, how will they regard their own achievements? Will they say, "My power and the might of my hand have gotten me this wealth" (Deuteronomy 8:18), or will they acknowledge that they are not entirely in control of their own fate?

How much of success should be attributed to one's own efforts, and how much is the result of other forces, forces beyond one's control? The Talmud (*Moed Katan* 28a) relates that one's "length of life, number of children, and material prosperity do not depend on one's merit, rather on one's '*mazal*' [good or bad fortune], as in the lives of Rabbah and Rabbi Chisda." It then presents the following contrasts between the luck of these two great rabbis:

Both were saintly rabbis; one master prayed for rain and it came, and the other master prayed for rain and it came. Rabbi Chisda lived to the age of ninety-two; Rabbah lived to the age of forty. In Rabbi Chisda's house there were sixty weddings, at Rabbah's house there were sixty funerals. At Rabbi Chisda's house they gave the finest of breads to their dogs, and there was some left over; at Rabbah's house there was barely enough plain bread for the human beings.

The existence of other forces impacting upon one's life *does not* nullify one's obligation to struggle and persevere. Upon being banished from the Garden of Eden, Adam was told that he would now have to support himself "by the sweat of his brow" (Genesis 3:19). Thus, humanity was not allowed to rely on miracles and had to labor for its survival. We are obligated to work and struggle to perfect the world.

The rabbis referred to the tractates that dealt with agricultural practices as the tractates of "belief" (*emunah*). Farmers especially, despite their long hours and hard work, are aware that they cannot bring the wind and rain at just the most opportune moments. The rabbis assumed that working the land would naturally deepen one's belief in divine intervention and *mazal*.

Around the Shabbat Table

1. Regarding the verse "the eyes of God are upon the land of Israel," the Midrash asks, "But isn't God looking at and judging all of lands of the world?" The Midrash answers that all of the lands of the world are examined via Israel, thus the moral behavior of the Jewish people in Israel has ramifications for the entire world. Do you see the Jewish people's or Israel's effect on other nations?

2. In the present age, it is accepted that one's physical condition is influenced by one's emotional and psychological states. The Torah posits that not only do we live in a psychosomatic universe but also in an "ethical-somatic" world, in which the physical condition of the world is influenced by people's moral behavior. Would you agree with this premise?

3. Is there a danger in believing that everything depends upon *mazal*? How do you see the effects of *mazal* in your life?

SHABBAT LUNCH: Punishing Children

And you remember the way which the Lord your God led you these forty years in the desert, to humble you and to test you, to know what was in your heart .. and He humbled you, and caused you to suffer hunger ... you should know in your heart, that, *like a man chastises his son*, so the Lord your God chastises you. [Deuteronomy 8:2–5]

How exactly should "a man chastise his son?" What are the guidelines for punishing children? The book of Proverbs (13:24) affirms a simple, though provocative, rule: "He that withholds his rod—hates his child; and he that loves his child—chastises him at an early age."

Punishments should not be for the sake of the parent, to make the parent's life easier; rather, they should be for the benefit of the child. Limits must be set for children at an early age, to help them to establish worthwhile habits of behavior. Parents who spare the "rod" and do not set limits on the behavior of their children, may in the end, come to resent or hate their own children.

Rabbi Samson Raphael Hirsch writes that "If during the first and second years you let the child educate you, if you play the weakling and he the strong one, then do not imagine that it will be an easy matter in the third and fourth year to exchange the parts." Hirsch stressed that obedience should be the guiding force for parenting.

According to Rav Kook and commentaries on the *Zohar*, however, rather than obedience, independence of thought and a strong will should be developed during the years of childhood. Without a strong will, a child will not be able to effect a positive change (*tikkun*) in the world. "For if the child does not have a strong desire to receive, in the end, he or she will also not have a strong desire to give." Only if a child is willing to fight for its "cookies" at the age of 5, will it then be able to fight for social justice at the age of 35. Rav Kook writes that this drive of selfishness is similar to a fermenting agent; without this agitating force, grapes can never be transformed into wine.

Around the Shabbat Table

1. The Talmud states that a parent who strikes a grown child will provoke the child to strike back and therefore the parent has transgressed the rule of "one should not put a stumbling block before the blind" (*Moed Katan* 17a). Commentaries range in their determining of the age of a "grown child." Some assert that a child is not grown until he is financially independent, others consider marriage to be the primary criteria, while some state that as soon as the child has a sense of his own self and personal dignity he is beginning to be "grown." What do you think should be the considerations in deciding when a child is grown? What do you think might be nonphysical equivalents of "striking" a child?

2. The Talmud states: A person should always punish with his left hand and caress with his right hand (*Sanhedrin* 107b). The intention being that since one's right hand is usually stronger than the left hand, one's support and encouragement of the child should always exceed one's disciplining. Have you ever seen examples of discipline and encouragement occurring together?

3. With which approach mentioned previously, that of Rabbi Shimshon Raphael Hirsch, or Rav Kook, do you most identify? Can you recognize or appreciate the advantages of the other system?

Seuda Shlishit: Belief in God

And now, Israel, what does the Lord your God ask of you—but to fear the Lord your God . . . [Deuteronomy 10:12]

In this week's *parsha*, Moses asserts that the most basic demand of God from the Jewish people is to fear, or be in awe, of God. Primary to all behavior is an awareness of the power beyond the control of humanity.

On this verse, the Talmud (*Berakhot* 33b) observes, "Everything is in the hands of God, except the fear of God." All that a person owns, everything that a person has, may ultimately be taken away. Possessions, relationships, even knowledge, do not abide totally within human control. According to this statement of the Talmud, the *only* thing that one does remain within control is one's relationship and faith in God. One always has the freedom to decide whether or not to believe in God.

The Ba'al Shem Tov commented on the phrase: "Our God and God of our Fathers," found in the Prayerbook:

> Some people have faith because their parents taught them to believe. In one sense, this is satisfactory, as no philosophical argument will break their belief; in another way, it is unsatisfactory—as their belief does not come through personal search and knowledge.
>
> Others come to belief after personal struggle and research. Their conviction is in one way satisfactory, as they know God from their own inner experience; in another way, it is unsatisfactory—since if others demonstrate to them the fallacy of their reasoning, they may lose or weaken their faith.
>
> The most complete form of faith is the belief that is satisfactory in every way: when one believes both because of tradition and also through one's own reasoning. This is what we mean when we say: "Our God and the God of our Fathers."

Around the Shabbat Table

1. Which do you think is stronger—belief fostered by parental influence or through intellectual investigation?

2. Has your relationship with God been molded more by your parents' influence or through your own exploration?

3. Would your life be different if you had a greater, or lesser, level of belief in God?

Re'eh

FRIDAY NIGHT MEAL: Seeing and Being Seen

Last week's *parsha*, *Ekev*, presented many of the challenges and difficulties the Jewish people would face regarding the physical and material qualities of the Promised Land. This week's *parsha*, *Re'eh*, deals with the spiritual hazards of life in the new land.

The *parsha* opens with the warning "See, I am placing before you, today—a blessing and a curse" (Deuteronomy 11:26). The curse will result primarily from being influenced by the other religious practices already existing in the land. A people yearning to grow spiritually is vulnerable to the lures of false prophets, idolatry, and paganism, all mentioned in this week's *parsha*. False prophets may have remarkable powers; the *parsha* speaks of individuals gifted with clairvoyant powers. The Jewish people's lives will be fraught with spiritual temptations and pitfalls, and they must struggle to discern between spurious and authentic paths of spiritual growth.

How can the Jewish people ever know which is the true path? Amid the dangers and enticements present in the land of Israel, what will safeguard the Jewish people, ensuring that they receive the blessing and not the curse?

The *parsha* begins and ends with different forms of the same verb: "*See*, I am placing before you, today—a blessing and a curse" (Deuteronomy 11:26) and "Three times a year shall all your males *be seen* before the Lord your God *in the place which He shall choose*; in the feast of unleavened bread [Passover], and in the feast of weeks [Shavuot], and in the feast of booths [Sukkot]" (Deuteronomy 16:16). Three times yearly the Jews were obligated to come to Jerusalem, the place that God chose and where God wanted them to be. The quality of the "seeing" at the beginning of the *parsha* is dependent upon the "being seen" at the end of the *parsha*.

What helped to ensure that the Jewish people would not be swayed by false forms of spirituality? *The experience of Jerusalem.* Jerusalem unified the Jewish people and served as a national center in many realms. The Talmud (*Yoma* 12a) states that it was forbidden to rent out rooms in Jerusalem; no one was allowed to profit from living in Jerusalem. According to one opinion in the Talmud, although all of Israel was divided between the twelve tribes, Jerusalem was never divided between them. It did not belong to individual tribes or members of the Jewish people; rather, to all of them together. It both created and symbolized their unity.

During the pilgrimage holidays, Jerusalem was the national social center. The national Supreme Court (Sanhedrin), based at the steps of the Temple, functioned as the legal and political center of the people, and the Temple provided the religious center. All this occurred with the overt consciousness of "being seen." The effect of "being seen," by other Jews, as well as by God, would hopefully impede the development of misguided elements of the society and keep the Jewish people focused in the right direction.

Parents were obligated to bring even small children to Jerusalem during the three pilgrimage festivals. The mishnah debates at what age a child must be brought up to Jerusalem by its parents: *Beit* Shammai asserts that even a child who cannot yet walk, but is only able to ride on the shoulders of his father, should be brought to Jerusalem, while *Beit* Hillel offers a slightly older criterion—any child who can walk while holding the hand of its parent. Clearly, the mishnah is not relating to the intellectual or spiritual capabilities of these toddlers. Jerusalem is not something that should be understood cognitively, rather, it is something that simply must be experienced and seen, even at the earliest of ages.

Around the Shabbat Table

1.   The tractate *Chagigah*, which discusses the mitzvah of coming up to Jerusalem and "being seen by the One who is not seen," fittingly also contains the most mystical sections of the Talmud. It engages in a further play on the word *see*, and states that "Anyone who looks at (or speculates about) four things, it would have been *see*ming for him not to have come into the world:
     1.   what is above (heaven)
     2.   what is beneath (hell)
     3.   what is before (what happened before the world was created)
     4.   what is after (what will be after the end of days)."
     What is the problem with engaging in these questions? Would you add any others?

2.   Even after the destruction of the Temple, is there a value in visiting Jerusalem? How would you characterize the difference between a pilgrimage and a vacation?

3.   If you had to pick one place to impress values upon your child, where would it be? Why?

SHABBAT LUNCH: Saying a *Berakah*

One of the key words in this week's *parsha* is *berakah* (blessing).
The *parsha* begins with God's offering a blessing to the Jewish
people: "Behold, I set before you today a blessing and a curse"
(Deuteronomy 11:26)—and closes with a description of the three
annual pilgrimage holidays to Jerusalem, in which each person gives
to God "according to the blessing which God has given to him"
(Deuteronomy 16:17). In the Torah, a blessing usually refers to God's
bestowing gifts and prosperity upon the Jewish people. This expression is also extensively used in the Talmud; the first tractate of the
Talmud is called *Berakhot* (Blessings). In the Talmud, however, a
blessing did not commemorate God's actions toward the Jewish
people; rather, it usually denoted the words of a Jew expressed toward God.

What exactly is the saying of a *berakah* meant to achieve? What
is the source for saying a *berakah*?

In the midst of the Talmud's discussion dealing with the blessings recited before eating different types of food, it asks the following question: What is the source for saying a blessing before eating?
Where did this obligation stem from? After a lengthy debate on this
issue, the Talmud concludes—there is no particular biblical or historical source for this practice; rather, it is simply logical! In the eyes
of the Talmud, saying a *berakah* before eating is simply a matter of
common sense: "It is forbidden for someone to receive pleasure from
this world without saying a blessing beforehand" (*Berakhot* 35a).

The discussion of the Talmud continues and states:

> Anyone who receives pleasure from this world without first saying a
> *berakah*—it is as if s/he has taken pleasure from holy matters [illic-
> itly] . . . Rabbi Levi resolved a seeming contradiction in the Bible. On
> the one hand, the Bible states: "The whole world belongs to God"
> (Psalms 34:1) and on the other hand it says: "The heavens belong to
> God but the earth was given to human beings" (Psalms 115:16). How
> can these both be true? In fact, he answers, there is no contradiction

at all. Before one says a blessing, everything belongs to God, after one says a blessing, the earthly things are given to human beings.

According to this discussion, the saying of a blessing constitutes the conferring of possession or dominion from the domain of God to that of human beings. Through the saying of a *berakah* the earthly things move into the ownership of human beings.

Why was the saying of a *berakah*, which constituted the formalizing of this conferring of ownership, considered by the Talmud to be such a logical or natural human response?

Many of the blessings that are recited over food use the Hebrew word *borei*, Creator (i.e., *Borei pri hagafen*, "Creator of the fruit of the vine"). This particular word, *borei*, denotes creation *ex nihilo*. Notwithstanding humanity's significant creative powers, only God is able to create something from nothing. According to the Talmud, human beings should naturally be aware that they do not have this type of creative power. Since human beings are not able to create these fruits, vegetables, and so forth, therefore, they are not really theirs, and they do not have the right to eat them. Before eating, a blessing is uttered that serves to remind the individual that he or she could not have created this food, that its existence stems from the powers beyond human scope. This acknowledgment of the human being's limitations and the recognition of the source of the food is, according to the Talmud, sufficient to grant permission to partake of the food.

The blessing of prosperity that God bestows upon the world is reciprocated by the Jew's saying a blessing, expressing gratitude for this prosperity. A simple piece of fruit can serve as a means of connection between the physical and spiritual domains.

Around the Shabbat Table

1. The Talmud (*Berakhot* 40b) states that according to Rabbi Meir, prior to eating bread one could even bless by saying, "How nice is

this bread, blessed is the One (God) Who created it." What would you have said if you could have coined the blessings before eating?

2. Different blessings are recited after one eats. What do you think is the purpose of saying a blessing after eating?

3. What would you have wanted people to think about while eating?

Seuda Shlishit: "*Segula*"

For you are a holy people to the Lord your God, and the Lord has chosen you to be a "*segula*" to Himself, out of all the nations that are upon the earth. [Deuteronomy 14:2]

The word, *segula*, is one of the most difficult in the Torah to translate. Sometimes translated as "treasure" or "prized possession," sometimes as "exclusive" or "chosen," the word *segula* reflects God's unique relationship to the Jewish people. Commentators and philosophers, both Jewish and non-Jewish, have struggled to comprehend what exactly constitutes this singular status of the Jewish people.

Mark Twain wrote:

If the statistics are right, the Jews constitute but one percent of the human race. It suggests a nebulous dim puff of star dust lost in the blaze of the Milky Way. Properly, the Jew ought hardly to be heard of; but he is heard of, has always been heard of. He is as prominent on the planet as any other people . . . He has made a marvelous fight in the world, in all the ages; and has done it with his hands tied behind him. The Egyptian, the Babylonian, and the Persian rose, filled the planet with sound and splendor, then faded to dream-stuff and passed away; the Greek and the Roman followed, and made a vast noise, and they are gone; other people have sprung up and held their torch high for a

time, but it burned out, and they sit in twilight now, or have vanished
. . .

All things are mortal but the Jew; all other forces pass, but he remains. What is the secret of his immortality?

Martin Buber wrote:

> Israel will not fit into the two categories most frequently invoked in attempts at classification: "nation" and "religion." One criterion serves to distinguish a nation from a religion. Nations experience history as nations . . . In religions, on the other hand, salient experiences are undergone by individuals, and, in their purest and sublime form, these experiences are what we call "revelation." When such individuals communicate their experiences to the masses, and their tidings cause groups to form, a religion comes into being. Thus, nations and religions differ in the same way as history and revelation. Only in one instance do they coincide. Israel receives its decisive religious experience as a people.

Perhaps the Torah intentionally chose a word that is impossible to translate precisely, to describe a people who are impossible to define.

Around the Shabbat Table

1. A modern religious thinker, the founder of the Reconstructionist movement, Mordecai Kaplan, sought to replace the idea of the Jewish people having been chosen by God with that of a "covenantal relationship" in which not God, but the Jewish people choose, as they dedicate themselves to the creative possibilities of Jewish future and life. "Why cannot the faith in God's choice of Israel function today as it did in the past? The reason is not far to seek. It is because the form that this doctrine took in the past is out of drawing with our modern conception of God (that actively loves) and incompatible with our highest ethical ideals (that elevates one

nation over another)" (*The Meaning of God in Modern Jewish Religion*, p. 94). Do you identify with his concerns?

2. What do you think characterizes the uniqueness of the Jewish people? Do you more identify with the people or the religious dimensions of Judaism?

3. What do you think is the secret to the "immortality" of the Jewish people?

Shoftim

FRIDAY NIGHT MEAL: Going to War

O ne of the painful but inevitable realities of becoming an independent people in its own land is the specter of war.

Is there a Jewish approach to war? What should transpire in the mind of the Jewish soldier during combat?

This week's *parsha* states that:

> When you go out to battle against your enemies, and see horses, and chariots, and a people more numerous than yourselves, do not be afraid of them, for the Lord your God is with you and brought you out of Egypt. And when you are close to battle, the priest [*kohen*] will approach and speak to the people, saying to them, "Hear, Israel, as you draw near today to do battle against your enemies, do not let your hearts melt, fear not, and do not tremble, nor be terrified because of them, for the Lord your God goes with you, to fight for you against your enemies, to save you." [Deuteronomy 20:1-4]

This whole section is quite baffling. While one might have expected a "pep-talk" moments before battle, the opposite seems to have occurred. Again and again the powers and resources of the enemy are mentioned; their horses, chariots, and numbers are stressed; while the Jewish army is repeatedly admonished not to fear or tremble. Moses reminds them of a moment in history with which they are surely already familiar—the leaving of Egypt. How are they expected to overcome their fear and panic? Furthermore, when they are close to battle, the priest, rather than the leader of the army, gives them their final words of encouragement. How is this supposed to prepare the soldiers for their battle?

It may be virtually impossible to psychologically prepare soldiers for the actual moment of combat. Nevertheless, the Torah does not deny the preeminent emotion that every soldier feels moments before entering battle—the flash of fear. Rather than negate this emotion, the Torah directly acknowledges its existence. A soldier who does not recognize his fear beforehand is more likely to either flee in panic or overcompensate and become savagely barbaric once the fighting commences.

Yet how is it possible to overcome these emotions of fear and doubt? Reminding the Jewish people of the leaving of Egypt seems, at first glance, facile and irrelevant. Every schoolchild knows about the story of Passover. Why is the Jewish army being given a history lesson precisely at this moment?

The path to overcoming personal anxieties is through transcending one's own identity, through subsuming one's individuality into that of the larger collective destiny. The leaving of Egypt, Passover, marked the birth of the Jewish people. Moses and the *kohen* are not giving the Jewish army a history lesson at this moment. They are conveying to them that all of Jewish history is now dependent on their efforts. All the struggles and sacrifices that countless Jews have made will have been for naught if the Jewish people are now overcome. The Jewish army is not fighting for themselves alone. If they fail, if the Jewish people are defeated, then all those who preceded them have also been defeated.

First, the personal fear of the individual Jew is acknowledged, hopefully precluding reactions of hysteria or savagery. Then, the people are reminded that they are not fighting for themselves, or even for their current generation; rather all of Jewish history and survival is now dependent upon the outcome of this conflict. This reminder should help the soldiers transcend their personal concerns and inspire them to fight a moral and determined battle.

Around the Shabbat Table

1. This week's *parsha* lists four categories of soldiers who are exempt from military service in a war that is not for self-defense:
   1. A man who built a new house and has not yet lived in it;
   2. A man who planted a vineyard and not yet eaten of it;
   3. A man who has betrothed a wife and not yet married her; and
   4. A man who is fainthearted.

   What may be some of the reasons for the first three categories of exemption? Who do you think should be included in the fourth category?

2. During a war of self-defense, every available person is enlisted to fight. The mishnah (*Sotah* 8:7) expresses this idea by saying that "even a bride and groom must leave their wedding" to go to war. Why do you think the rabbis chose this example in particular?

3. What issues or circumstances would you be willing to fight for?

SHABBAT LUNCH: Escorting Guests

What happens when a slain body is found in an open area, between cities, and it is not known who killed him? Who must take responsibility for the tragedy? *All the elders of that city* that is nearest to the slain man, shall wash their hands . . . and say, "*Our hands* have not shed this blood . . ." (Deuteronomy 21:6, 7).

The Talmud (*Sotah* 48b) asks, "Does anyone seriously think that the elders of the city would have shed this person's blood?! Rather, they had to testify that they had not allowed him to leave the city without proper provisions and protection." The leaders have to take personal responsibility for any crime that occurs near their city; they must safeguard every traveler who leaves their city. The rabbis declared that anyone who does not ensure the safety of his or her guests and escort them when they depart is as if he or she has shed their blood.

Maimonides writes that the escorting of guests when they leave is a *greater* mitzvah than inviting them in. This assertion is surprising. The mitzvah of welcoming guests into one's home entails preparing food and providing a comfortable environment for the guest; it changes and may disrupt the normal family dynamic within the house. According to Jewish law, however, escorting guests out can be accomplished with a minimal number of steps. One does not need to accompany the guest to his or her destination, and Maimonides writes that even walking a handful of steps is worthy of great reward. Why is this mitzvah given such preeminent status?

From the vantage point of the guest, leaving the home and company of the host may symbolize a moment of great emotional vulnerability. The "shedding of one's blood" referred to by the rabbis is not a purely physical description, since one who embarrasses another is also deemed guilty of "shedding blood." A host must be especially conscious of the fact that the guest will momentarily be outside and alone, while the host remains inside within the warmth and comfort of the home.

The responsibility of the host does not end when the guest walks out the door. The manner of departure reflects the quality and bond of their whole time together. Will the visit end on a note of sharing or of separateness? By escorting a guest, the host makes a symbolic statement that "Though our time together has ended, I would like to extend it for just a few more minutes. I am willing to leave the comfort of my home to help you on your way."

In the book of Genesis, in the midst of a moment of prophecy, Abraham asks God to wait for him while he escorts his visiting wayfarers to their next destination. From this, the rabbis conclude that the escorting of guests is even greater than receiving a vision from heaven.

Around the Shabbat Table

1. When a slain body was found between several cities, three judges from the Sanhedrin (Supreme Court) had to leave Jerusalem (where the Sanhedrin met) to measure which city was closest to the slain body.Then the elders of the closest city had to wash their hands and proclaim that "Our hands have not shed this blood ..." (Deuteronomy 21:6, 7). How do you think that this affected the elders of that city? The judges of the Sanhedrin itself?

2. A host offers the guest food and lodging. How does the guest benefit the host? How does the host also benefit from escorting the guest?

3. What were your best and worst experiences as a guest? As a host? Why?

Seuda Shlishit: The Tragic Battle of Latrun

This week's *parsha* describes the preparations of the Jewish army just prior to going to battle. In the brief history of the state of Israel, there have been many successful and heroic military campaigns. Regretfully, there have also been tragic failures and losses. Perhaps the most tragic battle waged in recent history was in the War of Independence, when a force composed primarily of Holocaust survivors attempted to protect Jerusalem by conquering the fortress of Latrun, west of the Holy City. Portions of the battle are recounted in *O Jerusalem*, by Larry Collins and Dominique Lapierre:

> The situation in Jerusalem was so alarming that a disaster was inevitable if some way was not found to get help to the city. Ben-Gurion

was determined to find a way. "At last we had a state," he would later write, "but we were about to lose our capital." A search for recruits began.

They arrived on the S. S. *Kalanit.* Carrying over 2,000 survivors of the ravages of Europe, there were uniformly thin blue-eyed Poles, Hungarians, Rumanians, Czechs, Yugoslavs, and Russians. Their faces revealed painful pasts.

When the future officer of the battle of Latrun pleaded with Ben-Gurion to delay their recruitment, Ben-Gurion replied, "You can't judge, you don't know how serious the situation is. We need them all."

The men would spend barely seventy-two hours on the soil of the land they had dreamed of before being enlisted for the battle of Latrun.

The battle of Latrun began at four in the morning of Tuesday, May 25.

A pale sun climbing into a leaden sky overhead heralded the arrival of still another enemy, the cruelest the Jewish soldiers would face that morning. It was the hot, burning wind rolling up from the depths of the Arabian Desert to wrap Palestine in a mantel of fire.

Studying the battlefield, Shlomo Shamir (the commanding officer) realized that his first battle as an Israeli officer was lost before it had really begun. His forces were much too weak to take Latrun in a daytime frontal attack. The only thing left was to minimize his men's losses and suffering by organizing a rapid retreat.

Trapped by flying shrapnel, bullets, the withering heat, the dense smoke of the burning fields, tortured by thirst and clouds of mosquitoes, men collapsed of sheer exhaustion. Some were not able to get up. Others crawled and dragged themselves, pulling their wounded with them, trying to jump from one rock to another for cover.

In the terror of the Arab shelling, many of the immigrants had forgotten the few words of Hebrew hastily learned on their arrival. Their officer tried to gather some of them and lead them to safety. They were like frightened animals. "They didn't even know how to crawl under fire. Some of them didn't know how to fire the rifles that had been thrown at them a few hours before."

He saw the familiar face of a seventeen-year-old boy he remembered from the *Kalanit.* He was lying in a ditch, dying. "Oh," he whispered, "we must have disappointed you." Farther on, he came on a boy who had mimeographed a news sheet for him in a D.P. camp in Germany. Weeping, the youth was clawing through the weeds looking for the thick glasses without which he was helpless.

No one would ever know how many of those immigrants had purchased with their lives the right to enter their new country. In the confusion that had preceded that attack, there had been no time to compile accurate rosters for their companies. Officially, the Hagana would admit to seventy-five dead. Unofficially, its historians acknowledged years later that their losses had far exceeded that. The Arab Legion claimed that eight hundred of the attackers had been killed, clearly an exaggerated figure, but they did capture 220 rifles. Their own losses were insignificant.

Whatever the true figures, the new immigrants of Shlomo Shamir's Seventh Brigade suffered the bloodiest defeat an Israeli unit would receive in three wars with the Arabs.

Around the Shabbat Table

1. Perhaps unlike other nations, the Jewish people remembers its defeats as well as its victories. Many days are set aside during the year to commemorate times of national destruction. As painful as this may be, why do you think it is important?

2. The Torah and its commentators strive not to glorify warfare. Nachmanides comments that in battle, even the most kind-hearted of men become brutalized and undergo spiritual and emotional damage (Deuteronomy 23:10). These scars may endure long after the end of the war. Have you ever witnessed postwar effects on its participants? What do you think is the effect on the society as a whole?

3. What would you have done in Ben-Gurion's place?

Ki Tetze

FRIDAY NIGHT MEAL: Rescuing Captives

This week's *parsha*, *Ki Tetze*, opens with an extremely troubling section often referred to as "the taking of the beautiful woman."

> When you go to war against your enemies and the Lord your God has delivered them into your hands, and you take them captive, and you see among the captives a beautiful woman, and you desire her for a wife; then you will bring her home to your house and she shall shave her head and cut her nails and she shall take off the raiment of her captivity and shall remain in your house and bewail her father and her mother a full month. And after that you can be a husband to her and she can be your wife. [Deuteronomy 21:10-13]

The Talmud (*Kiddushin* 21b) points out that in this case the Torah is responding to human weakness. During war, soldiers may need to act aggressively and this may lead to a brutalizing of their nature. In this case, the Torah allows the man to take the captive woman, but he is not permitted to marry her immediately. He must wait one month before marrying her, and during this time he must witness and hear her agony. It is hoped this interim time period will arouse his mercy and kindness for her.

While this week's *parsha* deals with taking captives, other Jewish sources talk of the mitzvah of redeeming captives. The Talmud refers to the redeeming of captives as "the great mitzvah" (*Bava Batra* 8b). Maimonides writes that "the redeeming of captives takes precedence over the support and clothing of the needy. There is no mitzvah as great as that of redeeming captives, because the hostage undergoes all of the travail of the poor while also being endangered. One who refrains from saving a prisoner has transgressed on . . . 'standing on your brother's blood'" (Laws of Gifts to the Poor 8:10). The *Shulchan Aruch* (*Yoreh Deah* 252) codifies that every moment that one delays in redeeming a captive is like shedding his or her blood. Furthermore, though a Torah scroll is the most holy possession of a Jewish community, the Talmud states that one is allowed to sell a Torah in order to either further Jewish education or to provide the means for a wedding and marriage (*Megillah* 27a). The commentaries write that the selling of a Torah in order to redeem captives is so self-evident that it precludes mentioning.

Notwithstanding the significance of this mitzvah, the Talmud (*Gittin* 45a) proposes several qualifications to rescuing hostages:

"Captives should not be redeemed at an excessive monetary value—for the good of the world."

Why? What does "for the good of the world" imply? How could any reason supersede the general consensus that the hostage is both suffering and in a life-threatening situation? How could any financial value be considered excessive in comparison to a life that is endangered? The Talmud offers two possible explanations for not redeeming captives at any cost:

1. The raising of the money may prove to be an unbearable burden on the community.

2. If a great ransom is offered for the captive, this may serve as a stimulus for further kidnappings.

The legal authorities (Maimonides, *Shulchan Aruch*, etc.,) adopted the second of these reasons, positing the fear that capitulation to a ransom of this kind may serve as a precedent and encourage kidnapping, resulting in epidemic proportions of this crime. Though we must never be apathetic to the pain of the hostage, in this case, the redeeming of the captive may ultimately engender greater suffering for others within the community. Similarly, individual captives should not rescued by others, out of the fear that the remaining captives would consequently endure harsher treatment, though any individual captive may try to engineer his or her own escape.

In a famous case, Rabbi Meir of Rothenburg (1215–1293), the leading rabbi of German Jewry, was taken captive and imprisoned by the non-Jewish authorities. Emperor Rudolph I demanded a substantial payment from the Jewish community for his release. Rabbi Meir quoted the talmudic section mentioned previously and prohibited the paying of the ransom. Seven years later, he died in prison.

Around the Shabbat Table

1. Why do you think that the Torah would posit a mitzvah that is a concession to human weakness?

2. Maimonides (Laws of Kings 7:15) states that when one goes to war, one must not think of his or her own personal family but, rather, only of the battle at hand. Why?

3. Do you know of any contemporary prisoner exchanges? Did they follow the ideas outlined here?

SHABBAT LUNCH: Cynicism

> Remember what Amalek did to you on the way, when you came out of Egypt. How he met you on the way and attacked the hindmost of you, all that were feeble, when you were faint and weary; and he did not fear God. Therefore it will be, when the Lord your God has given you rest from all of your enemies … that you should blot out the remembrance of Amalek from under the heavens, you shall not forget. [Deuteronomy 25:17-19]

This week's *parsha* closes with an injunction never to forget what Amalek and his people did to the Jewish people on their way out of Egypt. Amalek's forces attacked the weakest and most feeble Jews, those at the rearmost of the camp. At the time, the Jewish people were traveling in the desert, possessing neither wealth nor land; Amalek could have achieved no material, political, or territorial benefit from their attacks.

What motivated Amalek to attack? Amalek's sole aim was to weaken the Jewish people.

Why did he want to debilitate this seemingly powerless people? The commentators characterize "Amalek" as one who does not believe in anything. God had destroyed Egypt through the plagues and had parted the Red Sea for the Jews, and for a brief moment in history, their faith in God was unwavering. Amalek wanted to weaken the convictions of the Jewish people. His attack shook their belief in a supremely caring God. The mystics note that the *gematria* (numerical value) of "Amalek" is the same as *safek*, "doubt." Amalek's attack introduced a moment of doubt into the beliefs of the Jews; that was his only goal.

Over 100 years ago, the hasidic leader Rabbi Tzadok HaCohen from Lublin wrote that "Amalek" is not to be understood exclusively as a specific person or people but rather as a quality that may manifest itself in all human beings. This attitude is best exhibited in the cynic. The cynic takes nothing seriously, finds nothing meaningful or sacred. The commentators remark that Amalek wanted the Jewish people to think that their deliverance had not been intentional but rather had occurred by chance.

Not only does this *parsha* instruct not to forget what Amalek did to the Jewish people, but in the strongest language it adds that "... you must blot out the remembrance of Amalek from under heaven. ..." Likewise, this quality of cynicism ought to be utterly removed from one's personality.

Around the Shabbat Table

1. The Midrash offers a parable to describe Amalek's attack on the Jews:"All the nations were afraid to make war on the Jewish people and then Amalek came and began to point the way. A parable—it may be compared to a boiling hot bath into which no living creature could descend. Someone came and jumped into it. Although he scalded himself, he cooled it off, and made it appear cold to others." How do cynics often "cool off" the enthusiasm felt by others?

2. Maimonides writes that the Jewish people had to fulfill three commandments upon entering the Land of Israel: to appoint a king, to eradicate the seed of Amalek, and to build the sanctuary. Why do you think he listed them in this order? How would the same mitzvot—appointing of a king, eradicating Amalek, and building a sanctuary—symbolically manifest themselves in the internal life of an individual?

3. What is the difference between healthy skepticism and cynicism? What makes people become cynical? How do you think that a person may overcome this tendency?

Seuda Shlishit: Dreams of Treasure

The *parsha Ki Tetze* is replete with misdirected desires. Rebbe Nachman of Bratzlav offered a classic parable for the confusion and surprise that often accompanies the search for happiness and fortune:

> A man once dreamed that there was a great treasure under a bridge in Vienna. He traveled to Vienna and stood near the bridge, trying to figure out what to do. He did not dare search for the treasure by day, because of the many people who were there.
>
> An officer passed by and asked, "What are you doing, standing here and contemplating."
>
> The man decided that it would be best to tell the whole story and ask for help, hoping that the officer would share the treasure with him. He told the officer the entire story.
>
> The officer replied, "A Jew is concerned only with dreams! I also had a dream, and I also saw a treasure. It was in a small house, under the cellar."
>
> In relating his dream, the officer accurately described the man's city and house. He rushed home, dug under his cellar, and found the treasure. He said, "Now I know that I had the treasure all along. But in order to find it, I had to travel to Vienna."

Around the Shabbat Table

1. What do you think that the images of the story—"the treasure, bridge, cellar, Vienna," and so forth—symbolize? What do you think is the message of the story?

2. The rabbis considered dreams to be the last traces of prophecy, forms of divine revelation. Why do you think that it was not revealed to the man in his dream that there was a treasure in his own house?

3. Have you ever searched for a goal that was actually nearby all the time?

Ki Tavo

FRIDAY NIGHT MEAL: The First Prayer Text

What is the first formal prayer of the Jewish people that appears in the Torah?

Many individual prayers are mentioned in the Torah. Isaac prays for his wife Rebecca to have a child. Jacob prays that he would return safely to Israel. Moses prays for the health of his sister, Miriam. But what is the first prayer, whose actual words are recorded, that is commanded to be recited by future generations? Not until almost the end of the last book of the Torah is a formal prayer determined and recorded for posterity—six verses declared upon the bringing of the first fruits (*bikkurim*) to Jerusalem.

This week's *parsha* instructs that:

And it will be, when you come in to the land, which the Lord your God gives to you for an inheritance, and you take possession of it and live there, that you will take the first of all the fruit of the earth ... and place it in a basket, and go to the place which the Lord your God will choose to place His name there. And you will go to the priest ... and say to him, "I profess this day to the Lord your God that I have come

into the land that the Lord swore to our forefathers that He would give
to us . . ."

And you will speak and say . . . : "My father was a wandering
Arammian, and he went down to Egypt and lived there with only a
few, and there became a great nation, mighty, and populous. And the
Egyptians dealt evilly with us, and afflicted us, and laid upon us hard
bondage. And when we cried to the Lord God of our fathers, the Lord
heard our voice and looked on our affliction, and our labor, and our
oppression. And the Lord brought us out of Egypt with a mighty hand,
and with an outstretched arm, with great terror, and signs and wonders, and He brought us to this place, and gave us this land, a land flowing with milk and honey. And now I have brought the first fruits of
the land, which You, God, have given to me." [Deuteronomy 26:1-10]

What is so uniquely special about the bringing of the first fruits
that the Torah saw the need to define exactly how the occasion
should be marked? All other prayers in the Torah have been personal,
spontaneous, and heartfelt. Why didn't the Torah leave the exact
words of this prayer to the discretion of the person bringing the
first fruits?

Only the farmer is commanded to mark his first fruits and bring
them to Jerusalem. No persons in other professions are required to
mark their first product or make this pilgrimage. Of all the many
trades and professions, farming is conceivably the most lonely and
restrictive. Day after day, dawn to dusk, the farmer works his field,
usually by himself. He is subservient to his land. Unlike those engaged in business or other professions, the farmer possesses minimal control over the forces of nature that affect his crops. He can
neither choose to "take a day off" nor hasten the growing process.
The farmer is also a slave to time. He lives in the present. His cycle
of time flows from season to season, dependent upon the vicissitudes of what nature may thrust upon him in any moment. If he does
not focus thoroughly on each present moment, his whole crop may
be lost.

The farmer may have worked alone, but he did not come alone
to Jerusalem. The mishnah describes how the farmers of each re-

gion would assemble and then parade in unison to Jerusalem. The residents of Jerusalem would leave the city to greet them, standing in their honor, and calling out, "Brothers, come in peace." Even the king would join the residents in greeting the farmers. Once a year, this most solitary toiler of the land would be royally welcomed by the masses and leaders of the Jewish people.

The farmer brought his first fruits to Jerusalem and escaped from his social solitude. Yet what might he be thinking about his experience? If he were allowed to say whatever spontaneously came into his heart, what might he say? "Thank you, God, for enabling me to successfully grow these fruits"? "Thank you for enabling me to come to Jerusalem"?

The six verses prescribed to him in this week's *parsha* preclude his focusing either exclusively upon himself or upon the present moment. These verses immerse him into the entire history of the Jewish people: "My father was a wandering Arammian, and he went down to Egypt and lived there with only a few, and there became a great nation, mighty, and populous. And the Egyptians dealt evilly with us, and afflicted us. . . . "

A social and historical drama is being played out in the mitzvah of the farmer's bringing of his first fruits. Through the numerous stages of this occasion—the parade with all the other farmers, the royal welcome into Jerusalem, the prepared speech recounting Jewish history—the farmer unites with both those of his present and past generations. Moreover, a nation is being taught how to care for all of its working members.

Around the Shabbat Table

1. The mishnah (*Bikkurim* 3:1) states that one would "go down into his field and look for the first fig, grapes, or pomegranate that had ripened, mark it, and say aloud, 'Behold, these are the first fruits.'" How do you think this ceremony might affect the farmer's entire experience of growing and harvesting?

2. What group of people or profession in your society is set apart or unappreciated? What could be done to alleviate this problem?

3. What would you consider to be the "first fruits" of your work? Where would you bring them? What would you say?

SHABBAT LUNCH: Controlling Happiness

> And all these curses will come upon you, and will pursue you and overtake you, till you are destroyed . . . Because you did not serve the Lord your God in happiness and with good heart . . . [Deuteronomy 28:45-47]

Curse after curse, enumerated in this week's *parsha*, will visit the Jewish people, if they do not serve God "*with happiness and a joyful heart.*" Apparently, *simcha* (happiness) is so central to life that its absence warrants the curses in *Ki Tavo*.

The Talmud notes the beneficial effects of *simcha*. To facilitate an atmosphere of friendship, several rabbis of the Talmud would open their classes with a moment of humor. The Talmud (Tannit 21a) relates that once a rabbi asked Elijah the Prophet if there were any personalities in the marketplace who were destined to inherit the "world to come." Elijah pointed to two jesters. For Elijah, bringing joy was a supreme value.

The Maharal writes that deep feelings of happiness occur when people achieve greater meaning and clarity in their lives. Human beings are essentially incomplete, and the most profound moments of happiness occur when they feel an increased sense of completion. If serving God does not result in a greater sense of meaning in life, then, writes the Maharal, something is seriously amiss. If serving God does not yield greater happiness, then something crucial has broken down in the very fabric of this relationship.

Notwithstanding the centrality of "serving God in happiness and with good heart," is happiness an ultimate value? Should people place a limit or be concerned with qualifying their own happiness?

Rav Kook noted that the verse (quoted previously) in this week's *parsha* referred to two separate and independent qualities of joy: "happiness" and "a good heart." He explains that "happiness" is a particular feeling, whereas a "good heart" refers to an overall emotional condition. Rav Kook was concerned that feelings of happiness may be forced or contrived. Sometimes, one may feel obligated to be happy and may consequently try to force these feelings. Rav Kook wrote that a coerced sense of happiness cannot foster a "good heart." Artificial smiles and compelled laughter may actually be deterrents to the nurturing of sincere happiness. The state of happiness of the individual must be harmonized with all of the other components of an individual's personality.

The Talmud (*Berakhot* 31a) relates that once at a wedding feast one of the rabbis thought that the other rabbis had become excessively joyful and, to restore a more serious mood, broke a precious glass. Rabbi Yochanon commented on the verses "when God has brought the exiles back to Zion, we were like those who dream. Then our mouth will be filled with laughter" (Psalms 126:1–2), that it is forbidden for someone to fill his mouth with laughter, considering the present condition of the Jewish people. Only "then," namely, when the Jewish nation will have returned to Israel, will we be allowed to rightfully experience unlimited joy. The happiness of the individual cannot be detached from national concerns and the overall condition of the whole people.

Notwithstanding the preeminence of happiness expressed in this week's *parsha*, its presence is but one factor amid the constellation of individual and national concerns.

Around the Shabbat Table

1. One of the reasons for the breaking of a glass at a Jewish wedding is to momentarily shatter the couple's blissful happiness and to return them to the reality of this world. For their happiness to be productive, to positively affect others, they need to be aware

of the "brokenness" of other people's lives. Otherwise, their happiness may actually become estranging. Have you ever felt alienated by someone else's joy?

2. According to the Talmud, Elijah the Prophet said that jesters would merit "the world to come." What other professions would you add? Did you ever have a teacher who employed humor in his or her teaching? What was the effect?

3. What was the happiest moment in your life? Do you think that *simcha* is essential to spiritual growth?

Seuda Shlishit: The Master Teacher

And Moses, with the elders of Israel, commanded the people saying, "Keep all the commandments which I command you this day. And it will be on the day when you will pass over the Jordan to the land which the Lord your God gives you, that *you will set up great stones, and cover them with plaster*. And you will write upon them all the words of this Torah ... " [Deuteronomy 27:1-3]

It was not sufficient that the Jewish people learned the Torah from Moses. They had to become actively involved in its actual writing and, moreover, even in the preparations for its writing. Why does the Torah find it necessary to inform us that the Jewish people were required to "set up great stones and cover them with plaster?"

The following story, which echoes this incident, is found in the Talmud:

Rabbi Chanina and Rabbi Chiyya became engaged in an impassioned argument. Said Rabbi Chanina, "Would you quarrel with me? If, God forbid, the Torah was forgotten by the people of Israel, I could recover it through my sharp powers of reasoning and analysis."

To this Rabbi Chiyya replied, "I could make sure that the Torah is not forgotten from the Jewish people. What would I do? *I would go*

and plant flax seed and (from the grown flax) I would weave nets
and trap deer ... from the deerskins I would make parchment scrolls.
On those I would write the Torah, and then go to a city which had no
teachers for the children; and I would teach five children to read the
Five Books of the Torah [one book each]; and I would teach the six
sections of the mishnah to six children [one each]. Then I would tell
them, 'Until I return this way, study and teach it all to one another'; I
would tell each one, 'Teach your learning to a friend.' This is what I
would do so that the Torah would not be forgotten among the Jewish
people."This is why Rabbi Judah Ha Nasi said, "How great are the deeds
of Chiyya!" [*Ketubot* 103b]

Commentators ask, "Why did Rabbi Chiyya need to declare that
he would personally engage in the whole process of planting the
flax, making the nets, making the scrolls, and so forth?" Why didn't
he simply state that he would go to the cities and teach the children? The deeds of Rabbi Chiyya were "great" because he understood
that every effort that a teacher invests in educating his or her students is crucial to the final process of teaching. Teaching is not simply conveying information; it is the venue for a profound experience
between the teacher and the student. The effort that Rabbi Chiyya
expended in planting the seeds and preparing the scrolls became
part of the whole learning experience, which helped to ensure the
ultimate success of his teaching.

The Jewish people set up great stones, covered them with plaster, and wrote the Torah on them themselves. They became part of
the entire process of learning Torah.

Around the Shabbat Table

1. The commentators disagreed as to what the Jewish people actually wrote upon these great stones. The Ibn Ezra wrote that the
   Jewish people listed all of the mitzvot (commandments) on them;
   Nachmanides stated that the whole Torah was written on them;
   the Talmud (*Sotah* 32a) held that they wrote the entire Torah in

all of the languages of the world. What do you think is the basis for their disagreement?

2.   There are a number of stages in Rabbi Chiyya's blueprint for education. What is special about each stage?

3.   Have you ever had a teacher like Rabbi Chiyya? What did he or she do?

Nitzavim/Vayelech

FRIDAY NIGHT MEAL: *Teshuvah*

The *parsha* of *Nitzavim* is always read on the *Shabbat* before Rosh Hashanah. Apropos for this time, its principal theme is *teshuvah* (change or return), the obligation to improve oneself. "And *you will return* to God . . . " (Deuteronomy 30:2). " . . . When *you will return* to the Lord your God with all of your heart and all of your soul" (Deuteronomy 30:10). In the first ten verses of Chapter 30, eight different forms of the word *teshuvah* are mentioned, as if to stress the importance of undergoing change and improvement.

The *parsha* itself states that:

"This *mitzvah* [*teshuvah*] which I command you today, is not hidden from you, nor is it far away. It is not in the heavens, that you should say, 'Who amongst us can go up and bring it to us, that we may hear it and do it?' Nor is it beyond the sea, that you should say, 'Who amongst us will go over the sea and bring it to us, that we may hear it and do it?' *But it is very near to you, it is in your mouth and in your heart, that you may do it.*" [Deuteronomy 30:11-14]

Though the mitzvah of *teshuvah* may be "very near" and even presumed, few acts in life are as difficult as changing one's behavior. The "Salanter Rebbe," one of the leading rabbis of the nineteenth century, continually stressed the need to scrutinize and work on one's life and is said to have remarked that "it is easier to learn the entire Talmud by heart than to change a single habit."

What motivates a person to change his or her life? What induces a person to consider altering long-standing patterns of behavior?

Dissatisfaction, regret, or anguish over previous acts may engender new patterns of action. Yet this week's *parsha* offers a different motivation for changing one's life.

The *parsha* begins with Moses stating, "Not with you alone am I making this covenant and oath, but with all those that stand here today in front of God, *and also with all those that are not here with us today*" (Deuteronomy 29:13, 14). Why does Moses make the special effort to mention those who are *not* present? What relevance do *future generations* have with this moment of reckoning for the people? What does Moses want the people to think about when he alludes to their future generations?

Change occurs not only through an examination of one's past life but also through thinking about one's future. Often, dwelling on past mistakes may yield feelings of failure and result in depression. Focusing on the future, on "what I want to become in my life," has the power to change a person's will and inspire the individual to greater accomplishments. Redefining where one wants to go, what one aspires to achieve, impacts present patterns of behavior. Rav Kook writes that "the yearning for all existence to be better, purer, more vigorous, and on a higher plane than it is" impels people to improve and refine their course of action. A deeper yearning and sense of responsibility for improving the world may, in fact, hasten its ultimate improvement.

Moses introduces the idea of *teshuvah* in this week's *parsha* by first deepening the awareness of the people that their lives will affect all future generations. They bear responsibility not only for their own decisions but also for the consequences of their decisions for time immemorial. They should not err and think that they alone will be affected by their present decisions; they must also consider *"those* that are not here with us today." The impact of this weighty obligation will hopefully propel the Jewish people to do their utmost to change and improve their present lives.

Around the Shabbat Table

1. This *parsha* is always read before Rosh Hashanah. Since time has no beginning or end, the idea of setting aside a day to mark the beginning of a year seems problematic. How can any specific day serve as a beginning or an end to a cycle of time? The Talmud answers this query by positing that Rosh Hashanah commemorates the sixth day of creation, the day on which the human being was created. Thus, it serves as a "birthday" for all of humanity. The blowing of the *shofar* replays God's breathing the breath of life into Adam, and symbolizes our power to "blow life into" or "recreate" our own lives. What do you usually think about when the *shofar* is blown? How would you "blow new life" into your own life?

2. What decision of your grandparents (or any previous generation) most affects you today? What have you done that you think will affect the lives of your grandchildren and future line?

3. Is there anything you are currently striving to change? Which change in your life during the past year are you most proud of?

SHABBAT LUNCH: Who Should Lead the People?

And Moses called to Joshua and said to him in the sight of all Israel, "Be strong and courageous, for you must come with this people into the Land . . . *you will lead them to inherit it."*
[Deuteronomy 31:7]

As the Torah draws to a close, Moses transfers the mantle of author-ity to Joshua. God had instructed Moses to appoint Joshua to take the Jewish people into the Promised Land. "Joshua, the son of Nun, who stands before you [Moses], he will go in [to the land], strengthen him, for he will cause Israel to inherit it" (Deuteronomy 1:38).

Over a thousand years later, during the rabbinic period, it was less clear who should lead the Jewish people. What is the process through which leadership should be decided? Inextricably con-nected to the determining of leadership and authority is the pro-cess through which law is decided. What is the process through which leaders are given the privilege and responsibility of deciding the law, while other potential leaders are rejected? A debate occurred between the two principle institutions of learning, known as the House of Shammai and the House of Hillel. The Talmud (*Eruvin* 13b) relates that:

> For three years (!) there was a dispute between *Beit* Shammai and *Beit* Hillel, the former asserting, "The *halachah* [Jewish law] is in agreement with our views," and the latter contending, "The *halachha* is in agree-ment with our views." Then a voice from heaven announced, "Both [of these opinions] are the words of the living God, but the *halachah* is in agreement with the rulings of Hillel."

The response of this "heavenly voice" is difficult to understand. If both opinions were, in fact, correct, then why was the *halachah* decided in favor of the *Beit* Hillel?

According to the Talmud, the school of Hillel was chosen because "they were kindly and modest, they studied their own rulings and also those of the school of Shammai, and they were even so humble that they mentioned the opinions of the school of Shammai before their own."

The resolution of the Talmud seems to border on the absurd. Certainly, these character traits of the school of Hillel are praisewor-thy, but are "kindness and modesty" the determining factors for deciding communal authority, leadership, and control? Should "kindness and modesty" be the determining factors in deciding law?

The Talmud's surprising answer sheds light on Judaism's unique approach to the nature and purpose of law. The message of the Talmud is that the goal of Jewish law is not simply to maintain "law and order," but rather to try and create a society of "kindness and modesty." The opinions of *Beit* Hillel were chosen not because they were more accurate than those of *Beit* Shammai, but because they were more likely to lead to the creation of a society that reflected the qualities known to be epitomized by *Beit* Hillel.

Around the Shabbat Table

1. Among the countless disagreements between *Beit* Shammai and *Beit* Hillel, two especially reflect their contrasting perspectives. (1) The Talmud (*Ketubot* 17a) asks, "How does one dance [i.e., what song should one sing] before a bride? *Beit* Shammai said that one should praise her in whatever she happens to be truly praiseworthy. *Beit* Hillel said that one should always say, 'A beautiful and graceful bride.'" (2) A non-Jew once came to Shammai and said to him, "Convert me and teach me all of the Torah while I am standing on one foot." Shammai rejected him outright. He came in front of Hillel, who said to him, "Whatever is hateful to you, don't do to your friend—that is all of the Torah, the rest is commentary, now go and learn it" (*Shabbat* 31a). Can you find a common denominator to their approaches in these two stories?

2. Despite their significant differences, the children of Shammai married the children of Hillel. What does this say about their arguments?

3. Do you think that Jewish law and practice has succeeded in creating a "kind and modest" people?

Seuda Shlishit: Margaret Mead's Visit

... the Lord your God will turn your captivity, and have compassion upon you, and will return and gather you from all the nations amongst whom the Lord your God has scattered you. If your outcasts be at the utmost parts of heaven, from there will the Lord your God will gather you, and from there will He bring you, and the Lord your God will bring you into the land which your fathers possessed and you will possess it ... [Deuteronomy 30:3-5]

During the early years of the State of Israel, hundreds of thousands of Jews, from scores of different countries and backgrounds, came to settle in the land. An extraordinary individual, Lova Eliav, was responsible for their resettlement and acclimation. In his book, *No Time for History*, he recounts a conversation between himself and the noted anthropologist Margaret Mead:

After three days of intensive touring, I returned Dr. Mead to Jerusalem. On the way, I questioned her: "Dr. Mead, please let me have your general impressions of the project you've seen, and rest assured that my colleagues and I are open to criticism. I must tell you that we ourselves are groping in the dark, trying to learn from mistakes of the past and to apply new ways and methods."

Dr. Mead looked at me with probing eyes: "Do you really want to hear my opinion?"

"Of course," I replied.

"Well, I think you're proceeding in this matter in a bad, wrong and disorganized fashion."

"So," I said, "perhaps you'll explain what you mean."

"Certainly, I'll tell you how I would have set about it. Here you are, planning the establishment of a few dozen new villages, a number of rural centers and a new town, and you propose to settle a myriad of Jews in them. These Jews come from the Atlas Mountains, the towns of Czechoslovakia, the mountains of Kurdistan, from Yemen, India, Romania and so many other lands. I've observed that not only don't these people speak a common language; socially and culturally they could come from totally different planets. Their sole common denominator, and I stress sole, is that they're Jews. Furthermore, and this factor is possibly no less important, these people are not farmers at all; only individuals among them, from Kurdistan and Morocco, have engaged in primitive farming, and it would be better for them had they not known the art when they came here. And you're thinking of transforming them, in a matter of a few years, into modern farmers within a developed and complex cooperative context, which in itself is a novel experiment in our world."

"Quite correct," I said.

"Well, Mr. Eliav," Dr. Mead said, "I'd have gone about it in the following way: first, I'd have appealed on behalf of your government, to the appropriate U.N. bodies and requested them to investigate all aspects of the subject."

"The U.N. bodies?" I wondered.

"Yes, the U.N. bodies. Once you'd appealed to them in writing, they'd answer you a few months later that they were acceding to your request, and would be sending a commission for an on-the-spot preliminary study of this weighty subject. Such a commission would be composed of representatives of the Food and Agriculture Organization, the International Labor Organization, the World Health Organization, and similar bodies. The distinguished commission would request a reasonable period of time for investigating the complex subject—say, three years. At the end of three years of ramified research, the commission would request a year's extension for writing its report. At the end of the extra year, you'd receive a report—a thick volume containing hundreds of pages. At the end of the book, under 'Conclusions and Recommendations,' only one line would appear: 'It cannot be done.'"

I had gradually caught on to the fact that Dr. Mead was pulling my leg, and now, at the end of her speech, I noticed the mischievous glint in her wise eyes.

"And so, Mr. Eliav," Margaret Mead concluded, "you went your own way. You didn't call on the U.N. and its bodies, nor did you wait for the advice of sociologists and anthropologists such as myself. And a good thing, too. This is a great human adventure, and may God bless you."

Around the Shabbat Table

1. Until the time of the Isaac Luria, known as the Ari, the leading kabbalist (mystic) of Tzfat in the sixteenth century, most Jewish thinkers understood the exile from Israel as a punishment. The Ari asserted that the Jewish dispersion to the "four corners of the world" was, in fact, a necessary step in the process of redemption. In his view, each nation has something unique to offer the world. The Jews would internalize the special qualities of the nations and then, upon their return, would bring these attributes to Israel. Israel would thus become a "human symphony," possessing characteristics of all of the nations. What qualities do you think the various national and ethnic groups bring to Israel?

2. The verse (cited previously) states that "the Lord your God will gather you in." Do you see the ingathering of the Jewish people to be primarily a human or a divine occurrence? Do you think Israel has succeeded in its "great human adventure" of accepting the Jews of the other nations?

3. In which nations has your family lived?

Haazinu

FRIDAY NIGHT MEAL: A New Name of God

With *Haazinu*, the second to last *parsha* in the Torah, the book of Deuteronomy and the entire Torah draws to a close. Moses' final speech is nearing its conclusion. *Haazinu* recounts the history of the world: from the moment of creation through the choosing of the Jewish people, until the end of days. At the beginning of *Haazinu*, Moses suddenly changes the style of his address to the people; he abruptly moves from prose to poetry. As if acknowledging the limitations of language, as if to say that he has exhausted whatever he could have said in prose, Moses now conveys his message with unprecedented creative language and imagery.

After a brief general introduction, Moses begins the poem by presenting a new name of God—*Tzur* ("Rock"). "[God is] the Rock, His work is perfect" (Deuteronomy 32:4). This name of God, never before mentioned in all of the Torah, is used three times in fifteen verses. The name *Tzur* is etymologically connected to the word *Yotzer*, "Creator," and reflects the enduring nature of God's creation. Like a rock, *Tzur* is permanent and unchanging. In this *parsha*, the expression *Tzur* is used interchangeably to refer to both God and to an actual, physical rock.

Why is a new name of God introduced now, at the end of the Torah? What did Moses want the Jewish people to think when confronted with this image of immutability?

The poem in *Haazinu* cites some of the most egregious failures of the Jewish people, including their frequent provoking and forsaking of God. In *Haazinu*, Moses castigates the Jews for being a nation devoid of counsel, without any understanding (Deuteronomy 32:28). Though God faithfully guarded them in the desert, they often forgot or betrayed this care and worshiped strange gods. Moses' poetic reproach of the Jewish people is aimed to impel them to become more trustworthy and constant in their belief. The expression *Tzur* highlights the Jewish people's inconstancy and fickleness, in contrast to the eternal stability of God.

Yet there is, perhaps, a subtle drawback or danger to framing their relationship with God in the language of *Tzur*, the language of changelessness. The recognition of the permanent and immutable nature of the world may arouse feelings of futility and emptiness. Is it possible to effect change in a world whose Creator (*Yotzer*) possesses rock-like qualities (*Tzur*)? Is the human being utterly powerless during his or her brief time in this world?

The Midrash boldly shatters this possible paralysis caused by a sense of futility. Regarding the verse "You [the Jewish people] *forget* [*t'shi*] the Rock which gave birth to you," the Midrash proposes an alternative explanation of the word *t'shi*: "weaken." According to the Midrash, the verse is to be understood as "You [the Jewish people] weaken the Rock which gave birth to you." In the language of the Midrash: "When the Jewish people do not comply with the will of God, they weaken the heavenly powers; when they follow the will of God, they strengthen the heavenly powers."

According to the Midrash, at the conclusion of the Torah the whole process of creation has come full circle. God, the Creator of the world, is now dependent upon the actions of humanity for the further development of the world. The immutable *Tzur* of the Torah has become the evolving God of the Midrash. God's creation has become the springboard for human creation, as God and humanity have become partners in both the physical and spiritual worlds.

Around the Shabbat Table

1. The poem in *Haazinu* recounts the critical moments in Jewish history. When you look at Jewish history, what would you consider its proudest moments? Its most disappointing moments?

2. With which name of God (King, Father, *Shechinah*, The Holy One, The Merciful One, Creator, Master of the Universe, The Endless One, Rock, etc.) do you most identify?

3. Does your relationship with God enervate you or empower you to action?

SHABBAT LUNCH: Finding the Good in Others

Give ear, Heavens, and I will speak, and hear, Earth, the words of my mouth. My doctrine will drop as the rain, my speech will distill as the dew, as the small rain upon the tender herb, and as the showers upon the grass. Because I will call on the name of the Lord: "Ascribe greatness to our God. *He is the Rock, His work is perfect, for all of His ways are justice, a God of truth without iniquity, just and right is He.*" [Deuteronomy 32:1-4]

This week's *parsha* is composed primarily of Moses' poetic song proclaiming numerous attributes of God. One of the qualities that Moses mentions is fairness: "His ways are justice, a God of truth without iniquity." Just as God is just, so, too, should human beings, acting in the image of God, resolve disputes justly, independent of the personalities or situations of the litigants. The Torah states that "You should not transgress in judgment, you should favor neither the poor nor the powerful, but you should judge your neighbor justly" (Leviticus 19:15). Judges are cautioned not to favor someone who may warrant their mercy; that is, they should not favor a poor person over a wealthy one, or an elderly person over a young one.

While objectivity is the rule in a Jewish court, in life in general, however, this may not be the recommended approach. According to rabbinic tradition, when faced with the possibility of judging an individual positively or negatively, one should *seek positive justification for another's actions* and not merely arrive at a conclusion based upon what one observes. On the verse "you should regard your companion *justly*," the Talmud states that "you should judge him *favorably*" (*Shavuot* 30a). What may be true in courtroom disputes is apparently not the rule concerning the rest of life.

Why should one make the conscientious attempt to judge another favorably? Why not simply try to judge someone fairly and accurately?

Every person possesses both positive and negative qualities or idiosyncrasies. When a person *likes* another, the tendency is to overlook less desirable attributes and to focus on the more attractive ones; similarly, when a person dislikes another, there is a tendency to focus exclusively on unfavorable habits. A Jew is commanded to like each person, as well as him- or herself, and thus should make the effort to judge another person, as well as him- or herself, positively.

Furthermore, the manner in which one judges another often evokes a similar response in return. The book of Proverbs (27:19) notes that "As in water—face answers to face, so too the heart of man to man." Just as water reflects back a person's image, so, too, emotions that a person extends to another evoke a like response. Focusing on the positive qualities of another helps to bring out and strengthen the desirable qualities in oneself and in others.

Around the Shabbat Table

1. The mishnah in *Pirkei Avot* (1:6) states: "Find yourself a rabbi, acquire a friend, and judge all people favorably." Is there a connection between these three ideas?

2. The Talmud (*Bava Metzia* 30b) comments that Jerusalem was destroyed because its judges ruled *exclusively* according to the letter of the law and did not temper their rulings with mercy. Why would judging purely according to the letter of the law be considered so terrible that it warranted the destruction of the Temple?

3. Is there anyone who consistently brings out the best qualities in you? How does he or she do this? What qualities do you think you evoke in others? What quality would you ideally like to evoke?

Seuda Shlishit: Jerusalem of Gold

The poem or song *Haazinu* recounts the history of the world, from the moment of creation through Jewish history until the end of days. In recent history, the song considered to be the most beloved and well-known in the modern history of Israel underwent significant changes before it reached its final version.

The song "Jerusalem of Gold," by Naomi Shemer, was written just months before the outbreak of the Six-Day War in 1967. The title and refrain of the song—"Jerusalem of gold, and of bronze, and of light, for all of your songs, I am a harp"—is based on a story in the Talmud in which Rabbi Akiva promises to give his wife a bracelet engraved with "Jerusalem of Gold," symbolizing their eternal love for each other. Naomi Shemer later reminisced that she wrote the song while reflecting both on the destruction of the city of Jerusalem, 2,000 years ago, and on the heavenly Jerusalem, waiting to be rebuilt.

Mountain-air as smooth as wine
And the smell of pine
Floats in the air at twilight
With the voice of bells.

And midst the sleeping wood and stone
Imprisoned in her dream
The city that dwells alone
And in her heart resides a wall.

Refrain: Jerusalem of gold, and of bronze, and of light, for all of
your songs, I am a harp.

How dried up are the wells of water
The square of the market place deserted
And no one visits the Temple Mount
In the Old City.

And in the crevices that are in the rock
The winds cry out
And no one goes down to the Dead Sea
By way of Jericho.

Refrain: Jerusalem of gold, and of bronze, and of light, for all of
your songs, I am a harp.

But when the day comes to sing to you
And to bind crowns upon you
I remain smaller than your youngest children
And the least of your poets.

Because your name burns the lips
Like the kiss of a heavenly spirit
If I forget you, Jerusalem
Who is completely gold.

Months later, after the regaining of Jerusalem and the Old City, Naomi Shemer added one more verse to her song:

We have returned to the wells of water
To the market and the square
A shofar is calling on the Temple Mount
In the Old City.

And in the crevices that are in the rock
Thousands of suns are shining
We will once again go down to the Dead Sea
By way of Jericho.

Around the Shabbat Table

1. King David, often remembered for his heroic battles, is also known as the "sweet singer" of Israel. The Talmud (*Sanhedrin* 94a) relates that God wanted to make King Hezekiah the messiah but refrained because he did not "sing" after the miracles that God had done for him. What is so important about singing? What personality qualities impel or hinder someone from singing? Have you ever experienced a spiritual dimension to singing?

2. What image most comes to your mind when you think of Jerusalem? What image do you find most compelling in Naomi Shemer's song?

3. What do you think is the most moving or powerful Jewish song? Why? What is your favorite Hebrew song?

Vezot HaBerakah

FRIDAY NIGHT MEAL: The "Unfinishable"

Vezot HaBerakah, the last *parsha* in the Torah, is the only *parsha* that is not read on *Shabbat*. Instead, it is read on Simchat Torah, the holiday commemorating the conclusion of the annual cycle of reading the Torah. On Simchat Torah, immediately after completing the Torah, we begin reading it anew, starting with the beginning of the first *parsha, Bereshit*.

Why is there a need to begin the Torah once again upon its conclusion without delay? The *parsha Bereshit* will be read in full on the next *Shabbat*. Why, then, do we read part of *Bereshit* on Simchat Torah and have a public celebration showing that, after finishing the Torah, we resume reading from the beginning immediately?

There is an inherent danger in the study of Torah: one might approach Torah study with the singular intention *of acquiring knowledge* and may be tempted to try to master its *content* and to regard it like a textbook whose goal is to impart information.

The Maharal wrote that the blessing recited daily before the studying of Torah does not say "*to learn Torah,*" but "*to engage in the words of Torah.*" If the blessing had been "to learn Torah," then the goal of study would have been to understand and master the content of the Torah. The expression "to engage in the words of Torah," however, shifts the focus from the comprehension of the Torah's content to the process of study itself. While certainly advocating the deepening of one's understanding of the Torah, the Maharal asserts that it is the *experience* of learning Torah that is unique. This experience should engender a heightened awareness of one's relationship with the transcendent, with the holy. The experience of study should thus be self-transforming, instilling greater insight into one's uniqueness and purpose in the life.

Since the Torah serves as the primary vehicle for generating a more profound awareness of the self and of the Holy, it must, by definition, be "unfinishable." There is no limit to one's relationship with God; accordingly, since human beings are created in the image of God, there can be no limit to their potential growth. The goal of learning Torah is *not knowledge of content* but rather the *insight and wisdom* that its content may yield. Knowledge is the mastery of amounts of material, whereas wisdom deals with one's relationship to the Eternal, to that which is not bound by time or place.

The holiday on which *Vezot HaBerakah* is read is called Simchat Torah—"the Happiness of the Torah." Many commentators understand that true *simcha* ("happiness") results from personal growth. The recognition that the Torah is "unfinishable" means that each individual possesses unlimited potential for personal growth, insight, and wisdom. This awareness should impel one to rejoice at the prospect of beginning the process of study and growth once again.

Around the Shabbat Table

1. Has your experience of learning Torah ever deepened your relationship with the transcendent or granted you greater personal clarity?

2. Is there any other book that you have read repeatedly? Why?

3. When you consider the whole Torah, which story or event stands out as the most meaningful? Which has had the greatest influence upon you? Why?

SHABBAT LUNCH: Knowing God

This week's *parsha* begins with the verse:"This is the blessing which Moses, the man of God, blessed the children of Israel before his death" (Deuteronomy 33:1) and ends with "And there never arose a prophet like Moses, *who knew the Lord face to face*" (Deuteronomy 34:10).

When God first interacts with Moses at the burning bush, he is shocked and overwhelmed (Exodus 3:3). According to the Midrash, *he turned his face away from the holy presence*, not daring to look at the bush itself. Much later, after the Jewish people's sin of the golden calf, Moses asks God to show him God's splendor. God responds by saying, "*You cannot see my face*, for no man shall see me, and live" (Exodus 33:20). Now, at the close of the Torah, as part of God's eulogy for Moses, it is disclosed that Moses "*knew the Lord face to face.*"

However these metaphorical expressions are understood, it is clear that Moses grew spiritually and developed his relationship with God during the course of the forty years between the event of the burning bush and his death.

Is it possible to "know" God?

In Maimonides' treatise outlining the Thirteen Principles of Faith, he notes that God transcends all human comprehension of time and space. According to Maimonides, even the quality of oneness that we attribute to God is essentially beyond human comprehension and is different than the quality of oneness that we understand. God exists, yet is basically "unknowable."

Abraham Joshua Heschel writes that "The mystery of God remains forever sealed to man ... All we have is an awareness of the mystery, but it is a presence that the mind can never penetrate" (*God in Search of Man*, pp. 61–62). An infinite abyss separates the human experience from the holy, crossed only through moments of revelation and prophecy.

Today, centuries after the close of the era of prophecy, how is it possible to deepen one's relationship with the transcendent? How can one still grow spiritually?

Heschel writes that "there are three starting points of contemplation about God: three trails that lead to Him. *The first is the way of sensing the presence of God in the world ... the second is the way of sensing His presence in the Bible; the third is the way of sensing His presence in sacred deeds*" (*God in Search of Man*, p. 31). Through observing the natural world, through learning, and through action, one may begin to fathom the mysteries of the ineffable. Each person may be intuitively drawn to one of these paths, yet ideally all three paths are experienced and serve to complement each other.

Moses experienced God in each of these three ways: at the burning bush he saw God's influence in the natural world, at Mount Sinai he deepened his relationship with God through his mind, and in his forty years of leading the Jewish people in the desert he came closer to God through his actions. Though the Torah states that "there never arose a prophet like Moses ..." (Deuteronomy 34:10), nevertheless, his achievements serve as an example toward which every Jew can aspire.

Around the Shabbat Table

1. Heschel wrote that "awe precedes faith; it is at the root of faith. We must grow in awe in order to reach faith." For Heschel, awe represented a way of looking at the world, "to sense in small things the beginning of infinite significance, to sense the ultimate in the common and the simple" (*God in Search of Man*, pp. 74–75). What do you think furthers a sense of awe? What impairs it?

2. Just as God is, in essence, unknowable, so, too, every human be-
    ing, having been created in the image of God, is also essentially
    unknowable. Do you think that Heschel's three pathways to God
    are also applicable to deepening relationships with other people?
    How is it possible to begin to fathom the mystery of oneself and
    others?

3. Which of the three paths for approaching God mentioned here—
    through the natural world, through the Bible, and through sacred
    deeds—most resonates with you? What has enabled you to grow
    spiritually?

Seuda Shlishit: Telling the Story

And Joshua the son of Nun was full of the spirit of wisdom, for
Moses had laid his hands upon him; and the children of Israel listened to him . . . *and there would never be another prophet in
Israel like Moses,* whom the Lord knew face to face. [Deuteronomy
34:9, 10]

About 200 years ago, the hasidic movement faced a similar crisis. Their leader, the Ba'al Shem Tov, had died and they needed a new
leader to guide them. The following story is told:

When the Ba'al Shem Tov had a difficult task before him, he would go
to a certain place in the woods, light a fire, and meditate in prayer, and
what he had set out to perform was done.

When a generation later the "Maggid" of Meseritz was faced with
the same task, he would go to the same place in the woods and say:
"We can no longer light the fire, but we can still speak the prayers,"
and what he wanted done became reality.

Again, a generation later, Rabbi Moshe Leib of Sassov had to perform this task. And he, too, went into the woods and said: "We can no
longer light a fire, nor do we know the secret meditations belonging
to the prayer, but we do know the place in the woods to which it all
belongs," and that must be sufficient; and sufficient it was.

But when another generation had passed, and Rabbi Israel of Rishin was called upon to perform the task, he sat down on his chair and said:"We cannot light the fire, we cannot speak the prayers, we do not know the place, but we can tell the story of how it was done."And the story that he told had the same effect as the actions of the other three.

Around the Shabbat Table

1. Why do you think that each leader did not convey to the next generation exactly what he did? Why do you think that in the last generation the story that was told had the same effect as the actions of the previous three?

2. Why do you think that leadership is so difficult to transfer, especially from the first generation henceforth? Do you know of any other movements (Jewish or general) that also struggled to pass down leadership to the next generation?

3. Have you ever tried to pass responsibilities of leadership to someone else? Were you successful?

Glossary

Abarbanel, Isaac (1437-1508)—Spanish biblical commentator, philosopher, and statesman.

Abba Hilkiyah—First-century sage; recognized in the Talmud for his righteous behavior.

Agnon, Shmuel Yosef (Shai) (1888-1970)—Hebrew author and Nobel Laureate in Literature.

Akiva, Rabbi (c. 50-135 C.E.)—Prominent scholar, teacher, patriot, and martyr who, despite beginning his studies at a mature age, significantly influenced the development of the *halachah*.

Arba'ah Turim—Major halachic work written by Jacob Ben Asher (1270?—1340). Its arrangement, simple style, and wealth of content made it a basic work in Jewish law; it opened a new era in the realm of halachic codification.

Ba'al Shem Tov (Israel Ben Eliezer) (c.1700-1760)—Founder and initial leader of *Hasidut* in Eastern Europe.

Bava Batra—Talmudic tractate dealing in partnership, sales, promissory notes, and inheritance.

Bava Metziah—Talmudic tractate dealing in losses, loans, work, and wage contracts.

Babylonian Talmud—38 tractates of rabbinic discussions among Babylonian sages from the years 200-600 C.E., addressing the Mishnah and midrashic and rabbinic lore, which became the basis of Jewish law and study.

Bar Kamtza—Figure in the talmudic legend involved with events leading to the destruction of the Second Temple; the mistaken invitee whose anger toward indifferent rabbis led him to incite the Roman authorities.

Beit Hillel—Major school of Oral Law exposition, founded by the scholar Hillel (end of first century B.C.E.-beginning of first century C.E.) and in existence until the beginning of the second century C.E.

Beit Midrash—The traditional hall of Torah study in yeshivot.

Beit Shammai—major school of Oral Law exposition, founded by the scholar Shammai (end of first century B.C.E.-beginning of first century C.E.) and in existence until the beginning of the second century C.E.

Beit Yosef—Comprehensive commentary on the *Arba'ah Turim* by Rav Yosef Caro (1488-1575), author of the *Shulchan Aruch*; pseudonym for Rav Caro himself.

Berditchev, Rabbi Yitzchak (c.1740-1810)—Hasidic rebbe from the third generation of *Hasidut* who emphasized the importance of spiritual joy and enthusiastic prayer.

Berakhot—Prayers and benedictions.

Buber, Martin (1878-1965)—Jewish philosopher and theologian

whose work addressed a broad range of subjects, from *Hasidut* to philosophy of dialogue.

Carlebach, Shlomo (1926-1994)—Rabbi and musician who spread a message of traditional Judaism and lovingkindness throughout the world by way of his guitar, voice, and caring heart.

Chafetz Chaim (Israel Meir Ha-Kohen) (1838-1933)—Rabbi, ethicist, and halachist, recognized for his extremely righteous, humble, and pious behavior; author of *Mishnah Berura*, an important modern halachic work.

Chaim, Rabbi of Volozhin (1749-1821)—Rabbi and yeshiva head; main disciple of the Vilna Gaon who founded the yeshiva of Volozhin, which would serve as a model for all subsequent yeshivot in the Lithuanian tradition.

Chanina Ben Dosa—First-century c.e. sage who lived in the lower Galilee; recognized in aggadic sources for his extreme piety and righteousness.

Chanina, Rabbi—Sage of Eretz Yisrael at the end of the third to the beginning of the fourth century c.e.

Charlap, Rav (1883-1951)—Rabbi, kabbalist, and halachist; one of Rabbi Kook's primary students.

Chiya, Rabbi—Sage from the end of the second century c.e. who immigrated to Eretz Yisrael from Babylonia; was regarded in his day as second in learning only to Rabbi Yehuda HaNasi.

Dessler, Eliahu Eliezer (1891-1954)—Rabbi, scholar, and proponent of the Mussar movement in Lithuania; the work *Mikhtav me-Eliahu* was compiled by his students from Rav Dessler's writings and lectures.

Din—The divine attribute of strict, uncompromising judgment of humanity; in contrast to *Rachamim*.

Elazar Ben Arach—Eretz Yisrael Sage from the end of the first century c.e., who after the destruction of the Second Temple followed his teacher R.Yochanan Ben Zakkai to establish the learning center and *beit din* at Yavne.

Eliav, Loba—Zionist leader; commander of immigration ships to Eretz Yisrael before the establishment of the State; instrumental in the Jewish settlement of the Negev desert.

Eliezer, Rabbi (Eliezer ben Hyrcanus)—contemporary and associate of Elazar Ben Arach, who, despite his great scholarship, struggled with his colleagues and eventually suffered excommunication.

Elisha Ben Abuyah, Rabbi—Prominent sage from the first half of the second century c.e., who came to renounce his faith in Judaism and to be known as *"Acher"* ("another person").

Eruvin—Laws of permissible limits on *Shabbat.*

Ethics of the Fathers—Tractate of the Mishnah composed of ethical teachings of the Sages.

Fromm, Eric—American psychoanalyst, philosopher, and writer who understood Jewish texts and practices to answer to timeless human psychological needs, including the modern condition of alienation.

Gematria—a hermeneutic rule for interpreting the Torah through the assignment of numerical values to the Hebrew letters.

Goren, Shlomo—Israeli rabbi and scholar; head rabbi of the Israeli army, who accompanied the troops in the Sinai Campaign and Six-Day War; author of key halachic responsa regarding observance for Israeli soldiers.

Gur, Motta—Israeli paratroop colonel in the Six-Day War, whose brigade was instrumental in battles to recapture the Old City of Jerusalem.

HaKohen, David—Student of Rav Avraham Isaac Kook, who edited and published some of his writings.

Halachah—Jewish law; lit., "The Path."

HaLevi, Rabbi Judah (ca. 1075-1141)—Medieval Spanish Hebrew poet and philosopher; author of the *Kuzari*, a Jewish polemic against Aristotelian philosophy, Christianity, and Islam.

Haman—Persian minister and enemy of the Jews, as accounted in *Megillat Esther*.

Hannanel, Rabbenu (Hannanel ben Hushi'el) (d. 1055/6)—Roman rabbi, talmudist, and halachic decisor; author of a highly influential commentary on the Talmud.

Hasidut—Revolutionary religious movement founded by the Ba'al Shem Tov in eighteenth-century Europe, emphasizing the importance of fervent prayer, inner awareness and devotion, and Lurianic Kabbalah.

Herzl, Theodore (1860-1904)—Father of modern political Zionism, whose writings and strong political leadership transformed Zionism into an organized worldwide movement.

Heschel, Avraham Yehoshua (1907-1972)—American philosopher and theologian who addressed fundamental problems of modern Western Jewish existence.

Hisda, Rabbi (c. 217-309)—Babylonian sage; frequently quoted in both the Jerusalem and Babylonian Talmuds; noted for extreme depth and thoroughness of learning.

Hoshen Mishpat—One of the four sections of the *Arba'ah Turim* and *Shulchan Aruch*, dealing with civil and criminal law.

Ibn Ezra, Abraham (1080-1164)—Spanish biblical commentator and poet.

Jaffa Road—Thoroughfare in central Jerusalem.

Joshua Ben Gamla—Rabbi mentioned in the Talmud.

Judah HaNasi (late second to the beginning of the third century c.e.)—Patriarch in post-Second Temple Eretz Yisrael and redactor of the Mishnah.

Judah, Rabbi (mid-second century c.e.)—Sage, student of Rabbi Akiva; major contributor to what would later become the Mishnah and *Tosefta*; noted for his pious behavior.

Kabbalah—Jewish mysticism.

Kamtza—In the talmudic legend regarding events leading to the destruction of the Second Temple, the friend of the party host who mistakenly does not receive his invitation.

Kaplan, Mordecai (1881-1983)—American rabbi and founder of the Reconstructionist Movement, who defined Judaism as an "evolving religious civilization."

Kook, Avraham Yitzhak Ha-Cohen (1865-1935)—First Ashkenazi chief rabbi of modern Israel; kabbalist and author who wrote prolifically on the meaning of Jewish and general religious existence in modernity.

Kotsker (Rav Menachem Mendel of Kotsk)—fiery Polish hasidic rebbe who demanded extreme sincerity and honesty from himself and his select circle of students.

"L'cha dodi"—Litergical poem, sung weekly at the outset of *Shabbat*; composed in the sixteenth century by the kabbalist Shlomo Alkabetz.

Lag ba'Omer—The thirty-third day of the *Omer* counting (determined from the second day of Pesach until Shavuot); a minor holiday to mark the end of the plague that killed 24,000 of Rabbi Akiva's students because, according to talmudic and midrashic sources, they did not appropriately honor one another.

Luria, Isaac (Ariz"l) (1534-1572)—Kabbalist whose innovation and school of disciples exercised an important influence on the development of Jewish mysticism.

Luzzato, Moshe Chaim (1707-1746)—Italian kabbalist, ethicist, and poet; author of *Mesilat Yesharim* ("The Path of the Upright"), a guidebook of spiritual ascent and one of the most influential ethical works in Judaism.

Maggid of Dovno (Yaakov ben Ze'ev Krantz) (1741-1804)—Preacher who held posts throughout Poland and Lithuania; he composed orations drawn from Jewish ethical, halachic, and kabbalistic literature.

Maggid of Mezridtch (Rav Dov Baer)—Main disciple of the Ba'al Shem Tov and his heir to the leadership of the Hasidic Movement.

Maharal (Judah Loew ben Bezalel) (1525-1609)—Author of important exegetical and philosophical works.

Maimonides (Moshe ben Maimon) (1135-1204)—Rabbi and philosopher; author of a comprehensive code of Jewish law founded upon the Talmud, the Mishneh Torah, and an important philosophical work, *Moreh Nevuchim*.

Megilla—Laws of Purim.

Megilla—scroll; the biblical canon contains five *megillot—Rut* (Ruth), *Shir Ha Shirim* (Song of Songs), *Kohelet* (Ecclesiastes), *Eicha* (Lamentations), and *Ester* (Esther).

Meir of Rutenberg, Rabbi (1215-1293)—German talmudist and halachist.

Meir, Golda—Israeli stateswoman who served as Israel's fourth prime minister from 1969 until after the Yom Kippur War in 1973.

Midrash—Rabbinic term for interpretive biblical study; alternatively, specific compilations of teachings that are products of interpretive biblical study.

Mishnah—Six orders of halachic rulings, opinions, and disputes, redacted for the first time by Rabbi Yehuda HaNasi in approximately the year 200 C.E.

Mishneh Torah—Early code of Jewish law by Maimonides (Rambam), which would exert a strong influence on all later halachic rulings and become the authoritative code in certain Sephardi communities.

Montifiore, Moshe (1784-1885)—English philanthropist who generously supported the development of Jewish settlements in Eretz Yisrael and Jewish welfare projects throughout the world.

Musaf—In the time of the two Temples, special, additional sacrifices offered on *Shabbat* and certain holidays; in the post-Temple period, an additional prayer stated in lieu of that sacrifice.

Nachman, Rebbe of Bratslav (1772-1811)—Hasidic rebbe; author of complex theological teachings and popular, allegorical hasidic stories.

Nachmanides, Ramban (1194-1270)—Spanish biblical and talmudic commentator.

Nazir—From the root meaning "to separate," or "to dedicate"; someone who vows for a specific period of time not to consume grape products, cut his hair, or touch a corpse; addressed in Numbers 6:1-21.

Nedarim—Vows.

Niggun—A song without words; traditionally sung fervently by hasidim while dancing or otherwise celebrating.

Peretz, Isaac Leib (1851-1915)—Polish Yiddish writer who was active in Polish Jewish communal activity and, as a liberal reformer, identified strongly with the uneducated, artisans, and laborers.

Pesachim—Laws of *chametz* (leavened bread) and *matza* and the *paschal* sacrifice.

Pirkei Avot—Tractate of the Mishnah composed of ethical teachings of the Sages.

Purim—Jewish holiday on the fourteenth (in some locations, the fifteenth) of the month of Adar, commemorating the Jewish victory against an attempted mass annihilation, as accounted in *Megillat Ester* (which is read publicly on the day).

Ra'avad (Rav Avraham ben David of Posquieres) (1120-1197)—French talmudist and halachist.

Rachamim—The divine attribute of a merciful, forgiving attitude toward humanity; in contrast to Din.

Radak (Rabbi David Kimchi) (1157-1236)—French author of important biblical commentary.

Rashi (Rabbi Shlomo Yitzhaki) (1040-1105)—French rabbi and scholar, who wrote brilliant, broadly accepted, and highly influential commentaries to the Bible and the Babylonian Talmud.

Rosensweig, Franz (1886-1929)—German Jewish theologian; though once on the verge of conversion to Christianity, Rosensweig would become a major modern Jewish thinker and advocate for Jewish literacy.

Ruzhin, Rabbi Yisrael (1797-1850)—Hasidic rebbe and leader; after incarceration by Russian authorities, he succeeded in fleeing to Sadagora, Bukovina, where he established an opulent hasidic court.

Salant, Rabbi (Israel Ben Ze'ev Wolf Lipkin) (1818-1883)—Lithuanian yeshiva head who founded the Mussar movement, a moral movement widely adopted within the yeshiva world.

Sanhedrin—Courts, criminal law, principles of faith.

Sanhedrin—The high political, religious, and judicial body of the Jewish people from Second Temple period until 425 c.e., composed of seventy-one elder scholars.

Sanz, Rabbi (Haim ben Leibush Halberstam) (1793-1876))—Hasidic rebbe and founder of hasidic dynasty; discreet and modest, he opposed the luxurious style of Rabbi Ruzhin's Sadagora hasidim.

Sassov, Moshe Leib (1745-1807)—Hasidic rebbe and teacher, known for his boundless love for the Jewish people.

Scholem, Gershom—Jewish academic scholar and authority on kabbalistic studies.

Senesh, Hanna (1921-1944)—Poet and Haganah fighter who, following *aliyah* from Hungary in 1939, parachuted into Nazi-occupied Europe in an ill-fated effort to rescue Allied POWs and organize Jewish resistance.

Sfat Emmet—Collected teachings of Judah Arye Leib Alter (1847-1905), Polish hasidic rebbe from the Ger dynasty.

Shabbat—The Seventh Day, observed as a day of rest from constructive activity in recognition of the Seventh Day of Creation, when God rested (Genesis 2:1-3).

Shemer, Naomi (1933-)—Israeli composer and lyricist whose song "Yerushalayim Shel Zahav" became the "theme song" of the Six-Day War.

Shimon Bar Yochai (mid-second century c.e.)—Rabbi and student of Rabbi Akiva; sentenced to death by the Romans, spent twelve years hiding in a cave with son Eleazar; figures prominently in kabbalistic lore.

Shmuel HaKatan—Sage from the early second century c.e. who was asked to compose the twelfth benediction of the weekday *Amidah*—"benediction concerning heretics"—due to his extreme modesty.

Shneur, Zalman (1887-1959)—Modern author of Hebrew and Yiddish poetry and fiction.

Shulchan Aruch (lit., "The Prepared Table")—Concise code of Jewish law by Rav Yosef Caro, first printed in 1565, which would become broadly accepted by world Jewry as authoritative.

Soloveitchek, Yosef Dov (1903-1993)—Talmudic scholar, yeshiva head, and religious philosopher; spiritual mentor to a generation of Orthodox Jews due to his mastery of *halachah*, intellectual sophistication, and interest in the philosophical and practical concerns of modern Jewry.

Sotah—A woman who is accused of adultery, as addressed in Numbers 5:11-31 and expounded in rabbinic literature and *halachah*.

Sotah—Talmudic tractate dealing with the laws of an adulteress, a murder when the perpetrator is unknown, and war.

Talmud Yerushalmi—39 tractates of rabbinic discussions among Eretz Yisrael Sages from the years 200-500 C.E., addressing the Mishnah, which would become a halachic source of secondary importance to the Babylonian Talmud.

Tarfon, Rabbi—Sage from the generation following the destruction of the Second Temple in 70 C.E.; noted for his humane character and methodical study method.

Temple, First—The central building for the worship of God in Jerusalem, which was built by King Solomon and destroyed by the Babylonians in 586 B.C.E.

Temple, Second—The rebuilt Temple, which stood from 516 B.C.E. until its destruction by the Romans in 70 C.E.

Tikkun—"Fixing"; a central concept in Kabbalah and *Hasidut* that concerns the spiritual repair of self and community and the nature of the Divine emanations.

Teshuvah—"Return"; the process of repentance as a vital component of Jewish spiritual life.

Twerski, Dr. Avraham—Contemporary rabbi and psychiatrist, specializing in drug addiction.

Tzadok HaCohen of Lublin (1823-1900)—Hasidic rebbe whose strong background in halachic study enhanced his hasidic teachings by providing a foundation in traditional, nonkabbalistic sources.

Vilna Gaon (Eliahu ben Shlomo Zalman) (1720-1797)—Spiritual and intellectual giant renowned for his mastery of and diligence in the precise study of Torah; virulent opponent of *Hasidut*.

Wolffsohn, David (1856-1914)—Second president of the World Zionist Organization; colleague and successor to Herzl, credited with successfully mediating between rival forces within the Zionist Movement.

Ya'akov Yosef of Polonye (d. c. 1782)—Hasidic rabbi and preacher, whose work *Toledot Ya'akov Yosef* was the first to formulate in an organized manner the fundamental teachings of *Hasidut*.

Yehoshua, A. B. (Avraham B.) (1936-)—Israeli writer of fiction and essays.

Yevamot—Talmudic tractate dealing with Levirite marriage; prohibited marriages; testimony regarding the death of a husband.

Yishuv—Settlement, usually in Eretz Yisrael.

Yore Deah—One of the four sections of the *Tur* and *Shulchan Aruch*, dealing with (among other topics) dietary laws, interest, ritual purity, and mourning.

Zohar—"The Book of Splendor"; seminal text of the Kabbalah.

About the Author

Aryeh Ben David graduated from Vassar College in 1977 and moved to Israel in 1978. He studied at Kollel Meretz in Mevaseret Tzion from 1982 to 1986, receiving rabbinical ordination from the Ariel Institute and the Chief Rabbi of Haifa in 1986. He is a member of the Senior Faculty of the Pardes Institute in Jerusalem, having taught there since 1986. He also served as the Educational Director of the Jerusalem campus of Livnot U'Lehibanot since its inception in 1993 until 1998. He lives in Efrat, Gush Etzion, with his wife, Sara, and their six children. Aryeh Ben David welcomes comments and can be contacted at aryehbd@netmedia.net.il